Erotic Coleridge

Erotic Coleridge

Women, Love, and the Law against Divorce

Anya Taylor

EROTIC COLERIDGE
© Anya Taylor, 2005.

All rights reserved. No part of this book may be used or reproduced in any manner whatsoever without written permission except in the case of brief quotations embodied in critical articles or reviews.

First published in 2005 by
PALGRAVE MACMILLAN™
175 Fifth Avenue, New York, N.Y. 10010 and
Houndmills, Basingstoke, Hampshire, England RG21 6XS
Companies and representatives throughout the world.

PALGRAVE MACMILLAN is the global academic imprint of the Palgrave Macmillan division of St. Martin's Press, LLC and of Palgrave Macmillan Ltd. Macmillan® is a registered trademark in the United States, United Kingdom and other countries. Palgrave is a registered trademark in the European Union and other countries.

ISBN 1–4039–6925–6

Library of Congress Cataloging-in-Publication Data

Taylor, Anya.
   Erotic Coleridge: women, love, and the law against divorce / Anya Taylor.
     p. cm.
   Includes bibliographical references and index.
   ISBN 1–4039–6925–6
   1. Coleridge, Samuel Taylor, 1772–1834—Relations with women. 2. Divorce—Law and legislation—Great Britain—History—19th century. 3. Coleridge, Samuel Taylor, 1772–1834—Marriage. 4. Poets, English—19th century—Biography. I. Title.

PR4483.T39 2005
821'.7—dc22
[B]   2005048678

A catalogue record for this book is available from the British Library.

Design by Newgen Imaging Systems (P) Ltd., Chennai, India.

First edition: December 2005

10 9 8 7 6 5 4 3 2 1

Printed in the United States of America.

For Mark Taylor

All thoughts, all passions, all delights,
Whatever stirs this mortal frame,
All are but ministers of Love,
And feed his sacred flame.
    Coleridge, *Love*, lines 1–4

Whatever flames upon the night
Man's own resinous heart has fed.
 W. B. Yeats, *Two Songs from
   a Play*, 2, 15–16

Contents

List of Abbreviations   ix
Acknowledgments   xi

1. Coleridge and Women's Psychology   1
2. First Loves and Flirting Verses   9
3. The Smoking Torch of Hymen   21
4. Blank Faces and Fear of Ruin   43
5. "Christabel" and the Vulnerability of Girls   59
6. Sara Hutchinson: Love and Reading   77
7. Hearkening to the Voices of Women   103
8. Divorce and the Law   125
9. "A Kite's Dinner"   145
10. Communities of Women: Developing as Persons   157

Notes   187
Index   211

List of Abbreviations

BL	S. T. Coleridge, *Biographia Literaria*, ed. James Engell and Walter Jackson Bate, 2 vols (London and Princeton, NJ: Princeton University Press, 1983).
C & S	S. T. Coleridge, *On the Constitution of Church and State*, ed. John Colmer (London and Princeton, NJ: Princeton University Press, 1976).
CL	*Collected Letters of Samuel Taylor Coleridge*, ed. Earl Leslie Griggs, 6 vols (Oxford: Oxford University Press, 1956–1971).
CM	S. T. Coleridge, *Marginalia*, ed. George Whalley and H. J. Jackson, 6 vols (London and Princeton, NJ: Princeton University Press, 1980).
CN	*The Notebooks of Samuel Taylor Coleridge*, ed. Kathleen Coburn et al., 5 vols (New York: Princeton University Press and London: Routledge, 1957).
EOT	*Essays on His Times*, ed. David V. Erdman, 3 vols (London and Princeton, NJ: Princeton University Press, 1978).
Friend	S. T. Coleridge, *The Friend*, ed. Barbara E. Rooke, 2 vols (London and Princeton, NJ: Princeton University Press, 1969).
Lects 1795	*Lectures 1795: On Politics and Religion*, ed. Lewis Patton and Peter Mann (London and Princeton, NJ: Princeton University Press, 1971).
Lects Lit	S. T. Coleridge, *Lectures 1808–1819 on Literature*, ed. R. A. Foakes, 2 vols (London and Princeton, NJ: Princeton University Press, 1987).
OM	S. T. Coleridge, *Opus Maximum*, ed. Thomas McFarland, with Nicholas Halmi (London and Princeton, NJ: Princeton University Press, 2002).

PW	S. T. Coleridge, *Poetical Works*, ed. J. C. C. Mays, 3 vols (London and Princeton, NJ: Princeton University Press, 2001).
RSL	Robert Southey, *New Letters of Robert Southey*, ed. Kenneth Curry, 2 vols (New York and London: Columbia University Press, 1965).
SHL	Sara Hutchinson, *The Letters of Sara Hutchinson, 1800–1835*, ed. Kathleen Coburn (London: Routledge & Keyan Paul, 1954).
SWF	S. T. Coleridge, *Shorter Works and Fragments*, ed. H. J. Jackson and J. R. De J. Jackson, 2 vols (London and Princeton, NJ: Princeton University Press, 1995).
TT	S. T. Coleridge, *Table Talk*, ed. Carl Woodring, 2 vols (London and Princeton, NJ: Princeton University Press, 1990).

Acknowledgments

I am grateful to colleagues who critiqued all or parts of this book, especially Elisabeth G. Gitter, Mark Taylor, Marilyn Gaull, Valerie Allen, and Beth Lau. Early versions of chapters 5, 6, and 8 were originally delivered at the Coleridge Conference in 2000, 2002, and 2004. Part of chapter 7 appeared in Ashley Cross's session on Coleridge and the Gendering of Creative Expression at the Modern Language Association meeting in 2002. Several editors of *The Collected Coleridge*, Jim Mays, John Beer, and Nicholas Halmi, have generously answered queries about details. Librarians at Columbia University, Yale University, John Jay College, the Rare Book Room at the New York Public Library, and the British Library Manuscript Room opened their collections. In my own college Jacob Marini, Basil Wilson, Gerald Lynch, Patricia Licklider, and Robert Crozier have helped in various ways to give me time and support for research and travel to conferences. I thank the PSC-CUNY Research Fund for funding my released time over several years. I thank *SEL Studies in English Literature 1500–1900* for permission to reprint "Christabel and the Phantom Soul" from volume 42, 4 (Autumn 2002) in a different form in chapter 5, and *The Wordsworth Circle* for permission to reprint parts of "Filling the Blanks: Coleridge and the Inscrutable Female Subject" from volume 33, 2 (Spring 2002) scattered through chapters 3 and 6. I thank Andy, Kristin, Jack, Luke, and Daniel Taylor; Nick, Dustin, and Courtney Taylor, and Jenny Pellerito for their companionship. I thank Mark Taylor for his humor and love over a long time.

Chapter 1
Coleridge and Women's Psychology

Coleridge is a philosopher, radical politician, theologian, and poet whose work and nature appear tragic. His philosophical struggles—linking subject and object, unifying the fragments of life, moving from skepticism to trinitarianism—appear to compensate for his loss of poetic power and to express his suffering with drug and alcohol addiction, anxiety, and despair. Overlooked has been a concurrent side of his personality: the man of joy, whose energy radiates outward to all his activities, the precocious and passionate lover, the devoted observer of women. To shift the balance from pitying Coleridge's failure to admiring his resilience, I consider his sensuousness, his amorousness, his desires and yearnings in love, his miraculous discovery of it, his loss ten years later, and ultimately his redefinition of love so that he can endure its absence. Eros impels his excitement about the body, his glee and pleasure, his melancholy, and his developing ethics of reverence for persons. Love is the force behind human imagination, as his stanza from "Love" in the epigraph to this book reveals, and the influence of this stanza, famous in his own time, reverberates in William Butler Yeats's lines, the other epigraph that affirms how love lives within, spreads outward, and generates human creativity.

For understanding love as a source of energy, J. C. C. Mays's long awaited and recently published three volumes of *Poetical Works* provide the key. Many of the newly discovered or newly ascribed poems are love poems of varying degrees of seriousness. In the light of these new love poems, suddenly some of the familiar poems look like love poems, too. Mays cites the discovery of Desmond McCarthy that

> Coleridge [was] one of the master love-poets. Not in the poetry of passion (he was incapable of passion); not in platonic love in the proper sense of that trivialised phrase, namely, the love which transcends its object, and becomes the worship of an ideal beauty; but in affection-love, the kind

which is a longing for the most delicate sympathy that is possible between human beings, accompanied by a recognition of each other's goodness. For this relationship he was born.[1]

McCarthy startles the reader by calling Coleridge "one of the master love-poets." But how can one be a "master love-poet" and also be "incapable of passion"? In what sense would he then be a love-poet, rather than merely a shadowy, dreamy, murmuring sentimental love-poet?

This book presents a case that Coleridge was "a master love-poet" and a passionate one. Through the poems, and then, as the poems irradiate letters, notebooks, and marginalia, it suggests that Coleridge was more attentive to the physical attractions of other people than we had previously thought. The man who admitted that "I could have loved a servant girl had she only and entirely loved me," and that he was made for love, reveals his physicality in his blushes, in his pulsing meter, in his eye for the details of women's appearances and ear for the varieties of their songs. Along with his famous knowledge and fluency came a watchful and engaged love of other persons, that grew into his philosophy of reverencing the individuality of his neighbor. For him, being married to the wrong person was the major disaster of his life, but it did not stop him from loving women.

My study pursues Coleridge's desires through love songs, love letters, love dialogues, love rondos, love outcries, love delusions, love consolations, love advice, and love aspirations—love poems that together achieve the plan he announced "to write a *series* of Love Poems—truly Sapphic, save that they shall have a large Interfusion of moral Sentiment & calm Imagery on Love in all the moods of the mind" (*CN* 1064; Dec. 1801). It shows that Coleridge the dreamer was also a vigorously physical man, a close observer of female beauty and flesh, and that his many early sensualities were diverted in too shallow a channel by a hasty marriage and separated from the spirit in a way that he found disruptive to his wholeness of being. This study will illuminate his interest in female behavior, female distress, and the causes of this distress in constricting social conditions, the vulnerability induced by the position of girls in families, and the laws against women's freedom. It shows him searching, too late, for a full connection with women that would unite body, intellect, and soul. The new love poems and poems about women in Mays's volumes of poetry cast an erotic light on more familiar poems newly seen to be love poems. Indeed, the love poems overflow the confines of this book.

The large array of poems to and about women crowd out the famous manly poems like "Rime of the Ancient Mariner" and "Fears in Solitude," and change the focus and reassess the meaning of well-known poems toward womanly themes. Keats's friend, George Felton Mathew asked after reading "Christabel": "And shall it be considered unlawful for Coleridge to pay his addresses to more than one muse? or for the children of his imagination to be not only sons, but daughters?"[2]

Coleridge's physicality appears in the vigorous metrical throb of his verse, his emotional reactions to words and sights, and in the many corporeal metaphors of his prose that ground his theories in his acute experience of the physical world, even in his precise and often repulsive descriptions of his own bodily functions. With a similar intensity he watches women's faces and breasts, and he hears women's intonations, songs, poems, and snatches of conversation in dialogue. He is alert to their presence. Even in old age, he blushes when he looks at women; he interprets the feelings in their harps, and thinks of music itself as female: "To a spiritual Woman it is music—the intelligible Language of Memory, Hope."[3]

As a young man Coleridge's eagerness was quick, and his haste made real waste of time and spirit. His enlistment in the military under the pseudonym of "Silas Tomkyn Comberbache" was a mistake that could be corrected by pressure from a military family that had already given two of his older brothers to the colonial empire. The mistake that could not be undone, however, was a hasty marriage in the only Protestant country in Europe where divorce was illegal.

Why did Coleridge submit to the will of Robert Southey, the Oxford undergraduate and hiking partner who helped him concoct his plans for a utopian settlement, who insisted that he was obliged to marry Southey's fiancée's older sister? This incomprehensible mistake, based on weakness, the need to please, enthusiasm for a pantisocratic utopia that had crumbled months before he said his inalterable vows at St Mary Redcliffe's church in Bristol, constricted his subsequent life choices. This mistake chartered his personal river of energy in a narrow direction, from which he struggled to emerge. Coleridge's passions are balked by the English laws against divorce, the harsh penalties to adulterous women, the impossibility for the middling classes of severing unhappy connections except by separation, a process in itself shameful for the man and humiliating for the woman.

These laws and the rhetoric surrounding them provide the cultural context of Coleridge's sorrow. To recognize these laws against divorce is to understand in a new way aspects of Coleridge's emotional life.

Because of the impossibility of second marriages, he had to struggle to achieve wholeness in love within the limits of his belief in chastity or at least loyalty, beliefs almost incomprehensible to many twenty-first-century readers. As Graham Davidson has said, we lack the vocabulary to describe this sort of restraint.

Many readers of Coleridge do not recognize that he could not legally divorce his wife. Even well-informed and sensitive readers use phrases like "his refusal to divorce his wife" as if divorce were an option for him.[4] The anachronistic notion that he can't bring himself to leave his wife and commit himself to Sara Hutchinson is one of the most damaging to Coleridge, coming from a culture two hundred years after his where divorce is more frequent than continued marriage. Ignoring this central obstacle would be like ignoring the tragedy at the core of *Anna Karenina*: that she married young to a much older and colder man whom she did not love, fell in love with Vronsky when she already had a son by her husband, and had no way out in a country that forbade divorce. In Tolstoy's novel, we are repeatedly told that the complex laws against divorce and the ruination of wives also become the ruin of Karenin himself along with the two lovers.[5] This same ruin hangs over Coleridge in his triangle, but he averts, though narrowly, Anna's despairing solution.

In addition to this often neglected law, Coleridge's own character traits block his happiness: drug and alcohol addiction, fears, passivity, a submerged desire not to be fulfilled, a self-defeating impulse so powerful that readers sometimes blame him for his failure to find a partner to love.[6] They charge him with not making the best of the marriage he has, with selfishness, with falling in love too late, with finding the right woman at twenty-seven when he should have found her at twenty-two. He is in good company in his discontentedness and yearning. One does not need to limit the field of comparison to the major Romantic writers, Wordsworth aside, whose passions did not produce happiness. No one would mock Jane Austen, John Keats, or Letitia Elizabeth Landon for failing to achieve love. One reason Coleridge is mocked is because he mocks himself, partly wailing, partly ironical about that wailing, and because he analyzes his failures of character in notebooks that he thought would be private and in a few much discussed poems like the verse letter to Sara Hutchinson.

Despite the documented reality of his suffering, Coleridge also describes a large set of connections to women as friends and associates. He seems to know, write to, and talk to more adult women than most men of his class, era, and occupation have time for in the bustle of all-male schools, clubs, newsrooms, and raucous dinners. (P. B. Shelley might be offered as a rival, but his advocacy and practice of free love and multiple childbearing partners makes his associations suspect.) Coleridge's serious desire for unity in love may link him with D. H. Lawrence, as John Beer has suggested, but his respect for women as people and his wit set him apart from this twentieth-century saint of an ultimately impersonal Eros.

As lonely as he may seem in some lights, Coleridge also lived in a flutter of female attention unusual in one innocent of Byronic enticements and bereft of Wordsworthian domesticity. Many women in his own milieu and many American women in the years after his death cared for and about him. When he watched the "meek" baby Mary Wollstonecraft Godwin at "Catacomb-ish" play on William Godwin's floor (*CL* 1, 553), she also listened to him; she would later call him "the most imaginative of modern poets" and, as Beth Lau has demonstrated, would model her novel *Frankenstein* step by step on his narrative poem.[7] He prided himself that the "genius" Mary Robinson (as he called her [*CL* 1, 562 and 575]) wrote him a deathbed farewell thanking him for nourishing her creativity (*CL* 2, 669); Ashley Cross has developed their intricate dialogue of mutual support in her "From Lyrical Ballads to Lyrical Tales: Mary Robinson's Reputation and the Problem of Literary Debt."[8] Late in his life Coleridge, Mrs. Gillman, her sister, and several nubile women talked about love and yearning, travelling together to Ramsgate to keep up the dialogue.[9] Across the Atlantic, as Joel Pace and Chris Koenig-Woodyard have recently found,[10] Rhoda Newcomb in daily letters plied her transcendentalist son Charles with Coleridge's ideas, providing a missing link between the English Coleridge and his New England disciples.

Such affinity with the misunderstood Coleridge persists even now in the face of evidence indicating his essentialist notions of the feminine, belief in his superiority to most women, and mockery of a "feminine" and trivially gallic style.[11] Anne Fadiman admits to belonging to a generation of American women who keep Coleridge's name on their screen savers and wish that they had changed the course of literature by loving him as he should have been loved.[12] Women past and present knew Coleridge from his published or spoken words, ardent words that made them forget his sometimes stout anatomy, his large lips, moist eyes, and flabby carcass of a face (*CL* 1, 259–260), in some lights sensual, in others self-indulgent and weak. His lingering charm to doddering female scholars like myself is mysterious, and lies in his attentiveness to women's bodies and expressions, his physical vitality, his hilarity, his recognition of the difficulties inherent in women's lives, his own difficulties in love and willingness to express them openly, and his humility toward being a person.

Coleridge's physicality with regard to male friendship just shy of homosexual love has been lusciously revealed by Gurion Taussig. Taussig sees in letters to and from the confirmed bachelor Thomas Poole especially, but also to and from Southey and later Washington Allston, gushes of fellow feeling that sound erotic. These gushes sometimes reproduce the mother and child bond, and sometimes use images of swelling, throbbing, and even "tumescence."[13] Coleridge's expressions of passion in the 1820s to Thomas Allsop, twenty years his junior, will be just as passionate, when he writes, for instance, "I think only of it and you, or rather we are one and the same, and I live in you" (Sept. 24, 1821). Taussig finds evidence of Coleridge's denigration of women in a few isolated phrases—indeed very nasty ones—but focused, I suggest, not on women in general but on individual women of the petty, thwarting kind. When he finds that his friend Washington Allston's wife is yet another narrow-minded wife like his own, but worse than all the Fricker women put together including the "nibbling Martha" in being an ignorant American, he is so furious that he likens her to " 'a little Hydatid'—that is, a watery cyst caused by the larval stage of the tapeworm!" (cited Taussig, p. 323), a metaphor akin to his frequent likening of Sir James Mackintosh to a dung beetle. Such a wife sadly dims the glowing memory of the two artist/philosophers, free of their wives, strolling in the Belvedere gardens and discussing Plato, art, and poetry, while generating almost identical portraits (Taussig, pp. 316–319). I suggest that the author of "Kubla Khan"—one of the poems that led Camille Paglia to discover a pagan gush of eroticism in Coleridge[14]—has outbursts of desire directed toward many potential lovers along the spectrum of humanity, for he is tolerant as well as curious about homosexual love, which he tells Southey is a "bagatelle," "a fashionable levity" in many countries less punitive than England (*CN* 1, 1637).

Any study of Coleridge's expressions of love grows out of the biography, criticism, gender studies, and philosophy of personhood, whose circles of inquiry overlap. Among biographers, Richard Holmes pays particular attention to Coleridge's love life and dignifies its seriousness. Early memoirs by Sara Fricker Coleridge, collected by Stephen Potter and sympathetically narrated by Molly Lefebure; by Sara Hutchinson, first edited by George Whalley; and by Sara Coleridge Fille, recently reprinted by Bradford Mudge, record Coleridge's connections to women from their points of view. Kathleen Coburn placed Coleridge's notes on women next to his ethics of reverencing the individual, demonstrating the cohesion of these topics. Among critical writers, J. Robert Barth and Anthony Harding trace Coleridge's ideas about love as a spiritual ladder and a unifying force in creating community, the Christian Coleridge loving Jesus and thus learning to forgive himself his own trespasses, and the civic Coleridge irradiating love through a range of secular associations. John Beer displays how Coleridge can pursue an argument when he writes poems, that "poetic intelligence" can be as cogent as prose. Tim Fulford gives Coleridge's outrage at the trial of Queen Caroline center stage, as also his lament for the death of Princess Charlotte in childbirth, direct and indirect victims of a cruel and hypocritical royal patriarchy. Julie Carlson discovers the importance of female dynamism in Coleridge's plays, and explores in the notebooks later views on affinities with women. Anne Mellor argues that Coleridge like other male Romantics sees the world in a different light from women Romantics, whereas Beth Lau discovers parallel concerns among women writers of the period like Austen and Mary Shelley and male writers including Coleridge. One of the first to pronounce Coleridge a sensual enthusiast, Camille Paglia glimpses his surging passions between the lines of the great supernatural poems. Attending to persons generically, Thomas McFarland and Mary Anne Perkins show Coleridge seeking grounds to establish persons as sacred, based on their access to divine reason. Jean Bethke Elshstain returns these inquiries to Kant's original meditations, where Kant does worry about the difficulties for women and other dependent beings in sustaining personhood. McFarland and David Clark focus on the human impulse of yearning and craving for completion in another human being, an erotic if not necessarily sexual drive. My gratitude to these overlapping studies as well as to many other works that appear in the text and the endnotes does not prevent me from occasionally modifying particular points and larger implications in these writings.[15]

I follow Leigh Hunt's assessment that Coleridge was not "a spirit, all head and wings," but "very corporeal," "very fond of earth," very fond of dinner, sex, and drink. Hunt calls his mind "a mighty intellect put upon a sensual body" but denies that he "was a sensualist in an ill sense." "He was capable of too many innocent pleasures to take any pleasure in the way that a man of the world would take it. The idlest things he did would have had a warrant. But if all the senses, in their time, did not find lodging in that humane plenitude of his, never believe that they did in Thomson or in Boccaccio."[16] Love vibrates through his being, and is not at odds with thinking. Real love generates his theories of love and his pursuit of love in religion. As the two epigraphs to this book assert, love for Coleridge is the source of imagination, art, joy, and civilization. It generates "human plenitude."

Chapter 2
First Loves and Flirting Verses

The young Samuel Taylor Coleridge (STC) overflowed with songs, anacreontics, and sportive glees. Several Devonshire belles, who had previously blushed unseen, have come to the surface in J. C. C. Mays's new texts. These girls inspired his passions and verses in the years before he met his future wife in August, 1794, and for many months thereafter. Jenny Edwards, the daughter of the school nurse or matron, received his early sonnet "Genevieve." Since Coleridge spent "most of the school year 1789–90 in the school sick-ward," he had ample time to hear her singing, and to see her "breast with pity heave" (*PW* #17), and he remembered her in Malta as the victim of a false love letter sent by cruel classmates (*CN* 2619). A would-be dandy at 17, he begs his brother George for "a good pair of breeches" since the one he has is all scribbled on with sonnets and epigrams and "not altogether so well adapted for a female eye." The current pair, with shiny fabric, would incur "the charge of Vanity brought against me for wearing a Looking Glass" (May 26, 1789; *CL* 1, 5). The female eyes noticing his breeches may be those of the Evans sisters, but other girls responded to him in spontaneous meetings. Mays says that Coleridge met Fanny Nesbitt on the coach running between Exeter and Tiverton in July 1793, leading us to imagine the lively flirtations on such a ride, coach rides that he describes with rollicking humor in poems as he crisscrosses the West Country.

Miss F. Nesbitt received provocative poems, including ones that dared to place a cupid hidden in a thorny rosebud "On lovely Nesbitt's breast." Caught in the cleavage, the little cupid at first struggled to escape "and stamp'd his angry feet." When Cupid realized where he was, he "thrill'd with deep delight" and "fix[ed] [his] Empire here" (*PW* #56, l. 12, 16, 19, 24).[1] "Cupid Turn'd Chymist" (#57) develops the flirtation. Bold references to Nesbitt, the Beauty of Tiverton (addressed by her last name like "Prism!" in Oscar Wilde's "Importance of Being Earnest") include images of the "steaming Cauldron" bubbling with sighs and "soft Murmurs of responsive Love." "Kisses" abound, as the poet breathes "on Nesbitt's lovely lips" (#57, ll. 16, 18). Nesbitt's attractions suffuse a night of drinking; Coleridge blushes as he chants "An Extempore":

> Ten thousand Blushes
> Flutter round me drest like little Loves
> And veil my visage with their crimson wings. (#58)

Nesbitt inspires "Absence: A Poem," dating from August of this rapturous summer of 1793; "Nesbitt's charms" rouse the "magic alchemy" and "trembling string" of this long lament:

> No lovelier maid does love's wide empire know,
> No lovelier maid e'er heav'd the bosom's snow.
> A thousand loves her gentle face adorn,
> Fair as the blushes of a summer morn. (#60, ll. 38–42)

The rapture of being near Nesbitt "swells my secret breast!"

> A thousand loves around her forehead fly,
> A thousand loves sit melting in her eye:
> Love lights her smile—in joy's red nectar dips
> The opening rose, and plants it on her lips. (ll. 43–46)

Nesbitt may not be as clever as she is beautiful; signs of simple-mindedness creep in to the praise:

> Tender, serene, and all devoid of guile,
> Soft is her soul, as sleeping infants' smile!
>   She speaks! And baffled art repines to see
>   Th'unweeting triumph of simplicity!
>   She speaks! And hark that lip-bedewing song! (ll. 47–53)

The poet is astonished to hear her speak; he imagines that she embodies the "triumph of simplicity"; the soft infantile smile anticipates the pliable Christabel's. Mays's headnote to "The Absence" shows that at the time of his marriage to Sara Fricker two years later, Coleridge worked to disguise this early passion by backdating the poem and reassigning its kisses.

However brainless, Nesbitt has enticing lips, which allure the poet again in a later poem "To a Painter":

> And her lips a bank of *kisses*,
> Where laughing Love might gather *blisses*,

>Ripen'd by a breath as sweet
>As when flowers with west-winds meet. (#62, ll. 15–18)

The painter can "breathe along the canvass warm / An *Angels Soul* in *Nesbitt's* kindred Form!" (ll. 25–26). These poems are youthful adaptations of Anacreon, plump with conventional raptures about lips and breasts. They reveal a Coleridge more precociously amorous than we have imagined, one year before his meeting with Sara Fricker.

Fanny Nesbitt sometimes yields to Ann Bacon, Elizabeth Boutflower, or the excitingly named Miss Dashwood Bacon. In the presence of Miss Dashwood Bacon Coleridge's muse becomes "A *Child* of *Nature*, as she feels, she sings, / And while her rude hand roves the lyre along, / Th' attuned heart-string vibrates to the Song—" (*PW* #63, ll. 10–12). All four Devonshire belles, and others besides, were among the party of ladies who scrambled up the embankment to creep into the cave of the pixies in the summer months of the year 1793. They follow the "youthful Bard," the author, up to his lair in the earthen embankment, to "flash our faery feet in gamesome prank" (*PW* #64, l. 64). With "MIRTH of the loosely-flowing Hair" (l. 100), like Bacchantes, they surround the excited bard and participate in joyful activities.

In these early years, Coleridge was enchanted by the family of his Christ's Hospital friend Tom Evans. Mrs. Evans and her "lov'd Progeny," especially Mary Evans, inspire poems and letters. They seem to be addressed as much to the mother and sisters as to Mary, to an ebullient garrulous household where STC was welcome and awaited, fit audience for his puns, epigrams, doodlings in math books, and "odelings." One is elegantly directed to Mary: "I cannot forebear filling the remainder of *this* sheet with an Odeling—tho' I know and approve your aversion to *mere prettiness*, and tho my tiny love ode possesses no other property in the world. Let then its *shortness* recommend it to your perusal—by the by, the *only* thing, in which it resembles you: for Wit, Sense, Elegance, or Beauty it has none" (Feb. 13, 1792; *CL* 1, 28). Intimate and charming, he teases her about her stature, while praising her adorable peculiarities.

These few surviving letters to members of the Evans family of mother and girls reveal Coleridge's innocent sense of play, his sensitivity to others, his humor, and his easy flow of original metaphors. Who could resist the invitation to sit in the front row of the theater of his life, to see his "whole heart laid open like any sheep's heart" (p. 21), to hear his "laughing Nonsense" (p. 55), to hear the "twit twat-twat twit" of his violin lessons (p. 50), to giggle about a very heavy "Mrs. Barlow" (p. 51), to hear the story of the skinny mathematics teacher who fell into a bog of chickweed (49), to hear him laugh about wine party-goers falling into gutters (31), tooth problems, his cat, the arduous examinations, flower pots, pint pots, and chamber pots (p. 24). The sense of connectedness is established in direct dialogue: describing some ghosts, he turns to Mary: "at least those material and knock me down Ghosts, the apprehension of which causes you, Mary (valorous girl, that you are!) always to peep under your bed of a night." And in the same letter, directly to her, he teases: "I hate to *buy* sticking plaister, etc. What is the use of a man's knowing you Girls, if he cannot *chouse* you out of such little things, as that? Do not your fingers, Mary, feel an odd kind of titillation to be about my ears for my impudence?" (Feb. 13, 1792; *CL* 1, 26–27). Anticipating an attack for his early form of political incorrectness that assumes women are in charge of bandages, he imagines her very direct reaction: her fingers ready to smack him for demeaning remarks about girls and her hands "black and blue" from boxing his ears (p. 25). References to her bedtime habits, her "ease and energy," her "beautiful little leg" (p. 22) keep alive for us two hundred years later the physicality of his noticing with amusement and tenderness her short body, her activities, and her vivacious physical responses to him.

Swiveling his perspective, he reminds her of his own physicality: "It has been confidently affirmed by most excellent judges (tho' the best may be mistaken) that I have grown very handsome lately.—Pray—that I may have grace not to be vain" (p. 25). He mocks the stiffness of her salutations—" 'Believe me your sincere friend' "—"as dry as a stick, as stiff as a poker, and as cold as a cucumber"—and prefers his own "old God bless you" (*CL* 1, 24). He speaks to Mrs. Evans, Mary, and Anne, as if he is present, warm and alive, holding before his eye and ear their very faces, bodies, and tones of voice. He is a subtle quoter and imitator of the tones of other people's speech (anticipating James Joyce in this regard, as in many others). He quotes Mrs. Evans's accent to her: "Your Advice. La! It will be so charming to walk out in one's own *garding*, and sit and drink Tea in an arbour, and pick pretty nosegays . . . Foh! Oh! 'Twill be very *praty* to make water . . ." (*CL* 1, 24). With similar affection, intimacy, and humor, Keats imagines the newly Americanized speech of his sister-in-law Georgiana, getting a little so–so with her Kentucky neighbors, and shifts into girl talk, which already then included the "feminine intensive": "so" and "La!"

Physicality and presence buzz in Coleridge's descriptions. Women are bright eyefuls and warm armfuls. He notices their heft, dress or undress, and foibles. He tells Mary Evans, "I was in company the other day with a very dashing literary Lady. After my departure a friend of mine asked her her opinion of me. She answered—'The best I can say of him is, that He is a very gentle Bear.' What think you of this character?" (p. 26). The whole scene is physical: he admires the "dashing literary Lady"; he lets his desired friend Mary know that he notices this lady and she him; he records the lady's response to him, and the presence of others, and he asks Mary to muse on his being a gentle bear. Does this imply that he is large, bulky, cuddly, affectionate, and warm? He surely wishes Mary to think of his physical presence, to see him in the round from different perspectives. To Mary's sister Anne he confesses "I have seen no female in the whole course of the day, except an old bedmaker belonging to the College—and I don't count her one, as the bristle of her beard makes me suspect her to be of the masculine gender" (p. 30). The moment several months later when he saw the Evans girls from a window and hid back behind the curtain, heard that they came back looking for him, and was unable to come out and say hello, mortified that Mary had chosen another, is excruciatingly physical; we read it and blush for his awkwardness and shame.

His travel records are further enlivened and eroticized by his noting to Southey how "a most lovely Girl glided along in a Boat—there were at least 30 naked men bathing—she seemed mighty unconcerned—and they addressing her with not the most courtly gallantry, she snatched the Task of Repartee from her Brother who was in the Boat with her, and abused them with great perseverance & elocution. I stared—for she was elegantly dressed—and not a Prostitute" (Jul. 6, 1794; *CL* 1, 83), letting us know that he can tell one from another. He admires her ease amid naked men and her jaunty, bold repartee. To Henry Martin two weeks later (Jul. 26) he describes more women easy with naked men in rivers and pools: these are themselves naked and swimming among naked men: "a number of fine Women bathing promiscuously with men and boys—perfectly naked!" Marveling at their freedom from prudishness, he supposes that "the citadels of their Chastity are so impregnably strong, that they need not the ornamental Outworks of Modesty" (Jul. 22, 1794; *CL* 1, 83 and 93). The glimpses of naked British ladies, one elegantly dressed gliding among 30 naked men who are bantering with her, and the others swimming happily naked among equally naked men gives us an enchanting picture of British summer merriment and of Coleridge enjoying these views, appreciating the women—"most lovely Girl" "fine Women"—, and imagining a society where men and women were naked, free, and non-predatory.

Admiration for sensuous women continues in Germany five years later when he watches women waltzing. His description, originally sent in letters home to his wife, appears in purloined pages in *The Amulet* of 1828 (*SWF* 2, 1478–1479). In this voluptuous round and round, he watches a strong easy German woman "laying her arm, with confident affection, on the man's shoulder, or (among the rustics) around his neck"; he describes "a very fine tall girl, of two or three and twenty, in the full bloom and growth of limb and feature," "pretty lasses, not so tall as the former, [who] danced uncommonly light and airy," and a seventeen-year-old "with a full-blown rose in the white ribbon that went round her head, and confined her reddish-brown hair." Even ragged boys and girls waltz, and a three-year-old girl and a baby "whirl round and round, hugging and kissing each other, as if the music had made them mad" (*SWF* 2, 1478–1479).[2] Since the days of Caesar, German women had lived on equal terms with men, in admirable companionate marriages; Coleridge had praised this equality as early as *The Watchman* (1796).[3] As late as 1818 in a lecture on medieval poetry, he borrows from Schlegel praise of German womanhood.[4] Perhaps he finds that women who feel free and confident like the English women swimming or boating or the German women waltzing are more pleasing to watch than constricted and conforming women.

Coleridge's pleasure in women's language, forms, and oddities, his awareness of their physicality whether short, fat, or hirsute, his eagerness to address them and hear their retorts, even to be boxed on his ears when he rouses them to an early form of feminist indignation, are salient qualities of his youth.

Though most readers do not imagine it, Coleridge also participates in a chortling manliness that we usually associate with the letters and satires of Byron.[5] As quick as he was to notice that the elegantly dressed woman watching the naked men was not a prostitute, so is he amused by how long it takes him to scan in his memory the women of his past. For instance, he writes Humphrey Davy about how he is scouring his brain to recollect a woman named either "Hayes" or "Taylor":

> I went first thro' all the *virtuous* Women, I had ever known, as far as my Memory would assist—but it was all Blank. Then (& verily I, a Husband & a Father, & for the last seven years of my Life a very Christian Liver, felt oddly while I did it) then, I say, I went as far as memory served, through all the loose women I had known, from my 19th to my 22nd year, that being the period that comprizes my Unchastities; but as names are not the most recollectible of our Ideas, & the name of a loose Woman not that one of her adjuncts, to which you pay the most attention, I could here recollect no name at all—no, nor even a face nor feature. I remembered my vices, & the times thereof, but not their objects. (May 20, 1801; *CL* 2, 734)

The loose women have neither names nor faces but only bodies used as the "objects" of his pleasures; even to think of them now makes him feel disloyal to his family. He describes this manly exploitation of faceless female bodies—Ladies of Lubricity, as he calls them in Malta (*CN* 2621) in retrospect. But he can also shift around and see this stream of faceless and nameless women from their points of view and imagine sympathetically how their predicaments arose. Two poems, which we examine in chapter 4, show his concern for the fragility of young women's reputations, especially in the theatrical world. Once they fall prey to the many skulking predators lying in wait, their names will no longer be "recollectible." Only "Sal Hall," a girl about town in his college years, was vivid enough to retain her name.

His ogling never seems predatory. He watches with sympathy and interest, and in the case of the many poor girls abandoned to beg because of warfare and economic disaster, he expresses his outrage at their plights. Both Coleridge and Southey write in dismay about the exploitation of girls. Southey writes about a young woman who strangles her baby.[6] Coleridge laments the impoverished "little Girl with a half-famished sickly Baby in her arms." He quotes her voice begging at the window of an inn, in a description bristling with disgust at the gap between classes, and imitates ironically the "lingering Remains of Aristocracy" in the voice of Joseph Hucks, his traveling companion: "It is wrong, Southey! For a little Girl with a half-famished sickly Baby in her arms to put her head in at the window of an Inn—'Pray give me a bit of Bread and Meat'! from a Party dining on Lamb, Green Pease, & Sallad—Why?? Because it is *impertinent & obtrusive*!—I am a Gentleman!—and wherefore should the clamorous Voice of Woe *intrude* upon mine Ear!?" (*CL* 1, 83). The intonations of careless wealth sound harshly against the little girl's humble plea. He gives us the sounds of the voices, and needs no further preaching. Rich women and poor women form distinctly different species of human beings. Years later (March 24, 1801) he writes to Poole, "Consider for a moment the different Feelings with which a poor woman in a cottage gives a piece of Bread & a cup of warm Tea to another poor Woman traveling with a Babe at her back, & the Feelings with which a Lady lets two pence drop from her Carriage Window, out of the envelope of perfumed Paper by which her Pocket is defended from the Pollution of Copper" (*CL* 2, 711). With sharply observed physical detail, especially the perfumed paper shielding the dainty fingernails from the touch of filthy lucre, Coleridge shows in female behavior the class division of his country—"one rioting & wallowing in the wantonness of wealth, the other struggling for the necessarys of Life."

Coleridge's vivacious ability to imagine the situations of other people transforms his new friend Robert Southey, future poet laureate, dogged historian of the Iberian peninsula, and one of the radical writers briefly planning the utopia in Pennsylvania. Before the advent of Coleridge, Southey writes lugubrious and repetitive cadences in his early letters to Grosvenor Charles Bedford, harping on money, ways to succeed, his suffering, the cruelty of his relatives (his father's brother rejecting his request for help, his aunt insulting the low class of his beloved and ejecting him from her home), the cruelty of the powers-that-be (incarcerating his father for debt and letting him die of a broken heart), his terrible bad luck, his rage and impatience with Oxford. No humor leavens this pain. After meeting Coleridge, however, a miraculous transformation of his style occurs. The sentences shorten and zip along; bent for action, the periods are less morose; some tinge of emotion for Coleridge especially, and a little for Edith, enters. In extolling the plans for emigration to America, he is excited about being with Coleridge, and the two men are taking along our "beautiful females" for breeding purposes in the new world. The individual women figure very slightly in his exultation, for they sound much more like a herd of cows that will multiply in the "easy" climates along the American river. Coleridge's vitality is infectious.

Even when ostensibly engaged to Sara Fricker, Coleridge continues to write verses to attractive girls. In September 1794, Coleridge joined with his Christ's Hospital friend Francis Wrangham in a poetic courtship of the Brunton sisters, Ann and Eliza, singers and actresses from Bristol. In a tangle of intertextual amusement, Coleridge translated Wrangham's *hendecasyllabi* to Elizabeth (the more famous of the theatrical sisters), calling it "your exquisite Brutoniad"; to his translation he adds his own ending in praise of Ann ("A Sister Form of mirthful Eye"), announcing proudly: "I have my Brynton too!" (*PW* #79 and #80, l. 12). Their attentions to the Bruntons were reciprocated: Mr. and Mrs. Brunton importuned the young poet to join them for dinner and often for tea; as Coleridge writes Southey, "The young Lady and indeed the whole Family have taken it into their heads to be very much attached to me. . . . The Father (who is the manager & Proprietor of the Theatre) inclosed in a very polite note a free Ticket for the Season—The young Lady is said to be the most literary of the beautiful, and the most beautiful of the literatae" (Sept. 26, 1794; *CL* 1, 109). Bruntons were the rage in several letters and poems, making Coleridge's "Heart forget it's duties & it's cares" (Oct. 9, 1794; *CL* 1, 110), even as Coleridge promised Robert Southey that he was just about to write Sara Fricker, had done so, or would soon. Once he began praising Ann Brunton he could only be tugged away by "An Host of Elephants." The unspoken or implied commitment to Sara Fricker that Southey insisted upon had not shuttered Coleridge's roaming eye; he was still the twenty-one-year-old looking for whatever caught his male gaze.[7]

In a poem associated with his love for Mary Evans but worked on later in 1798, "Lewti; or The Circassian Love-Chant" (poem #172), Coleridge explores the coming and going of early passion, the contradictory insights into the mystery of the loved one—treacherous, kind, never kind, and perhaps not unkind—in the oscillations of the refrains, and a voyeurism verging on the ridiculous. Two slowly moving swans remind the poet of Lewti's breasts, hidden away in a leafy labyrinth at night. He wishes so intently to see her breasts that he is willing to die for this sight:

> VOICE of the Night! Had I the power
> That leafy labyrinth to thread,
> And creep, like thee, with soundless tread,
> I then might view her bosom white
> Heaving lovely to my sight,
> As these two swans together heave
> On the gently swelling wave.
>
> . . . .
>
> I'd die indeed, if I might see
> Her bosom heave, and heave for me!
> Soothe, gentle image! Soothe my mind!
> Tomorrow Lewti may be kind. (*PW* #461; ll. 69–75; 80–84)

The obsessive circling of these desires will later merge with his feelings for his later love, Sara Hutchinson. The poem ends its troubling fluctuations with a vision of the naked breasts hidden among leaves, the furtive poet mad to see, and a reciprocal vision in Lewti's sleeping brain of the poet lying dead from the accomplishment of his wish.

His emotional upheavals reach frenzy just after his twenty-second birthday. He wails to Southey as he copies out the unsigned letter from Mary Evans that urges him to abandon the pantisocracy project and brims with love for him. His love for Mary Evans revives when he learns that he is losing her to a richer man (and one moreover connected to the West Indian "trade," a slaver, that is, representing the corruption of his loved one's early moral values). He frequently attends the theater with Miss Brunton, "whose Exquisite Beauty and uncommon Accomplishments might have cured one passion by another" (Oct. 21, 1794; *CL* 1, 113). He cannot bring himself to obey Southey's orders to write warmly to

Sara Fricker. He is tormented by a turmoil of desires and panicked indecision. What Mary Evans writes reveals the intellectual and ethical agreement that Mary and he had developed and that Coleridge would look for in future relationships, and more specifically the understanding of the meaning of Mary Wollstonecraft's *Vindication*: that women must rise up from vanity and trivia and become persons with principles that they act on. Evans writes that she, who "thought in all things alike" with Coleridge, finds "Women in general vain—all of the same Trifle: and therefore little and envious—and (I am afraid) without sincerity—: and of the other sex those, who are offered and held up to my esteem, are very prudent and very worldly" (*CL* 1, 113).

Their mutual suspicion of trifling and small-minded women and prudential and worldly men indicates that they developed their values by talking and reading together: "She was VERY lovely, Southey! We formed each other's minds—our ideas were blended—Heaven bless her! I cannot forget her" (Nov. 3, 1794; *CL* 1, 123). Begging her to tell him if she is indeed engaged to Fryer Todd, smothering his passions since he has no "establishment" to offer her, thinking she liked him only as a brother, he praises her:

> Were you not possessed of a Mind and of a Heart above the usual Lot of Women I should not have written you sentiments, that would be unintelligible to three fourths of your Sex. But our Feelings are congenial, though [our] attachment is doomed not to be reciprocal. (early Nov. 1794; *CL* 1, 131; letter 71)

Acknowledging his loss of her (Dec. 24, 1794), he tells her and Southey (letters 76 and 77) that she can never be torn from the sanctuary of his heart. To Southey he cries out, "Southey! My ideal Standard of Female Excellence rises not above that Woman. But all Things work together for Good. Had I been united to her, the Excess of my Affection would have effeminated my Intellect. I should have fed on her Looks as she entered into the Room—I should have gazed on her Footsteps when she went out from me" (*CL* 1, 145).

These sensuous phrases—his eye feeding on her, his excess of desire effeminating his mind, buckling his knees, making him weak and distracted—indicate a physical and spiritual connection that cannot be replaced by suddenly marrying another woman, who will become "the Instrument of low Desire." To minimize this early love as a school boy crush or an idealized illusion fails to take account of its multiplicity (intimate in humor, thought, physical attraction, and feeling) and its depth.

Readers who think that Coleridge had contempt for women often refer to his comments in Shakespeare lectures (to a crowd that included many women) that all men wish to marry women without character and that Ophelia and Desdemona would be ideal wives.[8] Since one committed suicide and the other allowed herself to be falsely accused and murdered, surely STC is joking, as he often did in the heightened atmosphere of applause and uproar when his lectures were fashionable. But, before she betrays Hamlet to her father's plot, Ophelia is a model girlfriend. Indeed, in her last letter (Oct. 21, 1794) begging Coleridge not to go to America, Mary Evans speaks with the voice of Ophelia, " 'O what a noble mind is here *o'erthrown*. Blasted with Exstacy'!" (*CL* 1, 112). Neither insane nor suicidal, this Romantic Ophelia knows her old friend well enough to call him to his senses and to remind him of his affinities with the noble Hamlet. STC picks up this quick allusion based on their adolescent discussions about Shakespeare's tragedy, and cries out "I loved her, Southey! Almost to madness," as if he were Hamlet leaping into Ophelia's grave knowing that all is lost. The parallel between Ophelia and Hamlet and Mary Evans and Coleridge is not in the suicide, but in the intense early closeness, the sallies of wit and literary allusion, and his being too unreliable (Hamlet a prince, Coleridge a pauper) for her to set her hopes on marrying him.

Beginning with Mary Evans, his favorite women are readers and talkers, and he relishes being able to tell them what their often lax schooling has omitted, trying to do so in engaging ways without pomposity. He believes in education for girls, and lectures about it, though he adds finishing school touches that would be unpopular in our day, such as how to greet a husband cheerfully, how "to know the art of blessing in marriage," how "to distinguish the real charities of life from the selfishnesses disguised under them," and how to care for children.[9]

We see later how persistent were the values that Mary Evans and Coleridge shared. Ironically, having both failed to act on these values in choosing a life partner, they shared the same marital fate. Stephen Potter says of their meeting in midlife that Mary Evans was "now as tragically married, and fixed in as complete a misalliance as himself" (xxxi).

These are just the few letters to and about girls that escaped the burning of every scrap from bundles of letters that threatened his wife's respectability. These and the poems that Mays has discovered reveal the vivacious and eager-eyed man that he was on the verge of becoming. When he married on Oct. 4, 1795, these many songs and poems were hidden away, the girls' names were changed to "Sara," except those transcribed in common place books in provincial homes, evidence—lost until now—of his youthful ardor.

Coleridge realizes late in life that he had learned to hide from his powerful emotions and that their suppressed power deflected its glow onto other topics. He tells his beloved friend Thomas Allsop how his eloquence became a disguise of passion rather than an expression of it:

> My eloquence was most commonly excited by the desire of running away and hiding myself from my personal and inward feelings, *and not for the expression of them*, while doubtless this very effort of feeling gave a passion and glow to my thoughts and language on subjects of a general nature, that they otherwise would not have had. I fled in a Circle, still overtaken by the Feelings, from which I was ever more fleeing, with my back turned toward them.[10]

He realizes that his own language glows because of the banked up feelings within. He knows that he is a man of desire, passion, and enthusiasm, "Happily made, but most unhappily thwarted" (*PW* #332). Allsop tells his children in gathering his memories of Coleridge for them, that

> Of all the men, ordinary or extraordinary, I have ever known, Coleridge was the one in whom the *child-like*, the almost infantile, love and joyance, giving birth to or rather intermingled with perfect sympathy and identity of feeling, most predominated. His mind was at once the most masculine, feminine, and yet *child-like* (and, in that sense, the most innocent) which it is possible to imagine. (Allsop 2, 175–176 [1824])

Allsop captures an image of Coleridge's multiplicity and warmth when he was lovingly engaged. We recall that Leigh Hunt describes his "humane plenitude." Defending him against cruel detractors, praising his "sweetness, gratitude, and innocence," citing from his many writings (to prove that he had not wasted his time and talent), and steering clear of any reference to his tangled erotic life, James Gillman writes: "In his early life he was remarkably joyous; nature had blessed him with a buoyancy of spirits, and even when suffering, he deceived the partial observer." Like a comic actor, his gaiety covered a melancholic heart, but he "retained even to his latest hours" "the same childlike simplicity which he had from a boy."[11] "Childlike" "joyance" and "buoyancy" characterize the man whom both Allsop and Gillman loved.

Chapter 3
The Smoking Torch of Hymen

> The Torch of Love may be blown out wholly; but not that of Hymen. Whom the flame, and its cheering Light and genial Warmth no longer bless, him the Smoke stifles—for the Spark is inextinguishable save by Death.
>
> *CN* 4110

This fertile playfulness of life and verse—joyance, buoyancy, pleasure—might have gone on forever. Who does not lament the series of steps—day by day, hour by hour—that led to the caging of this free and gallant spirit? Who does not feel the encroachment of Robert Southey's small, hard, prudential will as it bore down on Coleridge, forcing him to take his own leavings and breaking his spirit?

Coleridge's sudden marriage to the most outspoken and opinionated of the five poor fatherless Fricker girls from Bristol was an error in judgment that will always remain a mystery. He hardly knew her; poems written before marriage show that he didn't like her much and that she did not welcome him warmly. She had her heart set on marrying her childhood friend Robert Southey, who had introduced her to Coleridge, his petulant hiking companion from Cambridge. Southey wrote Grosvenor Bedford that he and the Fricker girls were raised together. Mark Storey shows that Robert Southey and Sara Fricker played as children. Molly Lefebure describes Southey and Sara playing in spite of his snobbish aunt, and corresponding intimately. It is to Sara Fricker that Southey writes when his aunt disowns him, not to her sister Edith, his betrothed, for Sara is closer to him and readier to understand him (Oct. 18 and 25, 1794; *RSL* 1, 84–85 and note 2). His letters to Sara Fricker (Oct. 18 and 25, 1794) describe Edith as a lily of the valley, lovely in humility (p. 84), too humble to endure, as her later depression, chronic sickness, silence, and hypochondria will attest. "Edith is not well" and "Edith is better" are frequent refrains at the endings of his letters early and late. Sara, he believes, is made of stronger stuff and can respond to him. However, quite suddenly, Southey decided to marry Sara's younger, more passive and pliable sister Edith, stunning Sara Fricker. Her dismay can be seen twenty years later in her daughter's memoirs: "R. S. . . . corresponded with mama before his marriage . . . He had a friendship with mama first."[1]

By persistent pressure Southey made Coleridge feel that he was obligated to Sara Fricker after a few conversations and for breeding purposes on the Susquehanna, but he was passing on his own obligations and his own guilt to the bewildered and reluctant Coleridge. Richard Holmes suspects that "there may well have been some element of soothing his own guilty conscience in the brotherly rigour with which he soon pressed her suit with Coleridge."[2] Thus, as Coleridge takes Sara on the rebound from Mary Evans and reluctantly gives up the pleasures of multiple flirtations, so Sara takes Sam on the rebound from the far more compatible Southey. That Southey and Sara Fricker developed a sprightly and joking relationship in Coleridge's long years of absence after 1804 (when Sara and Southey were in their early thirties) is not surprising in that they had been dear to each other since childhood.

The interlocking marriages were ideological rather than personal. Three couples connected by three Fricker sisters formed the core of the pantisocracy scheme to build a communal family group on the banks of the Susquehanna. This ideal community was to be built on the principle of "aspheterism," which Coleridge defines as the "abolition of property." Although the pantisocrats planned to share money and work, they seem not to have intended to share their wives. Newly wed and still excited, Coleridge reviles those radicals who follow William Godwin's *Political Justice* in deeming "filial affection folly, gratitude a crime, marriage injustice, and the promiscuous intercourse of the sexes right and wise."[3] Coleridge argues with John Thelwall about marriage and sexual promiscuity. He asks

> one question only—Why should you not have intercourse with *the Wife* of your friend?—From the principles in your *heart*—Verily, Thelwall! I believe you—on your *heart* I should rest for my safety! But why not, I repeat, seduce my Wife from me?—Because it would be *criminal*? What more do we mean by *Marriage* than that state in which it would be criminal to tempt to, or permit, an act of inconstancy? But if criminal *at one moment* criminal always: in other words, *Marriage is indissoluble*. (*CL* 1, 213; letter 127)

Marriage must be based on principles in the heart not on magical priestly ceremonies or claims of property. In confining "the appetites to one object," marriage should become affectionate. In these early months of his marriage he imagines that the value of marriage can be immediately visible by comparing the face of a married man with the face of a "whoremonger" (p. 214). In this period of enthusiasm for married comfort, Coleridge does not advocate the easier divorces, more fluid families, free love, and shared "property" that have been the cornerstones of many utopian communities. Later letters from Southey and Rickman suggest that Coleridge did advocate easier divorces, but at this time he believes that marriage is "indissoluble" not by virtue of law or religious vows but by virtue of the constancy of the heart. Sadly, when the heart turns elsewhere, or the one object of love ceases to feel sympathetic, this "indissoluble" union of hearts dissolves.

Many of Coleridge's biographers treat his hasty marriage as unimportant, humorous, imagined, exaggerated. Molly Lefebure believes that he and Sara were ecstatically in love, and their marital happiness was ruined only by his increasing dependence on opium. It is indeed comical to think of Southey charging down to London, looking for Coleridge in the Salutation and the Cat pub, not finding him, and finally sniffing him out and dragging him back to Bristol to fulfill what Southey thought were Coleridge's duties to Sara Fricker but were in fact Southey's own duties. Humorous or not, this pressure and his submission to it were nearly the death of Coleridge's soul, and he thinks of the event in terms of spiritual loss, even in terms of his own personal "Fall of Man": "In an evil hour for me did I first pay attention to Mrs. Coleridge" (Feb. 17, 1803; *CL* 2, 929). We will see that this union mars the rest of his life.

Early poems reveal that Coleridge felt a negative emotional charge between them before their marriage and even in its early and often sexually vigorous months. In registering the presence of Sara Fricker, Coleridge's verse harps on her disapproval. In "The Kiss," the first poem written directly for her and not adapted from poems to her predecessors, he already notes her recalcitrance:

> One kiss, dear Maid! I said and sigh'd—
> Your scorn the little boon denied.
> Ah why refuse the blameless bliss?
> Can danger lurk within a kiss? (*PW* #76, ll. 1–4)

What a falling off from the ever kissable Nesbitt! The last stanza of this poem introduces the complex negative aura of his future bride:

> In tender accents, faint and low,
> Well-pleas'd I hear the whisper'd "No!"

> The whisper'd "No"-how little meant!
> Sweet Falsehood, that endears Consent!
> For on those lovely lips the while
> Dawns the soft relenting smile,
> And tempts with feign'd dissuasion coy
> The gentle violence of Joy. (ll. 21–28)

Hoping that "no" does not mean "no," the suitor presses on against coyness and "feigned dissuasion" to accomplish the "gentle violence" of kissing. Does he force these kisses upon her? "The whisper'd 'No!' " is uttered twice in the first poem written in August 1794 exclusively for the woman who in fourteen months will be his wife, even as other women continue to receive happier homages. This repeated "No," this refusal to kiss, forecasts a lifetime of struggle against his wife's negations, which he will call her "dyspathy," and which will grow over the years into the "constant dread in my mind respecting Mrs Coleridge's Temper" (*CN* 2398).

In July 1795, engaged to Sara, still capable of wriggling out of his commitment if he dared, Coleridge examines that frown. "Lines in the Manner of Spenser" (*PW* #111) mythologizes a quarrel that arose when Coleridge overslept an early morning meeting with her. He seeks peace by an imagined exotic riverbank:

> For o! I wish my SARA's frowns to flee,
> And fain to her some soothing song would write,
> Lest she resent my rude discourtesy,
> Who vow'd to meet her ere the morning light,
> But broke my plighted word-ah! False and recreant Wight! (ll. 5–9)

Sara's frowns seem ineradicably fixed, even before their marriage. The guilt for missing the appointment is intense and proportionate to the girl's anger. His excuses follow: he could not sleep for thinking about her; LOVE, in malicious mood, believed that Coleridge had received too many smiles recently, and determined that he should "ken her alter'd mien!" (l. 23); working him "woe," the laughing Elfin sends a blissful dream of Sara smiling:

> My SARA came, with gentlest Look divine;
> Bright shone her Eye, yet tender was its beam:
> I felt the pressure of her Lip to mine!
> Whisp'ring we went, and Love was all our theme— (ll. 37–40)

So enchanted was he by the joys of his dream vision of Sara

> That I the living Image of my Dream
> Fondly forgot. Too late I woke, and sigh'd—
> "O! How shall I behold my Love at even-tide!" (ll. 43–45)

His dream imagining that Sara might smile at him prevents him from meeting the real Sara. Now Sara—affronted, impatient at these excuses—is really frowning, and he dreads meeting her later in the evening. Delusion and reality circle in a sequence of missed cues, misconceptions, and resentments. The frowning face is more and more clenched, reinforced by Coleridge's fear of that frown, reluctance to encounter it, and repeated postures of apology.

Coleridge continues to watch Sara Fricker's face with trepidation in "The Eolian Harp" (*PW* #115). Here his opening observation of her "pensive" face and the concluding "reproof" by her "more serious eye" (l. 49) are again separated by a dreaming tranquillity where he imagines the two of them as one—only in his dreams. In "The Eolian Harp" the frowning Sara invades the arena of his philosophy, reining in his speculations and bidding him to "walk humbly with my God" (l. 52). It is hard to imagine the marital dynamics in which one of the great thinkers of the Romantic era, who won the Craven prize for Greek odes at Cambridge University and thought deeply already as a boy about Plato, Plotinus, and Ficino, is commanded by an uneducated young woman to reject his Platonic visions as "shapings of the unregenerate mind." Equally surprising is his willingness to revise his thoughts and to record and obey her rebuke.

Watching her face for disapproval and dispraise as well as for tears, gloom, and the "dark disliking eye" ("Ode to Sara, Written at Shurton Bars," *PW* #116) is the subject of much of his verse addressed to his wife. The references to her suggest his alert attention to her "boding fears" (l. 9), her sullen loneliness, the "trifles" that weigh on her, and the ominous recognition of her "Void within" (l. 18). He still hopes that in the storm "To me your arms you'll stretch" (l. 74), that she will accept "my kisses chaste and meek" (l. 80), and that her sighs and tears might eventually respond to him—"shall make your rising bosom feel / The answ'ring swell of mine!" (ll. 82–84). The sense of a gap between them that he yearns to cross gives this ode to Sara a melancholy wistfulness:

> How oft, my Love! With shapings sweet
> I paint the moment, we shall meet!

> With eager speed I dart—
> I seize you in the vacant air,
> And fancy, with a Husband's care
> I press you to my heart! (ll. 85–90)

He imagines meeting her, he darts forward, he grasps at emptiness, and his husbandly embrace is only in his fancy. He seems to have forgotten the Fool's words when King Lear dreads his daughter's disapproval: "Thou wast a pretty fellow when thou hadst no need to care for her frowning" (*King Lear* 1, 4, 182–183).

What does this frown mean on the face of a person one must live with? A frown is not a voice, or explanation, or argued disagreement. It is a generalized mask of disapproval—an expression of what Coleridge calls the "dyspathy" of women, where even a kiss is a no, even if the no is unintentional or automatic. The frown marks a habit of judging adversely, of disgruntlement. A face that silently registers fixed discontent cannot encourage dialogue. It does not await or initiate communication or seem ready to "listen." It would not stimulate sallies of humor, feeling, or thought. It would repel easy spontaneous outbursts.

The human face is at the center of the philosopher Emmanuel Levinas's hope for the holiness of being. Levinas speaks of our reaction of wonder at seeing its uniqueness, based no doubt on the image of the infant gazing with love at the unique, irreplaceable face of the mother feeding him. But Levinas does not specify the expression on this face, he does not venture to explore the countless unpleasant and downright unholy looks possible when the face is animated by inner emotions like anger, pettiness, cruelty, or indifference. An unpleasant face evokes no sense of sanctity at all and, far from saving the person from harm, might in fact arouse an urge to harm. In addition, a face can assume false expressions, smiles that disguise evil intentions or indifference, the "feign'd dissuasion coy" of his wife's negation. Thus, when Coleridge writes poems to his wife he confronts even before marriage an alienated face, barely masking disapproval.

Was there any aspect of the man she married that Sara Fricker Coleridge actively liked and approved? Stephen Potter, editing her letters, reads in her words "the importance of this marriage failure in the study of Coleridge,"[4] this meeting with a void of personal response, a frown of discontentedness. We read her letters in search of the feelings that lie behind the frown and in search of the sorrow that we assume she must also have suffered. In his introduction Potter points to Southey's overbearing imposition of duty and thence to Coleridge's developing bitterness at performing such an important personal act at the behest of another. Potter sees "the friendly affectionate references to his wife" stopping in February 1797 (xvi). He sees that the death of baby Berkeley and Coleridge's refusal to return from Germany were "the end of an era for Mrs. Coleridge" (xix). Her letters to Thomas Poole begin by lamenting this beautiful baby's death in 1799, and then for the decades between 1807 and 1834 concentrate on asking Poole for money, wondering where her husband is and when he might be coming back, gossiping enviously about rich people, complaining about her troubles, praising Robert Southey, bragging about her children, and jeering at her husband's work.

Her favorite words are "respectable" and "prudent." About her husband she writes, "I am shocked at the description he gives of the jovial parties, their [German] manners and their Mirth must be excessively disgusting" (March, 1799); with glee she reports, "The Lyrical Ballads are not liked at all by any" (April 2, 1799; p. 5). Dorothy Wordsworth begs Catherine Clarkson "to report something of the fine things said of him by the fine folks, for she would fain persuade us he is a perfect clown, at least in his *appearance*" (Jun. 27, 1806; L, *MY*, 2, p. 51). In April 1816 in a letter exalting Southey's greatness in enduring the death of his son Herbert she reports the rejection of Coleridge's play and shows surprise at his "fit of despondency" (p. 48). "You will also be sorry for another thing respecting him—Oh! When will he ever give his friends anything but Pain? He has been so unwise as to publish his fragments of 'Christabel' & 'Koula Khan' [*sic*] Murray is the publisher & the price is 4s 6d—we were all sadly vexed when we read the advertizement of these things" (p. 48). As Potter quips, she is "the only critic who has preferred 'The Lay of the Laureate' to 'Kubla Khan' " (xxvii). While she knows the book's price, she doesn't bother to know the spelling of her husband's famous poem. Only once does she pay close attention to a poem of her husband's, that is, "A Wanderer's Farewell" addressed to the two sisters Mrs. Mary Morgan and Miss Charlotte Brent. Sara notes that the poem "abounds with gratitude to these young Ladies, and bitter complaints and woful murmurings at his own unhappy fate!" (Potter, p. 10). His fit of despondency and his woe are risible to her.

At Coleridge's death she does write her final letter to Poole on black-bordered paper. But the letter describes for three pages Southey's nobility in bringing his wife, her sister, Edith to her madhouse (pp. 180–182). She then mentions a visit to the Gillmans and describes their sadness at Coleridge's death in the third person with an incredulous and almost sarcastic tone:

> [L]ast week I paid a short visit to the Gillmans, they are both in indifferent health and bad spirits: they find it difficult to reconcile themselves to their loss: nineteen years, they say, in the daily habit of seeing & conversing with such a being as he whom they deplore cannot be easily forgotten. They have erected a Tablet in Highgate Church expressive of their love & reverence for the departed. (p. 182)

She does not use Coleridge's name, she distances herself entirely from the Gillmans's grief "for the departed," and seems to find it unbelievable that they would feel for "such a being as he whom they deplore" or even would "say" that they do, as if their emotions were fraudulent. The black border proclaims that she is now a respectable widow; the contents of the letter refer to her husband only through the indirect words of people who cared for him.

Two revolutionary writers whose works Coleridge knew by heart, John Milton and William Godwin, had defiantly warned against incompatibility in marriage as a danger to personal development. Milton's warning participates in his advocacy of free and knowing choice, in his study of biblical precedent, and in his own sorrow in marriage. Godwin's warning places the dangers of marriage in a materialist context, arising from the empiricism of the century following Milton.

Coleridge tells Daniel Stuart that "I cleave with head, heart and body" to Milton's partisan ideas, specifically in the "*Morals*" of "the Treatise in favor of Divorce."[5] In that powerful tract of 1643 Milton argues that adultery should not be the only grounds for divorce but that mental and spiritual incompatibility is equally dangerous to the development of a person's soul. Influencing Coleridge's very phrases, Milton writes of the tyranny of "household unhappiness", of the "drooping and disconsolate houshold captivity without refuge or redemption," of "antipathy . . . wearisomeness and despaire," and of "loneliness," which expressly countermands God's decision that Adam should not be alone, the original reason for providing Adam with a mate.[6] Milton uses the word "dejection" to describe the emotional paralysis that breaks down the spirit of an unhappily married man, and sometimes prompts him to "piece up his lost contentment by visiting the stews or stepping to his neighbours bed" (p. 247). He says that the law "provides all for the right of the body in marriage, but not for the wrongs and greevances of the mind," a bias that seems to view human beings as "brute beasts" whose sole interest is "the satisfaction of an irrational heat" (pp. 248–249). He wonders how chaste men are supposed to judge the characters of the modest virgins they meet, when sometimes the veil of modesty covers mere dullness; he finds it unjust that promiscuous men should be able to test the characters of their potential wives and freely reject them when warranted. Once married, the innocent husband discovers that "to all the more estimable and superior purposes of matrimony [his wife's mind is] uselesse and almost liveles" (p. 250), and he learns to dread the wasteland that will be the rest of his life. Similar complaints about the mental and spiritual loneliness in unhappy marriages recur in Coleridge's laments, for he learned from Milton "that mariage is a human society, and that all human society must proceed from the mind rather then the body, els it would be a kind of animal or beastish meeting" (p. 275).

When Coleridge comes in late 1809 to list why men of genius often choose the wrong women, Milton is at the top of the list. The causes apply as well to his own temperament as a man of genius: for men of genius have "quick sensibility of mind and body," a tendency "to form an ideal in their own minds," "Quick sense of Honor, dread of their own conscience, which makes them often persevere if once they have payed marked attentions, or payed direct addresses, even after their eyes have been opened—in cases where Men of the World would feel no scruple and anticipate no Blot on their characters," and "more sensibility than the generality of even well-educated men & therefore, what they have more opportunity to see they feel more deeply" (Dec. 1809; *CN* 3648). What he does not know about Milton's marriage he supplies from his own experience, assuming that both the unhappily married geniuses felt a "dread of their own conscience" after paying "direct addresses" to women whom they already knew were inadequate and whom "Men of the World" would have dropped without a qualm.

As he cleaves with head and heart to Milton's argument, so Coleridge comes also to recognize the truth of Godwin's arguments against marriage as property, although he disapproved of the general coldness of Godwin's philosophy. Godwin's vision of married life would chill any prospective bride or groom:

> Cohabitation is not only an evil, as it checks the independent progress of mind, it is also inconsistent with the imperfections and propensities of man. It is absurd to expect that the inclinations and wishes of two human beings should coincide through any long period of time. To oblige them to act and to live together, is to subject them to some inevitable portion of thwarting, bickering and unhappiness. This cannot be otherwise, so long as man has failed to reach the standard of absolute perfection. ("Of Property," p. 101)

Although Coleridge disagreed with Godwin's rejection of "all attachments to individuals," he learned too late the truth of his remarks about the dangers of marriage when it was a mistake, when it forced the married persons to "shut their eyes upon realities, happy if by any perversion of intellect they can persuade themselves that they were right in their first crude opinion of their companion" (p. 102). Thwarting, bickering, and unhappiness Coleridge would have in abundance; he dreaded "domesticating with" his wife. Dorothy Wordsworth watches them together for many years and describes the gulf between them: "striving to bring Mrs. C. to a change of temper, and something like communion with him in his enjoyments [,] he is now, I trust, effectually convinced that he has no power of this sort"; he has come face to face with "the utter impossibility of producing powers and qualities of mind which are not in her."[7] By such incompatibility the character of each partner is warped, and the chief goal in life, to develop as whole persons, is cankered.

Struggling against the pressure that Southey is exerting to force him to marry a woman he does not love, Coleridge tells him that to have sex without love would be using the woman as a thing, polluting his own soul as well as hers. Coleridge writes Southey that he can rise above the selfish pang of the loss of Mary Ann Evans, but that marrying a substitute woman whom he does not love is abhorrent: "to marry a woman whom I do *not* love—to degrade her, whom I call my Wife, by making her the Instrument of low desire—and on the removal of a desultory Appetite, to be perhaps not displeased with her Absence!—Enough!—These Refinements are the wildering Fires, that lead me into Vice. Mark you, Southey!—*I will do my Duty* (Dec. 29, 1794; *CL* 1, 145). Eyes wide open, he enters a marriage that he foresees will be whoredom mixed with indifference. He predicts accurately that once his desultory appetite is satisfied, he will be "not displeased" with separation from a person whose feelings and values are alien. He foresees the corruption of his own soul, and the degradation of hers. Sex with a woman whom he does not love pollutes her and him, turns her into a thing for his use, and him into an animal grossly pursuing his lusts. Both souls are stunted; both partners are debased. Curiously, although their marriage seems to be based on sex alone, and they seem to conceive quickly when they cohabit, Coleridge notes to himself that she is sexually cold because she sees herself through the "Ears & Eyes of others" and has formed no "*real Self*," that they can be naked together, and bathing together, and yet "all as cold & calm as a deep Frost" (Aug.–Sept. 1801; *CN* 979), quite different from the stolen embraces of a warm Sara Hutchinson, recorded, perhaps significantly, in the same month (Sept. 1801; *CN* 985). He watches the separation of body and soul in his marriage, knowing with Milton that in the eyes of the law the only estrangement that matters is physical. He will develop fully his theory of the dangers of "soul-murder" thirty years later in his letters to Thomas Allsop on marriage.

Whereas Coleridge shared many values with Mary Evans, as we saw, short of her decision to marry a man enriched by the West Indian "trade," he and Sara Fricker had from the start very different values. Detractors have reason to rage at Coleridge's leaving his wife and sons, at his refusal to return from Germany at the death of his second son Berkeley, at his never knowing his daughter, at his inability financially to support his family, and at his letter telling his wife as politely as he could "that in sex, acquirements, and in the quantity and quality of natural endowments whether of Feeling, or of Intellect, you are the Inferior. Therefore it would be preposterous to expect that I should see with your eyes, & dismiss my Friends from *my* heart, only because you have not chosen to given them any Share of *your* Heart" (*CL* 2, 888). Indeed, our attempts to understand this marriage are further baffled by the many expressions of warmth in Coleridge's letters to his wife, his "dearest, dearest Sara!—my Wife & my Love, & indeed my very Hope," as he struggles to come back to her as "a confident and affectionate husband" (*CL* 2, 890). Though they know they are unsuited for each other, sometimes they seem to jog along together at peace.

In the absence of information about the private struggles within their marriage—aside from Coleridge's references to his wife's "ill-tempered speeches," "freezing looks," "screams of passion," and "the sentiments which I held most base, ostentatiously avowed" (*CL* 2, 876)—we can glimpse the hostility by indirection. That is, we can look at Southey, the man whom Sara Fricker Coleridge admired and had hoped to marry, and measure Southey's difference from Coleridge, who was very briefly his close friend.

Such triangulation will allow us a previously unnoticed view into this marriage. We can look at Southey's humorless misanthropic letters maneuvering and complaining; we can look at Coleridge's powerful attack on his values, and his several portraits of the man whom his wife urged him to emulate. If this kind of person is her beau ideal, clearly they have incompatible values.

Southey's spirit is misanthropic and disapproving before he meets Coleridge. To his school friend Grosvenor Bedford, he writes of his "gloomy prospect" and "calamity," (37), of being surrounded by "fools" and deceivers (36) of a "weight on this heart" (39) of "the wretched debasement of society" (40), his somber childhood without playmates

(150), his aunt's "mischievous fondness" in forcing him to sleep with her (150). In response to such letters, Coleridge admonishes Southey for his indignation, and probes its underlying psychological source, urging him to love other people more generously:

> Southey! I must tell you, that you appear to me to write as a man who is aweary of a world, because it accords not with his ideas of perfection—your sentiments look like the sickly offspring of disgusted Pride. Love is an active and humble Principle—It flies not away from the Couches of Imperfection, because the Patients are fretful or loathsome. Why my dear very dear Southey! Do you wrap yourself up in the Mantle of self-centering *Resolve*—and refuse to us your bounden Quota of Intellect? Why do you say, I—I—I—will do so and so—instead of saying as you were wont to do—It is all our Duty to do so and so—for such & such Reasons. (Jan. 19, 1795; *CL* 1, 149)

Hatred of individual people, of London, which Southey calls "a diabolical city," and of all the systems of the world shows a proud and egotistic outlook. By contrast, Coleridge advocates and practices love, enthusiasm, tolerance, and humor. His many very real sorrows (especially in his childhood exile in London) are transformed into hilarious adventures so as not to burden others, a far cry from the habitual disgruntlement of his friend.

In a quick and melancholy ceremony Southey married Edith: "My Edith returned home at night, and I slept as usual at Cottles. The next day we parted."[8] In tears, his marriage unconsummated, he left the next day for six months in Portugal to obey his mother who wanted to break up this unsuitable match with a poor fatherless girl, even though she knew it had already happened. Southey wrote Grosvenor Bedford (Nov. 17, 1795) that he did this to provide for Edith, but that she kept her own name in case he did not return alive. For six months, he did indeed flirt with the various girls provided by his uncle to catch his attention, claiming that he talked to these girls about Edith (105–107). His departure broke up the pantisocracy plan and infuriated Coleridge, who lost Mary Evans, who was stuck with the woman whom Southey had demanded he take to America, and who was appalled at Southey's willingness to accommodate his mother and uncle in their immoral demands for the sake of an inheritance that in fact ultimately did not appear, though that consequence did not change the moral status of the self-promoting desertion of the plan. Coleridge's disgust at such prudential compromising roars in his prose: "Southey! . . . you are *lost* to *me*, because you are lost to Virtue" (Nov. 13, 1795, *CL* 1, 163). In page after raging page Coleridge details Southey's abandonment of pantisocracy in favor of selfishly preserving his own money and own annuity. "And was not this your own Plan? The Plan, for the realizing of which you invited me to Bristol—the plan, for which I abandoned my friends, and every prospect & every certainty, and the Woman whom I loved to an excess which you in your warmest dream of fancy could never shadow out?—Why I returned from London, when you deemed Pantisocracy a DUTY . . . what then were our circumstances?" Calling Southey's motives "weak & shadowy and vile," he shouts: "O Selfish, money-loving Man! What Principle have you not given up? . . . O God! That *such a mind* should fall in love with that low, dirty, gutter-grubbing Trull, WORLDLY PRUDENCE!!" (Nov. 13, 1795; *CL* 1, 170–171). Southey manipulated others, betrayed the utopian plan for his own interests, and then blamed the failure of the plan on Coleridge's "indolence."

Even Sara Fricker rebuked Southey for this injustice, exclaiming, "What a Story!" (Potter, p. 172). Years later, contemplating the wreck of his life, Coleridge writes, "O Southey! Southey! an unthinking man were you—and are—& will be" (*CL* 3, 74).

"Startled" by the lies of her old love, who had betrayed her as well by choosing her sister Edith over her, Sara may occasionally have glimpsed Southey's hypocrisy. Since Coleridge was open and "free from all contriving," she may also have known about the love for Mary Evans that Southey had forced him to abandon. (We will see later that he was frank about his love for Sara Hutchinson and his right to pursue it.)

If this is the man whom his wife favors over him for his prudence, his materialism, and his concern for how he appears to the world—all qualities that Coleridge will charge his wife with in the next years—if she greets him with merry comedy and her husband with frowning disapproval, Coleridge has good reasons to shun her as a pollution to his soul's wholeness.

Eleven years later, when the marriage is over, these small-minded, prudential qualities have become entrenched with little likelihood of change. Coleridge cannot bear to encounter them. Fraught with anxiety on his return from Malta, delaying week after week his trip from London to Keswick, Coleridge dreads domesticating with his wife as much as he dreads telling her that he does not wish to domesticate with her. With Mary Lamb begging him to write Sara or she will do it for him, with Wordsworth and Charles Lamb writing each other about his unhappiness, he finally arrives after an absence of almost three years. He finds that his wife is more like Southey than before: he writes the Wordsworths that he sees his wife's character, her "mere selfish desire to have a *rank* in life and not to be believed to be that which she really was, without the slightest wish that what was should be otherwise, was at the bottom of all. Her temper, and selfishness, her manifest dislike of me (as far as her nature is capable of a *positive* feeling) and her self-encouraged admiration of Southey as a vindictive feeling in which she delights herself as satirizing me &c. &c . . ." (Nov. 19, 1806; *CL* 2, 1200). These words suggest that Sara wants to *be* a married woman but not to improve or change herself, that she dislikes him as a person, and laughs at him either in front of others or behind his back, that she retaliates for his absence by loudly admiring Southey for all the qualities that Coleridge does not have.

To come from an international arena where people admired him to a house in a remote mountain town where the few smug and entrenched inhabitants make fun of him cannot have been cheering. On her part she thinks his looks improved, but finds that "in 3 or 4 days he is gone!" unwilling to see that associating with her makes him flee. The selfish desire to have a rank in life is one aspect of her concern with appearance and not substance; though she "has fully agreed to" the separation, "she breaks out into outrageous passions, & urges continually that one argument (in fact the only one which has the least effect upon her mind) that this person, & that person & every body will talk." (Dorothy Wordsworth quoting Coleridge to Lady Beaumont Dec. 3, 1806; headnote to letter 637 *CL* 1, 1203). Sara has no argument based on her love for him, but only "that it will not look *respectable* for her" (to his brother George, Apr. 2, 1807; *CL* 3, 8).

Although at this very time Southey and Rickman gossip about Coleridge's frequent advocacy of easy divorces, as we see later, no surviving letters reveal Coleridge himself making such an argument in general, but only saying that he himself can no longer live with a woman who so mocks and unsettles him. In many ways his wife is an admirable person tutoring their children and making ends meet; he thinks they part "the best of friends," and soon after parting they correspond amusingly about the behavior of Hartley getting repeatedly lost in the same field, and other peculiarities of their children. "If my wife loved me, and I my wife, half as well as we both love our children, I should be the happiest man alive but this is not—will not be!" (*CL* 2, 774–775).

This foray into Southey's moral qualities serves as an oblique approach to the secrets of a tumultuous marriage that is otherwise blotted from the records, an eradication that follows naturally from the concern with respectable appearance desperately pursued by the socially and financially marginal Frickers. It casts light on Sara's parallel moral qualities, in that she came to align herself with Southey, one of the causes of her estrangement from her husband but also one of the results of it. They were two peas in a pod.

Whether Sara Fricker was infected by Robert Southey's prudentialism, found an answering mirror of her own in his, or developed hers alongside his in similar circumstances as poor fatherless children in Bristol, Coleridge sees his wife as a microcosm of a certain kind of women's society of self-promoting, calculating acquaintances (*CL* 1, 562). He writes in his notebooks as late as Dec. 1812–June 1813, when he had long stopped cohabiting with his wife, that male friendship is often disrupted by "the influence of Wives, how frequently deadly to Friendship—by direct incroach, & perhaps intentional plans of alienation—chilling Effect of prudential anxieties" (*CN* 3, 4175).

Near the bottom of Coleridge's moral hierarchy is prudence, the trait encouraged in William Paley's ethics and in the careful actions and accountings of the expanding commercial classes. Prudence has a long history of positive values: moderation, circumspection, thrift, and self-control. But for Coleridge prudence registers its negative meanings in self-seeking, self-advancing, avoiding dangers and dangerous company, averting risk, amassing things, hoarding, calculating before acting, subduing ebullience. These negative aspects of prudence stifle the free spirit.

Coleridge associates them with Southey and also with his wife and her family's need for care and money; his wife's understandable criticism that he has not provided for the children born of their sporadic unions; the concern for appearance and reputation. He describes not only the obviously unpleasant "ill-tempered speeches," "freezing looks," and "screams of passion," but also "the sentiments, which I held most base, ostentatiously avowed" (*CL* 2, 876). Toward the end of his life one of these "base" sentiments—prudence—as an individual personal characteristic swells into a description of a whole acquisitive culture that he will call "fetishism" (*OM*, 126), where accumulations of external things and status define the human being rather than inward powers of love and imagination, a critique of materialism that expands into Dickens's universal disgust with acquisitiveness in *Our Mutual Friend*. When Coleridge judges others he values their honesty and disapproves of their schemes for self-advancement; in these values he bears a resemblance to the judgments made by Jane Austen's exemplary characters. With a slimmer figure and a more noble and self-contained hauteur, Coleridge might sound like Mr. Darcy deflecting Caroline Bingley in the Netherfield Drawing Room with his clipped and impersonal dictum: "Whatever bears affinity to cunning is despicable."[9] Opposing Paley's prudentialism, like Bentham's utilitarianism, Coleridge and Austen admire people who are open, generous, and unscheming. Like Blake, they believe that "Prudence is an ugly old maid, courted by incapacity." Unfortunately, as Blake's gendering of prudence confirms, many people who are closed, spiteful, and scheming are women, because women need to scheme to survive, their characters warped by social demands in constricted environments. The nugget of Coleridge's opposition to prudentialism is his own wife. As Mary Wollstonecraft taught him, "the grand source of female folly and vice has ever appeared to me to arise from narrowness of mind" (*Vindication of the Rights of Women, hereafter referred as VRW*, 144).

Nor could any wife, however willing to separate, enjoy the frequent references to Sara Hutchinson's presence in Grasmere, his plans to come in on a double horse with her (*CL* 2, 909), and his hope that the two Saras will both care for the new baby named Sara. From Coleorton, where Coleridge took Hartley to stay with the Wordsworths in the summer of 1807, he writes his wife that "All here love [Hartley] most dearly: and your name sake [SH] takes upon her all the duties of his Mother & darling Friend, with all the Mother's love & fondness. He is very fond of *her*—" (*CL* 2, 1205). And to Derwent Feb. 7, 1807: "Your dear friend, Sara Hutchinson, sends her Love to you!" (*CL* 3, 3). His free and open nature does not imagine jealousy (until it overwhelms him). He imagines that both women should love each other because he loves them both and they both love his children.

Molly Lefebure praises Sara Fricker Coleridge's imaginary language, tied up with her intimacy with Southey and rising to a flurry in the 1820s. She cites letters from Southey to his old school friend Grosvenor Bedford delighting in the amazing coinages of his sister-in-law and housemate: "And she asks me, how I can be such a Tomnoddycom . . . and calls me detesty, a maffrum, a goffrum, a chatterpye, and sillycom, and a great mawkinfort" (cited Lefebure, p. 21). Her coinages—"detestabumpus" and "figurumpus"—are so tightly packed in sentences as to be incomprehensible except to initiates and constant companions like himself, her first suitor. It is curious that Coleridge himself in writing to or about her mentions this private language only in one poem, humorous "Hexameter Lines to Mrs. Coleridge" in Feb. 1804, perhaps to demonstrate that he could join in if he wished:

> Yes! In my Dreams I beheld thee: the Cawl of incarnate Osiris
> Turban'd thy Head! Thy Knees with profitless fury assailing
> Curly-tail'd Gruntlets accus'd thee, O false & immane to this
>   Guest-friend!

> For lo! To those Knees there depended the Hide of their grunnient
> Mother
> Slain as she swill'd at thy Trough! (*PW* #342, ll. 4–8)

Lefebure suggests that this private language was a defense mechanism for relieving anxiety about her absent husband, her embarrassing social status, her poverty, and her dependency on her younger sister's husband's support, as well as being a sign of her good humor and vivacious courage (222–223). Coleridge may have reasons for ignoring it. Perhaps she uses it only with Southey and her own sons, and not with him; perhaps it represents a competitive use of words which challenges and possibly mocks his own verbal inventiveness, as if to suggest "I invent language every day and you do very little"; perhaps it annoys him with its continual unwavering flow of thoughtless distortions or its muddling of arcane knowledge that satirizes his own knowledge; perhaps it reminds him of the compatibility between his wife and Southey, both irritatingly smug, giggling at their private argot. For someone interested in the power of words in rhythmic form to control, absorb, and magnetize (as in his own "Christabel" and "The Three Graves") this exclusive magic circle of private lingo rankled. Hearing the two of them cheerfully chirping together, knowing that in many ways Southey stood for values of opportunism, materialism, and hypocrisy that he loathed and that his wife admired, surely helped to make him feel alien. Painfully, his son Hartley also caught the infection of Southey's language. Late in life Coleridge annotates the writings of his estranged son and notes that Southey's coyly clever style has infected his son's: "It is this petulant ipse dixi smartness & dogmatism in which as in a certain Mannerism, a sudden *jerkiness* in the *mood*, and *unexpectedness* of Phrase, something between Wit and Oddity, but with the latter predominant, the Peculiarity certain, the felicity doubtful, [that] he has *caught* from Southey . . . that annoy and mortify me in Hartley's writing" (*CM* 2, 54, 5).[10] During his long absence Coleridge's wife and older son have learned Southey's estranging language; he himself is outside the perimeter of their distorted discourse.

In her eagerness to show how much her subject suffered, Lefebure provides the smoking gun for an alternative interpretation. Telling us that Sara Fricker told her daughter that Southey courted your Mama first, Lefebure says "This speaks volumes." Indeed, it speaks volumes for the view that Sara Fricker originally loved Southey, married his friend so as not to be left behind, preferred her prudential first love to his vivacious and unworldly friend, and may tangentially have nudged her own dull and heavy sister out of her first love's affections and into depression. (For the shadowy Edith must have suffered as she watched her prettier and more talkative older sister usurp her husband's attentions.) This man Coleridge's wife preferred, enjoyed laughing with, shared her special sassy "clever me" language with.

But Southey was one of the few people who liked Sara Fricker Coleridge. In *The Gang*, John Worthen examines the fellowship of Coleridge, William and Dorothy, and the Hutchinsons in the year 1802, finding that the only outsider to the group was Coleridge's wife, whose rages interrupted their intimate late night talks and whose petty domestic proprieties were a source of hilarity to the others, especially when Dorothy Wordsworth raided her closets and tried on her dresses like costumes. As late as 1816 Henry Crabb Robinson visits Keswick: "I did not like any of the three [Fricker] sisters. Mrs. Coleridge is a very unpleasant woman: she is not *handsome*, and her manners are obtrusive." In 1826 Sara Hutchinson writes, "We are *threatened* with a *visitation* from Mrs. Coleridge."[11]

The magic circle of the "*lingo grande*" and the "*ipse dixits*," a circle revolving around Sara and Southey, also involved the care of children over the months and years that Coleridge stayed away. When it came to supporting families, caring for sick children, and finding money to send the sons of his old friend Coleridge to university, Southey's prudentialism saved the day for both of Coleridge's sons. Southey's letters to friends in 1814 struggling to raise this money are brave and touching, even though he did not understand that Coleridge was not purposely idling but was helpless from sorrow, loneliness, and increasing dependency on opium and brandy.

Along with resenting his son Hartley's stylistic dependency on Southey, Coleridge also resented Southey's monopoly of his daughter Sara, although he was an absent father throughout her childhood. Away from his family he begs his wife for news of his little daughter: "You told me nothing about sweet Sara / tell me every thing—send me the ve[ry] *Feel* of her sweet Flesh, the very Looks & Motions of that mouth / O I could drive myself mad about her!— . . ." (Feb. 15, 1804; *CL* 2, 1062). This daughter wrote as much as she could of a memoir as she lay dying of cancer. Addressed to her own daughter Edith, named inauspiciously after Mrs. Southey (whose lifelong depression ended in a York asylum), she struggles to describe her father's visit that aimed to establish a parental connection to her. This page makes sad reading, especially as it ends in dieresis, an uncompleted figure that suggests her physical weakness, and also her inability to complete her meaning without sullying her father's memory, which she had come, at least philosophically, to revere:

> I slept with him, and he would tell me fairy stories when he came to bed at twelve and one o'clock.... I think my dear father was anxious that I should learn to love him and the Wordsworths and their children, and not cling so exclusively to my mother, and all around me at home. He was therefore much annoyed when, on my mother's coming to Allan Bank, I flew to her, and wished not to be separated from her any more. I remember his showing displeasure to me, and accusing me of want of affection. I could not understand why. The young Wordsworths came in and caressed him. I sat benumbed; for truly nothing does so freeze affection as the breath of jealousy. The sense that you have done very wrong, or at least given great offense, you know not how or why—that you are dunned for some payment of love or feeling which you know not how to produce or to demonstrate on a sudden—chills the heart, and fills it with perplexity and bitterness. My father reproached me, and contrasted my coldness with the childish caresses of the little Wordsworths. I slunk away, and hid myself in the wood behind the house.[12]

Coleridge's rage at the little girl for running to her mother shows his hurt feelings at being on the outside of the magic circle, his hopelessness at establishing affinities when he lived far away, and his own inability to take an adult perspective on the child's faithful love for her mother. He seems not to imagine that his easy play with the little Wordsworths, especially the mischievous Dora, would make her jealous, or that he intentionally provokes her jealousy in order to assuage his own. As he wrote longingly about "the *Feel* of her sweet Flesh," so he does drive himself "mad about her." In the coda to "Christabel" Coleridge admits to feeling similar rage at Hartley, whom he was also unable to direct and claim. In Coleridge's daughter's memoir, readers are also surprised to learn of Coleridge's strict preferences in the dress of girls—white dresses, a feminine cap, no red stockings: "he much liked everything feminine and domestic, pretty and becoming, but not fine-ladyish." When he does not like her dress as a little girl, he "set her down again without a caress" (*Memoir*, pp. 45–46).[13]

Sara Hutchinson provides a glimpse into the family, where Sara Fricker Coleridge appears purposely to inhibit her daughter. She argues that *Sara fille* is spoiled, vain, and indulged by her momma, her dependency a cause of her frailty. With a subtle swipe at Sara Fricker Coleridge's smothering lack of intellectual curiosity, Sara Hutchinson urges Sara *fille* to "rouze yourself—believe me 'quiet' and the presence of the same objects will not so speedily work your cure as change of scene & occupation." Later she writes in anger at both mother and daughter, one for oppressing, the other for allowing herself to be oppressed: "O how I do pity her! & hope that if she gets rid of her mother that she may turn out something useful before she ceases to be ornamental . . . I am vexed at her weakness" (*SHL*, 322–323). Finally, she rejoices in little Sara's freedom: "she I am glad to find has enjoyed good health ever since she left her Mother who *made her fancy* she was ill & unhappy" (*SHL*, 349). She implies that Coleridge's daughter Sara was sickly because her mother made her think she was, even going so far as to douse her with laudanum to make her sleep at unusual times when she would have preferred to stay awake. That home was suffocating for more people than just Coleridge.

Sara Hutchinson also describes a joyous Coleridge among the Grasmere children in 1803 (when most of his readers believe that he is suffering alone in his room):

> we are a nice round family you may think and when Coleridge's boys are here on a Saturday & Sunday a pretty noisy one—even now I hear C making racket enough for twenty with Sissy [Dora Wordsworth, aged four] below—he does tieze her in such a way for she cannot be too naughty for his taste; he calls her "beautiful Cat of the Mountain" & she is more like a cat with him than anything else—the moment he appears she puts on her airs—with every body else she is far more gentle than she used to be—she has been poorly & is much softened by it. (*SHL*, 12)

Romping, wrestling, making noise, larking with wild kids, delighting the woman he loves who listens upstairs as he probably knows, Coleridge can still experience delight.

Discussing the unhappiness within the marriage between Sara Fricker and STC is gossipy and frivolous by some lights, but it is significant because their unhappiness debases both their characters. Trapped in this marriage, he escapes for study in Germany, for month-long hikes, for work in London, Malta, and Italy, returning refreshed but immediately feeling sick again in her company. Coleridge cannot get space to develop his character. Coleridge lives with "the consciousness, that I was myself growing a worse man" (*CL* 2, 876). To see this daily bickering and thwarting on both sides is to understand why Coleridge pays attention to marriage in his writings throughout his life, because marriage determines personal development and ultimately the state of the soul when it enters the immortal future that he assumes awaits it. When the torch of hymen smokes instead of flaming, it suffocates, chokes, and blinds both partners (*CN* 3, 4110).

The argument of this chapter can be swiftly summarized. Coleridge marries precipitously at the bidding of others. He learns his wife's character too late, realizing that, far from the libertarianism that he had hoped for on the basis of her eagerness to join the pantisocracy adventure, the governing bent of her character was a calculating prudence congruent with Southey's, a tendency to look at externals, to value things, and to treat other human beings as things, that is, as means to an end. Poisoned by her values, he despairs of his soul, because he believes that on his choice of partner hangs his development as a human being and hers, and that just settling down, bearing it, cheating or living in sullen silence, is a wrong choice. In the way of destinies, he finds the right woman five years too late to do anything about it, given the peculiar English laws forbidding divorce that were in place until the Married Women's Property Act of 1857. While he admires many girls and women over the forty years between fifteen to fifty-five (in love as in verse he is precocious), he loves intensely the one woman whom he met too late, and her warmth, music, and personal integrity cast a glow over the women he loves after her.

Of all the Romantic male poets and prose writers, Coleridge is the most interested in women in themselves, not just in how he can use them, and his gradual steps toward recognizing that their personhood is established differently from men's is not as contemptible as it is sometimes perceived in an anachronistic view of his choices.

Coleridge is not a hypocrite like Percy Bysshe Shelley who preaches equality but practices freedom only for himself, dragging his wife around in climates where her babies die and she must share him with nursemaids and stepsisters and their babies by her husband. Coleridge does not abandon his wife, take half her dowry, and live lavishly amid harems like Byron. His love for Sara Hutchinson probably most resembles Keats's for Fanny Brawne, though he knows her better as a person and is happiest when working side by side with her, and no one makes fun of Keats, even of his late desperate poem "The Jealousies." Coleridge's interest in women is closest to Blake's, but Blake's comfort with his wife is palpable for he met her in time to marry her.

Nor does Coleridge use his women relatives as secretaries to his production line as Wordsworth does.[14] He does, however, share with Wordsworth an intense sexual response to women. This drive to pleasure, prominent in both their definitions of the purposes and methods of poetic rhythms, which both men compare to sexual intercourse, was ignored by their younger contemporaries. Shelley in "Peter Bell the Third" tweaks Wordsworth as "a kind of moral eunuch," a "Male prude" too timid to lift the hem of "Nature's shift."[15] However, readers who thought that Wordsworth sublimated his sexual drive in a generalized discussion of natural landscape were surprised to read his lusty love letters to his wife, long after the scandals of his youth—an affair with an older woman, a daughter out of wedlock, dangerous missions of espionage—that marked his robust stay in revolutionary France. These letters pulse with desire during a brief absence in London. On June 3–4, 1812 he writes to his wife that "the fever of thought & longing & affection & desire is strengthening in me, and I am sure will be beginning to make me wakeful and to consume me. Last night I *suffered*; and this morning I tremble with sensations that almost overpower me." His sentences become too arousing for a later reader and are scratched out, though the words "rapture" and "pleasures" can be deciphered. Wordsworth knows that Mary's thoughts about him lead her to "losing all sense of the motion of the horse that bears thee." He urges her to "speak for me to thyself, find the evidence of what is passing within me in thy heart,"

> in thy limbs as they are stretched on the soft earth; in thy own involuntary sighs & ejaculations, in the trembling of thy hands, in the tottering of thy knees, in the blessings which thy lips pronounce, find it in thy lips themselves, & such kisses as I often give to the empty air, and in the aching of thy bosom, and let a voice speak for me in every thing within thee & without thee.[16]

His memories of their sexual life together rouse Mary to a correspondent ardor, hinting that she shares with her sister Sara a Hutchinson family warmth. Both Wordsworth and Coleridge were more grounded in their bodies, their senses, and their hearts than their later reputations allowed. This physicality shows in their athleticism, their vigorous verses, their metaphors, and in their attractions to women, which will make them rivals for Sara Hutchinson in 1806, the subject of chapter 9.

Chapter 4
Blank Faces and Fear of Ruin

> The chariest maid is prodigal enough
> If she unmask her beauty to the moon
> *Hamlet* 1, 3, 36–37

Living with his wife and baby Hartley in the village of Nether Stowey, and traveling in and out of London, Coleridge continues to watch women of all classes and to describe their appearances to his friends. He pays attention to their dress, bodies, carriage, size, weight, even as he is learning to value their conversation. Faced with the dazzling surfaces of the Georgian and Regency female, his admiration often stopped short at the body. In convivial mode he laughed heartily at female shapes and peculiarities: heavy inking covers the name of someone whose wife is "a nasty hard-hearted, hatchet-fac'd, droop-nos'd, eye sunken, rappee-complexioned [old Bitch]" (*CL* 2, 880). Fat women amused him: "A superfluity of Beef! . . . Vulgarity enshrin'd in blubber!"[1] And breasts always caught his eye: "Blessed, blessed were the breasts!"[2] During the 1797–1802 years he wrote for the *Morning Post*, and charmed actresses, writers, and hostesses whose low-cut dresses provided a fleshy vista for his moist and protruding eyes. Indeed, given the eye-catching décolletages at the Bath Fashion Museum, it is remarkable that Coleridge alone talks about breasts; we should instead wonder why the other male Romantics rarely mention them. In this cosmopolitan interlude he dined at Charlotte Smith's house (*CL* 1, 571), and several times with Mr. and Mrs. Barbauld (*CL* 1, 577); he spent a night surrounded by the three Allen girls, innocently, he writes his wife (*CL* 2, 890), while arguing the case that no one can promise to love just one person for the rest of his life; any "warm & wide-hearted man" loves many people (*CL* 2, 887–888). He boasted of his fashions and flirtations and dared Sara to scratch out the eyes of his admirers (Feb. 24, 1802; *CL* 2, 789). He enjoyed calling Mrs. Inchbald and Mrs. Barbauld "the two bald women" (Allsop 1, 203). Watching women not only led to amusement but also to sympathy and thence to sexual arousal: "Sympathy itself perhaps may have some connection with this impulse to embody Feeling in action. The accumulation of these eye-given pleasure-yearnings may impel to energetic action/but if a woman be near, will probably kindle or increase the passion of sexual Love" (Feb. 1803; *CN* 1, 1356). "Eye-given pleasure-yearnings"—wonderful words that recall his own moist and protruding eyes—stir physical interest and at the same time emotional understanding.

In several rarely noticed poems from this period Coleridge observed women performing their roles in society. These poems investigate how women hide their characters in obedience to the requirements of deportment and subdue vitality to meet the expectations of other women, those "elderly young women that discuss the love-affairs of their friends and acquaintance at the village tea-tables" (*Friend* 1, 49), and of men assessing them as commodities. In an age of mass produced people, of course, women were not alone in following the demands of fashion to look and act alike. Men also adhered slavishly to "the Religion of the *Gentleman* . . ., the all-implying word of Honor—a thing more blasting to real Virtue, real utility, real standing forth for the Truth in Christ, than all the whoredomes & Impurities which this Gentlemanliness does most generally bring with it" (*CL* 1, 323), conformists whom he will late despise as "Fetich worshippers," who measure value in terms of things.[3] But while men shaped themselves as "gentlemen" for numerous reasons, women conformed in order to be marriageable, in a market that Mary Poovey has chillingly enumerated as an economy of male scarcity, a market that denatured women's humanity by imposing an enfeebling "modesty," and rendered them almost invisible.[4] As Sonia Hofkosh perceives in regard to Mary Shelley's story "The Invisible Girl," a girl reading amidst luxurious furnishings is seen as "always already materialized—but only as a fetish of herself, an image, a picture, or a 'living shadow.' "[5] Hofkosh's words might be read backward into Coleridge's positioning of inscrutable women amid their belongings, hiding their bodies, their voices, and their distinctive thoughts.

"On the Christening of a Friend's Child" (1797) prays for the safe delivery of Coleridge's Nether Stowey neighbor, Anna Cruikshanks, whose husband John was briefly Lord Egmont's agent before he went bankrupt. She was one of "a number of very pretty young women in Stowey, all musical—," as Coleridge wrote John Thelwall, adding "I am an immense favorite; for I pun, conundrumize, *listen* & dance. The last is a recent acquirement" (Feb. 6, 1797; *CL* 1, 308). Coleridge's sympathy for Anna during her difficult pregnancy leads him to pray,—"May the

Father & Lover of the Meek preserve that meek Woman, and give her a joyful and safe deliverance!!" (*CL* 1, 251). This fervent prayer for his neighbor down the road suggests that in the small village he knew of her struggles (or perhaps could even hear the cries) and wondered, as he often did, why God would let women suffer in childbirth: "the pangs which the Woman suffers, seem inexplicable in the system of optimism. . . . here are pains most horrible in consequence of having obeyed Nature" (Mar. 20, 1796; *CL* 1, 192). Indeed, his interest in childbirth leads him twenty-five years later to write a long review of two books on "Uterine Disorders" (*SWF* 2, 872–893), a compendium of operations on atrophied or cancerous uteri that are often botched by doctors so incompetent and stupid that they should be prosecuted. Celebrating Anna Cruikshanks, this "amiable" neighbor, this "sweet little woman [the] same size as my Sara," he hopes that her baby daughter will resemble her in body and spirit: "Dear Anna's dearest Anna!"

As passionately as he feels about the safe birth and survival of these females, his diction is unusually bland, his ten quatrains metrically predictable, his rhymes identical, coinciding with the meek redundancy that he praises:

> While others wish thee wise and fair,
>   A maid of spotless fame,
> I'll breathe this more compendious prayer
>   May'st thou deserve thy name! (*PW* #147, ll. 5–8)

Where William Butler Yeats will pray that his daughter would not be beautiful so as to spare the men whose hearts she might come to break, Coleridge prays that this baby girl will develop innocuous personal qualities—"Meek Quietness without offence; / Content in homespun kirtle" (ll. 13–14)—so as to avert the eye of adventurers who may attempt to ruin her.[6] He foresees a face "eloquently mild," a "green and rude" bud unnoticed at her full blown mother's side, "alike in place, shape, name" (l. 38), an ordinary female, calmly going about her duties in a provincial town, following her mother's footsteps: "Another and the same!" (l. 40). He imagines that if the new Anna is meek enough she will replace her mother so entirely that her mother's eventual death will go unnoticed. Like flower buds, these palindromic mothers and daughters seamlessly redouble. This interest in redoubling female identities persists in an 1807 poem, "To Two Sisters: A Wanderer's Farewell" and beyond.

In 1797, using floral images again, the poems, "To an Unfortunate Woman, Whom I Knew in the Days of her Innocence" and "Allegorical

Lines on the Same Subject" (1797), alert the girls to the danger of getting noticed:

> Gaily from thy mother-stalk
>   Wert thou danc'd and wafted high—
> Soon on this unshelter'd walk
>   Flung to fade, to rot and die. (*PW* #149, ll. 13–16)

Coleridge had already articulated the dangers in his early "Religious Musings" (1794–1796) foreseeing how the unwary woman may become

> The victim of seduction, doom'd to know
>   Polluted nights and days of blasphemy;
>   Who in loath'd orgies with lewd wassailers
>   Must gaily laugh, while thy remember'd Home
> Gnaws like a viper at thy secret heart! (*PW* #101, ll. 282–286)

Women might be free from such degradation—which is itself a many-layered fraudulence—by binding themselves to norms of chaste behavior, by keeping their heads down, but at a loss of personal uniqueness.

The interchangeability of provincial women, whose names can be the same or different so long as they are linked to a man by a possessive pronoun, is very different from the namelessness of the "loose women" whose bodies he recalls from the period of his "unchastities." Middle-class women purposely remain nameless so they will not be known or talked of, and therefore will not risk their reputations; "loose women" have lost their reputations and are nameless because no one now cares to remember their names. Women's anonymity surfaces in a playful poem adapted from Lessing in 1799. The second stanza of "Names" finds the lady answering:

> Ah! replied my gentle fair,
> Beloved, what are names but air?
> Take thou whatever suits the line;
> Call me Clelia, call me Chloris,
> Laura, Lesbia, or Doris,
>   Only, only call me thine. (*PW* #236, ll. 8–13)

The woman's voice relinquishes individuality. Names are "but air," though she may pun on "heir," hinting that only connectedness legitimates her. It is better to be "unkiss'd, and foully husbanded" (*CN* 604) than not husbanded at all. "O Women are hardly off!," he tells his notebook (*CN* 1708).

The words "same" and "alike" hint not only at charming modesty but also at obliterated selfhood. In these poems to inscrutably undifferentiated women, Coleridge describes a society that needs to teach girls to fear "soft the glances of the Youth / Soft his speech and soft his sigh" ("To an Unfortunate Young Woman at the Theatre," *PW* #148), to listen only to the voice of "Mother Sage of Self-Dominion," to tamp down the pleasures and vitalities of girlhood: "Inly arm'd, go, Maiden! go."[7] For a metrist capable of thrilling variety, the bland meter, conventional metaphors, and repetitive rhymes of these several poems contribute to an argument about sameness and "propriety" across generations that echoes Mary Wollstonecraft's far less veiled critiques of the meagreness of women's activities. Wollstonecraft rages, "If women are in general feeble both in body and mind, it arises less from nature than from education. We encourage a vicious indolence and inactivity, which we falsely call delicacy. Instead of hardening their minds by the severer principles of reason and philosophy, we breed them to useless arts, which terminate in vanity and sensuality" (*VRW*, p. 126, note 2). Girls are not raised to be agents of their own lives and immortal souls but anonymous and indolent pretty faces waiting to be chosen, bodies used as vessels for the continuity of lineage. Once they are chosen, however, their prettiness soon ceases to charm; character, good humor, and learning do not rise to fill the void.

Mary Wollstonecraft contributed more than we have thought to Coleridge's lifelong meditations about women. Wollstonecraft's *Vindication* not only advocates education and activity for women to liberate them from the seraglio, her well-known powerful argument, but also gives a reason for education that is alien to many of her fellow revolutionaries: that is, she advocates education because women have immortal souls that they have an obligation to perfect. She uses this spiritual argument often, writing, for instance, that "women, considered not only as moral but rational creatures, ought to endeavour to acquire human virtues (or perfections) by the *same* means as men, instead of being educated like a fanciful kind of *half* being" (124); she believes in the immortality of the soul (p. 142); she cites Anna Barbauld's poem "To a Lady with some Painted Flowers" as an example of how even this woman author deprives women of their dignity (p. 143); she asks, "where is the store laid up that is to clothe the soul when it leaves the body?" (144). "If women be allowed to have an immortal soul, she must have, as the employment of life, an understanding to improve. . . . or she was born only to procreate and rot" (155), or "to flutter our hour out and die" (191). Conditioned to please, to be passive, timid, dependent, and idle, women do not work to become fully human; they sink into brutes, and die unready for immortality. Wollstonecraft's belief in an immortal soul leads Coleridge to prefer her philosophy to her husband Godwin's.

In sum, "On the Christening of a Friend's Child," "To an Unfortunate Woman at the Theatre," "To an Unfortunate Woman" and "Names," examine the cloning of meek women, effaced by propriety, their glances conventionalized by fear for reputation. In each of these poems Coleridge sees the pretty face, but notices that the mask of feminine fashion is kept purposely blank. (Now we might say "botoxed.") Blankness may, however, be preferable to those fixed frowns he endures from his own wife.

Coleridge's early belief in reverencing the personhood of the Other is balked by this reduplicating sameness, which again calls into question the universal sanctity of the human face that twentieth-century philosophers hope will guarantee personhood and thus ensure humane treatment of others. Emmanuel Levinas writes that "[t]he face is not just another name for the personality. The face is the personality—but in its manifestation, its externalization and reception; in its original frankness. The face is of itself, and, if I may express it so, the mystery of all clarity, the secret of all openness."[8] But no such openness or frankness characterizes the female face in Coleridge's time. In a gallery of similarly opaque faces, few distinctive traits alert the gazing eye and utterances are muffled under the masks.

Coleridge meditates on the opaqueness of all faces, but particularly female faces, in the 1826 essay "Individuality" (in *SWF*, 2, 1336). He argues that much about the human person cannot be accounted for "or even described intelligibly because it has its source in that which is deeper than Intelligence . . . Take two lovely and interesting Faces—Mrs. Gillman's for instance and Mrs. Aders's (and to my notion there are few finer ones). You will find no difficulty in stating this and that feature, proportion, shade of color, in which the two faces differ, and by which you might enable a Stranger to distinguish the one from the other." But cataloguing the details of appearances is no guide to the being within. Coleridge asks his imaginary interlocutor: "Would the Sum total of all the describable or even visible differences produce in you that sense of the individual character of either face, which the Face itself gave you?—Certainly not." Enumerating the details does not reach "the Castle, the strong-hold" to which the person retreats. Women may look similar through sororal genetics, through fashion, through the need to obliterate oddities, but their character and will are hidden beneath the surface. Unlike Levinas, Coleridge has learned to look behind the face to the individual character, the stronghold of personal being. The very word *Person* suggests by its etymology that personhood is a sounding through—*per sonare*—rather than an appearance.[9] The face is a mask that blocks the flow of sound, and diverts attention to its surface.

Young women do not dare express themselves for fear of rousing the wrong kind of interest or being different from other young women. A brief poem sent to George Dyer recognizes the fragility of the body that protects the woman's soul from fracture:

> Chastity's a balsum—woman's but a glass—
> That, alas, how costly!—how fragile, this, alas! ("Balsamum in Vitro," *PW* #345)

Sometimes the body responds when the mind or face on top of the body does not concur. In "The Kiss and the Blush" (Apr.–May 1803) Coleridge admits to taking advantage of this body–mind schism, rousing anger from the face, but heat from the flesh below the throat:

> From off that delicate fair cheek,
>   Oh Maid, too fair, I did but seek
> To steal a kiss, and lo! your face,
>   With anger or with shame it glows;
> What have I done, my gentle Grace,
>   But change a lily to a rose?
>
> At once your cheek and brow were flush'd,
> Your neck and ev'n your bosom blush'd;
> And shame may claim the larger part,
>   In that smooth neck, and all above:
> But the blush so near the heart,
>   Oh! Let it be a blush of love.
> Pygmalion thus lit up with life
>   The statue that became his wife. (*PW* #330)

The sensuous poet keenly watches the color flush downward as he makes bold to kiss her, the anger of the face and the responsive blush of the upper body. If Mays is correct in dating this poem from 1803, the woman would not likely be his estranged wife, but perhaps another woman whom he wishes to bring to life from her marble self-control, another fragile glass that he yearns to break, however sympathetic he is in his thoughts.

The dangers of false suitors noted in the two theater poems become the subject of "The Ballad of the Dark Ladie: A Fragment." This dramatic dialogue probes the common situation of the abandoned girl who has believed her suitor's promises. Started in March 1798, spurting ahead when he fell in love with Sara Hutchinson, and developing in tandem with two related poems "Love" and "Christabel," the poem "was interrupted by griefs & darknesses of a less poetic description, and was never completed," as Coleridge explains in 1831 to an unknown recipient of a copy of the poem (*PW* #182, headnote). The young woman on the mossy river bank waits desperately to be summoned:

> And there upon the moss she sits,
> The **Dark Ladiè** in silent pain:
> The heavy Tear is in her eye,
>   And drops, and swells again.
>
> Three times she sends her little Page
> Up the castled Mountain's breast,
> If he might find the Knight, that wears
>   The Griffin for his Crest.
>
> The Sun was sloping down the Sky,
> And She had linger'd there all day,
> Counting Moments, dreaming fears—
>   O wherefore can he stay? (ll. 5–16)

When the Knight appears after keeping her waiting all day out of sight in the shrubbery, she kisses him, and "quenches" her fiery kisses with her tears. She is tormented by the gossip of women, presumably because her pregnancy has become noticeable:

> "My Friends with rude ungentle Words,
>   "They scoff and bid me fly to thee! (ll. 25–26)

Her reputation is ruined, she is humiliated, and she begs him to fulfill his promises:

> "My Henry! I have given thee much!
> "I gave what I can ne'er recall!
> "I gave my Heart, I gave my Peace—
>   "O heaven! I gave thee all." (ll. 29–32)

Henry, whom Coleridge calls "a solemn Scoundrel" in a penciled interpretation along the margin, changes the subject, saying that when evening comes he will secretly deposit her in one of his nine castles:

> "And thro' the Dark we two will steal
>   "Beneath the twinkling Stars!" (ll. 43–44)

Such a union under cover of darkness is not what the young woman had in mind: "The Dark? the Dark? No not the Dark?" (l. 45). Crying out against the Dark, she sounds as if she is being smothered or shoved into a cave. In her mind, even perhaps from inside her imprisoning castle, she imagines a bridal party that will never take place, a detailed dream that may continue as a delusion to soothe her solitary pregnancy.

Coleridge stops his poem in the midst of the young woman's vision of her wedding, as if the imagined scene would obsessively recur perhaps to the point of madness. Calling the poem a fragment may be his usual way to keep his readers from asking any more questions about yet another sensual narration.

Unfinished or not, the poem treats the all too common subject of seduction and abandonment, the subject of his fears for the young woman at the theater and for young shop girls like his sister Nancy sent to work in Exeter, and also the subject of letters about neighbors and daughters in real life. For instance, he writes Thomas Poole in 1801 about a Stowey youth who seems to have impregnated and then married the daughter of an angry old man named Symes.

> I cannot see that Bradley has committed any error at all—or has done any thing which I would not have done in his place. A lewd Boy & a wanton Girl mutually seduce each other; but the Boy is willing to repair the evil, & to marry the Girl. If he do not, the Girl is hunted by Infamy, & perhaps hunted by it into the Toils of Guilt & habitual Depravity. . . . You must know that Symes never would have consented to the marriage—& Bradley knew it—& if, Poole! You do not know that the young man did his duty in marrying the young woman, all I can say is that my moral system is more austere than your's. . . . Bradley saw that whatever Hubbub might at first be created, all would die away—Husband & Wife are Husband & Wife—and *warmth* of constitution is often connected with many excellent moral dispositions—the affair may have prevented her from being a Whore—& no doubt has prevented him from being, as the Stowey youths of his acquaintance all were, Whoremongers deep-died! . . . As to the clandestineness, &c &c—they were only steps of prudence—if it were right to do the thing, it certainly could not be wrong to do it in the only way in which it could be done without uproar & desecration. . . . P.S. You will see, I take it for granted that the Girl is with child.— (Oct. 31, 1801; *CL* 2, 772–773)

For an understanding of Coleridge's sexuality and of his sympathy for the general plight of girls this letter is crucial. He admits to a man who may have some level of homosexual yearning for him that he himself would have done just what the bold youth did. He believes that sex, pregnancy, and then a quick marriage were the only ways to get the job done that both the wanton girl and lewd boy wanted. He praises "*warmth* of constitution" as the generating force behind many moral qualities, with the underlying assumption that "warmth of constitution" is part of his own sensual nature. He promises to shake Bradley's hand "& say, *You* have acted, Sir! As a man, & a Christian."

Young Bradley contrasts indeed with that "solemn Scoundrel," the Knight of "The Ballad of the Dark Ladie" who hides his pregnant girlfriend in a dark castle or abandons her by the wayside "hunted by infamy," scoffed at by friends, with no way to survive but by "habitual Depravity." These are the "cruel wrongs" that "[b]efel the Dark Ladie." In the "Introduction to the Tale of the Dark Ladie," a draft that merges with the first part of the poem "Love," the poet promises his listener

> A sister tale
> Of Man's perfid'ous cruelty ("Love," #253; added lines, p. 606)

These cruel wrongs make up the plot of many a "tale of woe." Coleridge is not shy about addressing the common subject of rape and abandonment, even joking about a girl named Nancy who bears Will's *image* in her *heart* or "an inch or two *below*" (*PW* #244). He sees that girls have hard choices when they have choices at all. He lets "The Dark Ladie" end with the girl's cries and then silence, with the girlish dream of bridal festivity trailing off, echoing through the rest of her life her hopes for what might have been. This would be the situation of Lydia and Wickham in *Pride and Prejudice* if it were not for the forceful, munificent, and highly unlikely intervention of Mr. Darcy.

His own sister Anne, or Nancy, may have been in the back of his mind. Though Mays believes he did not think of her,[10] Coleridge laments her death in an early sonnet—

> How are ye flown, whom most my soul held dear? (*PW* 1 #25, l. 7)

and later recalls their closeness when he writes to Charles Lamb soon after Mary Lamb's attack of madness:

> I too a **SISTER** had, an only Sister—
> She loved me dearly, and I doted on her!
> To her I pour'd forth all my puny sorrows
> (As a sick Patient in his Nurse's arms)
> And of the heart those hidden maladies

> That shrink asham'd from even Friendship's eye.
> O! I have woke at midnight, and have wept,
> Because SHE WAS NOT!— ("To a Friend [Charles Lamb],"
> 1794, *PW* #100, ll. 12–19)

He was a conscious and lonely ten when she was sent away from home. James Engell has found in the family letters that on the death of her husband, Mrs. Coleridge not only sent her youngest son Sam away to Christ's Hospital charity school in London, specifically insisting that he not be allowed to come home for vacations and be licensed to the Royal Navy if he proved difficult, but she also sent away her only daughter, four years older than Sam, to work as a sales clerk in Essex. Nancy died there at the age of twenty (March 12, 1791) of tuberculosis.

The oldest Coleridge brother, John, from his camp in India admonishes his mother that she should not send Nancy out of the family. He writes his brother James to be sure that the two hundred pounds he is sending does go to provide for his sister, and that his mother be made to comply with his wish. In his impassioned letter he warns of the dangers in "binding her to a trade," especially when the remittances that he and Frank are sending home make it "totally unnecessary":

> Dear James, let me request that you will (should my sister be now in Exeter) urge everything that lays in your power for her being recalled back to her mother, where she may improve herself in every accomplishment that ought to adorn the fair Sex. By my honour, James, I would rather live all the rest of my days on Bread and Water than see my Sister standing behind a Counter, where she is hourly open to the insults of every conceited Puppy that may chuse to purchase a Yard of Ribbon from her, horrid Idea! chucked under the chin, etc. etc. too bad to mention. For God's sake get her back, don't let her go to destruction, as some others has, who shall be nameless, but you may guess.[11]

Referring to a ruined and therefore "nameless" half sister from their father's first marriage, John Coleridge provides a physicality of detail that seems to be a Coleridgean family trait. He envisions how his sister could be ruined like her half sister. Struggling to save her from his great distance a world away, trying to impose a respect for decency on his stubborn mother, he dies—a possible suicide—four years later, the second in a sequence of five sibling deaths. What Nancy did as she worked and trudged to her mysterious dwelling, who if anyone "chucked [her] under the chin, etc. etc. too bad to mention," who tended her as she died, and where she died, are facts shamefully unknown in a family of their status. Did the mother pocket the money, refusing to bring home her daughter and namesake? Here is yet another redoubling pair of Annes, but this one is far from bland: the brothers send this managerial mother their "duty," their love to everyone else.

Having a single sister four years older who cared for him when he was sick may have been significant for Coleridge in learning to feel for and speak easily to girls, as not having a brother was in his view the reason for "certain peculiarities in the character of his wife, Mrs. Southey and Mrs. Lovell," who formed part of the large and cohesive Fricker matriarchy.[12] But his own sister's solitude and lonely death, very different from Mary Lamb's protected life in the generous care of her brother, was an object lesson in the dangers for girls. It alerts him to the unusual pressures on them. He walks to the Unitarian Church in Taunton to perform the divine services for Dr. Toulmin, whose "daughter in a melancholy derangement suffered herself to be swallowed up by the tide on the sea-coast between Sidmouth & Bere.—These events cut cruelly into the hearts of old men" (May 14, 1798; *CL* 1, 407). Finding the graves of unknown sisters named "Bevan" and "Jones," dead at 19 and 21, and 5 and 19, he records their dates in his notebooks (*CN* 1, 1267), suggesting that such innocent female deaths were meaningful to him even if the girls were strangers.

In November and December 1802, Coleridge interrupts his powerful essays on Napoleon to track down a local fraud posing as an MP and seducing young women in the Lake District. He publishes two detailed and sometimes hilarious articles in *The Morning Post* called "The Keswick Imposter I and II." Drawing details of the imposter's bright eyes, strange hair patterns, gait, and hand motions from the police notice, Coleridge assails the man and the gullible country people who are impressed by his accent, name dropping, and manners as he pursues two or three girls with differing prospects, one of fortune named Miss D'Arcy (could Austen have seen this name in *The Morning Post* and adapted it for Darcy's sister preyed upon by Wickham and her nurse in the 1813 *Pride and Prejudice*?). The so-called Colonel Hope, sensing that he was about to be detected by the Irish gentleman who was protecting Miss D'Arcy, quickly settled on the poor Maid of Buttermere named Mary Robinson (a name resonating with memories of the seduced and abandoned actress and poet), whom he spirits to an imaginary wedding in Scotland and impregnates. Coleridge fiercely defends the Maid of Buttermere on the grounds that all the local gentry were likewise deceived by Colonel Hope: "Is there on earth that prude or that bigot, who can blame poor Mary? She had given her lover the best reasons to esteem her, and had earned a rational love by innocence and wise conduct. Nor can it be doubted, that the man had really and deeply engaged her affections. He seems to have fascinated every one in all ranks of society; and if Mary had remained an exception, it would have detracted more from her sensibility, than it would have added to her prudence" (*EOT* 1, 411). A tangled financial web, a mad escape over the passes to Langdale, a package of letters revealing his previous treachery and multiple counts of bigamy, and other "villainous schemes" (415) finally unmasked the imposter as John Hatfield, who was hanged—not for enticing girls to ruin—but for impersonating an MP, and mourned by several abandoned wives and children who were "left to die of poverty and a broken heart" (note 10, p. 416).[13] Coleridge's satire of the innocence and susceptibility of the villagers does not undercut his rage at the ease with which whole villages can turn against affectionate girls. A young woman recalls that Coleridge took her on his knee during the months of this scandal and "told her 'with a plaintive voice . . . the story of Mary of Buttermere'. . . and she long remembered 'his pallid face, his long black hair . . . the appealing tones of his voice—the earnest gaze,' the tears running down his cheeks" (note 10, p. 416). Coleridge planned a novel on the subject, but his fervor was channeled instead into the many poems upon the subject of abandoned girls that we have been noticing in this chapter. In his view, a woman who falls for a man "has given her lover the best reasons to esteem her."

Reading *Baldwin's London Weekly Journal* in Malta, he copies into his notebook the tale of a young woman seduced by a laborer on one of the canals near Lincoln: "she proved pregnant, the parish Officers *compelled* him to marry her. Within an hour he killed her, almost beating her Head from her body with the heavy club, he was known to walk with" (June 1806; *CN* 2863). Seduction, madness, infanticide, and suicide result from the social and emotional pressures on young women to hide their emotions, to be chaste, to be marriageable, to marry no matter whom.

The story of ruin is told over and over, as Coleridge's older, more worldly, brothers could predict in regard to their sister left alone in Essex. It is a story that Coleridge tells in many ways himself, in "The Dark Ladie," in "Christabel," in the story inside the story of "Love," where the poet tells the story and reverses the outcome to woo his lady, and late in life, giving the woman the upper hand and adding the pangs of jealousy, in "Alice du Clos, or the Forked Tongue: A Ballad." These poems intermingle and revise the themes of women's struggle.

In the aftermath of ruin, women destroy other women's reputations as fiendishly as men do. "Mean girls" have become a research interest in recent years, as their cliques humiliate other girls by passing secrets.[14] Coleridge may have remembered Thomas Gainsborough's large painting, "The Mall in St. James Park" (1783), where the groups of young women gaze at each other's attire—tilted hats, pointed shoes, lace, ribbons, and silks—all identical except for slight shadings of tint in hair and taffeta. These young women dress for each other and look at each other, intertwining their arms as they saunter, in the absence of men. Close up, the expressions on their faces, the judgmental sidelong eyes, and the superior smirks as they assess the appearances of others, are vicious, and, again, identical. Coleridge may have seen the next generation of these models (which Gainsborough actually copied from dolls) in real life, strutting down the lanes, suppressing their mocking titters.

Coleridge saw the power of smug social women in destroying Mary Wollstonecraft's reputation after William Godwin published his naively blunt story of her love affairs. Coleridge was disgusted, also, with the gossips' treatment of his friend Mary Robinson. In a remarkable letter to Mary Robinson's daughter, Coleridge urges her not to include profligate male poets in a collection in memory of her mother, for these men had sullied her mother's reputation. He speaks of Mary Robinson's chastity of soul, and dismisses the rumors about her well-known affairs as the work of male debauchés like Thomas Moore, Peter Pindar, and Monk Lewis in collusion with the "Calumny and the low Pride of women (who have no other chastity than that of their mere animal frames) [and who] love to babble of your dear mother" (Dec. 27, 1802; *CL* 2, 903–906). Despite her early notoriety, she is a blameless woman. Coleridge does not mention the contemporary cartoons of Mary Robinson, which Betsy Bolton has shown "used the trope of prostitution to domesticate and degrade the figure of Mary Robinson as a public woman."[15] The nastiness of idle women and "vulgar," "licentious" male writers destroyed Mary Robinson's reputation; they make Coleridge's heart "sicken" and his flesh "creep." Women as well as men busy themselves to harm women with genius, beauty, and a good heart, often pushing them over the edge into poverty and hunger. Coleridge knew that the chastity of the spirit was far more meaningful than the chastity of "their mere animal frames," echoing Milton's disdain for the common interest in the activities of bodies as opposed to the conversations of minds and spirits.

Obviously, men are predators. But is there some deeper problem, too? What is it about girls that makes them vulnerable to "the rude ungentle Words" of female "Friends" who jeer at their seductions and taunt them to seek shelter with their seducers instead of giving them comfort, as the Dark Ladie learns too late (ll. 25–28)? Why do girls attend to surfaces, to appearances, to reputation, and to the lies of scoundrels? Why do they not unite to defend each other? Modern psychologists examine the difficulties in the identity formations of girls: two hundred years earlier, Coleridge explores these vulnerabilities in the poem he is struggling with at this time: "Christabel."

Chapter 5
"Christabel" and the Vulnerability of Girls

In a social system where young girls are forced to deny their individuality to keep their reputations, where they often must marry old, ugly, or nasty men for economic reasons in the bargaining of fathers and suitors over land, dowries, and ranks, where if they do not marry they must scrimp and manage as obscure maiden aunts (as Sara Coleridge, the daughter, remembers her Fricker maiden aunts doing), or marginally haunt the houses of their brothers or go into stranger's homes as governesses, girls often go amiss. At puberty, the pressure of choosing or not being allowed to choose, of making a match, succumbing to adventurers, or being turned over to an unsympathetic, unloving, or even brutal man, not to speak of the unruly pressures of their own pubescent desires, can undermine the sturdiest of egos. Coleridge's sympathy with women's lives and his identification with the fragility of their boundaries as persons, leads him to explore this region of self-forming or self-losing. Pursuing the issues in poems to women who were seduced and destroyed, he begins in 1798 a long struggle to chart these disintegrations in his "Christabel," a poem that circles around and around the perils of young womanhood. It is significant that the poem hears the heroine being silenced, crying out briefly for justice, then being abandoned, a pattern that began in "The Ballad of the Dark Ladie" where the girl's last words cry out against incarceration in the dark.

"Christabel" is Coleridge's longest poem, his least revised, the most satisfying to himself as its preface indicates, and his most troubling to readers. It is a poem that can drive readers "mad" or make them feel "stupid."[1] From its opening—"Tu-whit!—tu-whoo!"—, its lulling, almost lobotomized repetitions—"Is the night chilly and dark? / The night is chilly but not dark"—, its shifting narrative voices, and its metrical hesitations and forward rushes,[2] it lures listeners into its twilight. Coleridge's opening section does to listeners what Geraldine does to

Christabel: leaves them anxious and ungrounded. Critic after critic has tossed interpretations into the poem's "Dark fluxion, all unfixable by thought."[3] Each interpretation seems to work as well as the next, even if the interpretations are contradictory. Some see the heroine Christabel initiated into love;[4] some see her as a more or less innocent Eve falling into the snares of a demon from preternatural realms or a Satan;[5] some see the poem as having no meaning besides the complex contradictions of language and voice,[6] as a Blakean examination of divided states of body and soul,[7] as a dream or many dreams with condensed or displaced images,[8] even as a meditation on Rousseau.[9] Hazlitt called the poem "Obscene"; Tom Moore thought its gaps showed incompetence.[10] How do we cope with this tumult of uncertainty?

As one more reader transfixed like a "three year's child" by the rhythms of this disturbing poem, I wish to see Coleridge's deliberate (and perhaps even gleeful) construction of mystery in "Christabel" in the context of his wider investigation into the lives of women, set in the context of philosophical and psychological studies that apply to men also. The poem can be seen as a thought-experiment, enacting ideas that he elaborates in other poems and prose writings. To set "Christabel" in the context of these ideas is not to thin out its maddening density, but to reduce its isolation.[11] As a thought-experiment, "Christabel" is a germ of future thought; it initiates Coleridge's continuing work on the development of the human person, on how selves are made and lost. The poem narrates incidents in the emotional life of a young woman; it shows her acting and being acted upon; its segments—written at different times—circle backwards to address questions that had been left unanswered. The poem, part of Coleridge's lifelong meditation on the vulnerabilities of will and agency, is in many ways a female version of "The Rime of the Ancient Mariner."

Some of Coleridge's concerns emerging early and taking different emphases throughout his life provide an encircling context to help explain the purposes of "Christabel."

The first element of the context that bears on "Christabel" is Coleridge's belief in the necessity of preserving a distinction between persons and things at a time when human beings were increasingly tabulated as numbers, averages, and groups. Coleridge argued against the use of a vocabulary that would reduce persons to things to be used, means to an end. Fully aware that persons are not always coherent to others or to themselves, that persons fragment and lose control, and that persons allow themselves to be used as things as their dependencies require, Coleridge advocates in different ways at different times the sacred distinction between persons and things;[12] the necessity of not using others as things;[13] or not letting oneself be used by abdicating the will.[14]

A second context for gaining perspective on "Christabel" is Coleridge's interest in the interplay of souls and bodies, spirits and selves, in metamorphoses that merge substances. Such a flow of identities is familiar to contemporary American film-goers, who have watched the fusion of bodies and souls in Steve Martin and Lily Tomlin's "All of Me," but in Coleridge's day this interplay also had mesmerizing possibilities; ghosts, revenants, and diabolic possession were common superstitions, the topics of early anthropological research, and frequent invaders of dreams. Coleridge's plan to publish "Christabel" with an essay on the "Praeternatural" may have aimed to justify his use of such spiritualistic traditions to render human emotions.[15] For Coleridge, such porous perimeters can be intimate, as when he writes his young friend Thomas Allsop "Let's exchange Souls" (*CL* 5, 164); at other times they are frightening, as when he describes "the absence of a Self . . . the want or torpor of Will" that is the "mortal Sickness" of his son Hartley (*CL* 5, 232). In his late *Opus Maximum* he finds the word for a soul that evaporates for want of a connection with others: this is "the phantom soul" (*OM*, 124–125).

Related to these contexts is the biographical reality that one of the most influential and brilliant men of the Romantic age saw himself as weak and empty and that he proliferated images for his own absence of personhood. We saw this collapse when he capitulated to Southey's demands that he marry Southey's first girlfriend even though both men knew that there was no love between them. Nine years later (1803) he analyses this weakness to Southey himself, confessing, "A sense of weakness—a haunting sense, that I was an herbaceous Plant, as large as a large Tree, with a Trunk of the Same Girth, & Branches as large & shadowing—but with *pith within* the Trunk, not heart of Wood/—that I had *power* not *strength*—an involuntary Imposter—that I had no real Genius, no real Depth/—/This on my honor is as fair a statement of my habitual Haunting, as I could give before the Tribunal of Heaven/ How it arose in me, I have but lately discovered/ Still it works within me/ but only as a Disease, the cause & meaning of which I know/" (Letter 509, *CL* 2, 959). Watching himself experience this inner absence, he plays with botanical metaphors to amuse Southey with the spectacle of his insignificance.[16]

These fluctuations of power and weakness Coleridge often formulates in terms of gender. In "To William Wordsworth" (1807; *PW* 2, #401), Coleridge calls Wordsworth "Strong in thyself, and powerful to give strength" (l. 103), and describes himself as "passive" (l. 96) and "absorbed" (l. 111). Marlon Ross shows that Coleridge, abased before Wordsworth's masculinity, "assumes a 'feminine' position in order to attain a distinctively 'masculine triumph',"[17] a needy self-abasement that Donald H. Reiman explores as a continuation of Coleridge's adoring and resentful relation to his older brothers.[18] In a positive sense, Coleridge aspires to the androgyny that he finds in Shakespeare rather than to the masculine singlemindedness of Wordsworth, though Diane Hoeveler sees the androgyny in "Christabel" as a negative force.[19] In part because of his sense of himself as yielding, Coleridge is engrossed in the lives and feelings of his many women friends, who by nature or nurture must learn to yield; these affinities come to the surface in "Christabel."

Coleridge's search for "the cause and meaning" of feelings of emptiness takes him deep into child psychology. Why do some children develop a strong identity and others wither and collapse at the slightest trauma? While notes from 1796 already suggest a project on infants and infancy (*CN* 1, 330), his fullest analysis of infant selfhood comes late in the 1820's, when he dictates to Joseph Henry Green his great *Opus Maximum*. In Part 2 of the *Opus Maximum* he examines mother and child bonding and argues that the nursing child who gazes at its mother's face does not gaze a mirror but at an Other, whom the child learns to love and subsequently leave.[20] A crisis of some kind occurs to startle the child into a separate identity. "The child now learns its own alterity and sooner or later, as if some sudden crisis had taken place in its nature, it forgets hence forward to speak of itself by imitation, that is, by the name which it had caught from without. It becomes a person; it is and speaks of itself as 'I,' and from that moment it has acquired what, in the following stages, it may quarrel with, what it may loosen and deform, but can never eradicate—a sense of an alterity in itself, which no eye can see, neither his own nor others" (*OM,* p. 132).[21] If this bonding or the crisis that disconnects it do not occur, the child grows into a thing grasping after a world of things that will always recede. He or she becomes the "Mad Narcissus" of Coleridge's age and of our own. The "Mad Narcissus" is the active side of "The Phantom Soul." Coleridge's scrutiny of early infant learning is revolutionary, 120 years in advance of John Bowlby and D. W. Winnicott. His interest in the formation of infant identity may inform the thought-experiment of the poem "Christabel" with its insistence on the girl's motherlessness, need, and vulnerability; the poem surely leads on to his later meditations on lack of self.

A last element of the context for "Christabel" is also related to the previous ones: it is Coleridge's lament that the yearnings that impel men and women cannot be satisfied. They lead to a chasm that he calls "self-insufficingness." The hunger for love cannot be adequately returned in this world and so provokes imaginings of unearthly love. Yearning, craving, hunger, and need come increasingly to explain both loneliness and the aspiration to spiritual life; this "want" spreads through "Christabel" and many later poems.[22] In his 1826 essay "On the Passions" Coleridge specifically relates this hunger to puberty; he plans to quote from King John, from the Greek tragedians, from Dante, Chaucer, Shakespeare and Ben Jonson to "prove Grief to be a Hunger of the Soul" (*SWF* 2, 1438 and 1451).

These ideas and many others, modified or recharged over time, converge on "Christabel," and take specific form in a "character" who is imagined as growing and ceasing to grow. Coleridge's principles surround the poem; the poem embodies the principles, and at the same time suggests their limitations. The poem and the principles that it embodies are rooted in Coleridge's affinity with women.[23]

These surrounding preoccupations will cast a "peculiar tint of yellow green" ("Dejection: An Ode," *PW* # 293, l. 29) on the poem we are gazing at. If we see "Christabel" as one specific experiment furthering Coleridge's work in distinguishing between persons and things, in showing how the souls or spirits of one person pass in and out of another person in the form of dream-like phantoms, in understanding selves as fluctuating between strength and weakness and male and female, in exploring infant psychology for its formative moments of developing identity, and in yearning for an ever-receding completion, we will be hard put to find the joy and sexual rapture that many critics have seen in the poem. We will see it instead as a companion piece to the "Rime of the Ancient Mariner." Where "The Rime" encapsulates one form of Coleridge's obsession with will, action, guilt, penance, perpetual torment, and the glimmer of blessing, "Christabel" hides at its center a different sort of pain. The poem in all three of its segments spins inward to an intricate knot of need, yearning, self-obliteration, and merging. It struggles with non-being and emptiness, the "horrible solitude" and "self-inquietude" of the notebooks (*CN* 257), the reaching outward of the letters, the analysis of human development in the *Opus Maximum*. It catches in rhythms a deep and mournful emotion which "must pine" in words, struggling to escape (*CN* 2, 2998). Coleridge places this almost incommunicable emotion in the hidden life of a young woman, in a poem that Julie Carlson calls "Coleridge's most remarkable statement on women, gender, a subject's coming-to-sexuality, and his or her formation by generic forms."[24]

Readers who find joy and exhilaration in sexual initiation concentrate on part one, lines 220 to 264. They see a young woman on the verge of puberty venturing forth, defying her father, his walls, his guards, his rules, and his morbidity, acting on her own, inviting a young and unknown woman hospitably to her castle chamber, and making all the moves that will accomplish her own, suddenly upsurging, sexual desires. I think that we would all agree that these are the occurrences in the first part of the poem from lines 23 to 225. Susan Luther calls Christabel's "martyrdom" "the psychological death which she must undergo in order to experience the life of mature adult emotional functioning." Jonas Spatz emphasizes the importance of the "sexual maturation" "as the basis of love and a happy marriage." H. W. Piper finds "enlightenment and joy as well as suffering in it"; John Beer also affirms a positive fulfillment in sexual initiation. Camille Paglia exults in the "erection" of female power in the poem as a whole and throughout Coleridge's libidinous work.[25] These interpretations focus on the moment of entry, the initiation, the "liminality" of the narrative.[26]

It is certainly true that Christabel assertively wills her own adventure up to line 230. She leaves the castle at midnight on her own will. She is not prevented by guards or nurses from leaving the walls and going alone into a deep forest. She is left alone to do as she wishes; no one notices her absence or cares for her, despite the tag "whom her father loves so well." She may or may not have a fiancé for whom she prays. The mysterious glittering female Geraldine, who moans and arises from the other side of the oak, may be a projection from a dream, an aspect of Christabel's personality, a witch, a young victim of gang rape, a specter of nature and fertility. Christabel actively courts Geraldine and invites, leads, and even carries her over the threshold as if she were her bride, saving her from the taboos that guard the entrances to the castle, determined to hold onto this one potential companion. Christabel moves in stealth, urging Geraldine to secrecy, and evades the mastiff bitch, the warning flames, and her father's closed door. She intoxicates her guest with wine made by her dead mother, softening her up for whatever purposes she intends. This is the opening, the crossing of the threshold and return over the threshold. It seems to promise release.

But the effects of this initiation undercut any hope of joy. The silencing and transformation in lines 265–278 of part I; in the conclusion to part I; in part II, lines 381–392, 451–474, 589–635; and in the conclusion to part II constitute the Ovidian and Dantean metamorphoses of the poem. Like Ovid's tale of Philomela and Dante's canto 25 describing the thieves absorbing each others' substance and being,[27] these sections show one person being absorbed and obliterated by another and then made to bear the imprint of the inner life of the other. The sexuality of the event is peripheral; it is one image for many kinds of intersubjective exchange and transformation. What occurs is a loss of self, from which there is no escape because there remains no one inside to cry out "from the inmost" (*CN* 3353).

Coleridge is deliberate in presenting what he later calls "an extremely subtle and difficult" idea (*TT* 2, 245). Once inside her bedroom the girl's adventurous will seems to shrivel, whereas the visitor's will swells to overpower it. Geraldine struggles with the dead mother's hovering spirit for control of the body or soul of Christabel. Shifting her voice into a hollow reverberant supernatural vehicle, Geraldine intones:

> Off, Woman, off! this Hour is mine—
> Though thou her Guardian Spirit be,
> Off, Woman, off! 'tis given to me. (ll. 211–213)

Geraldine, a ventriloquist or improvisatrice, assumes numerous voices, sighing in sweet weakness, speaking to spirits, summoning powers, vibrating magical force. Her different voices multiply, while Christabel's go mute. Geraldine swells up and Christabel becomes the shell that two women—the bodiless mother and the excessively embodied love-object—try to enter. This exchange of power occurs by the means of commands; through the sight of flesh, variously described as old, withered, reptilian; through physical touch; through the spoken incantation; through an unspoken but implied sexual act; through lying beside each other asleep or just before sleep. Jack Stillinger shows that the variants in this otherwise quite stable text work to smudge these shocking details.[28]

While the aftermath of this exchange of power has sometimes been read positively, as a successful recapturing of the lost mother, the recuperation of neglected infancy, or a bland peace following initiation into mature sexuality, in my view the descriptions point to a sinister overtaking: the resigned obedience ("So let it be!") as she strips down to "her loveliness"; the agitated features that give no hint of the "many thoughts mov[ing] to and fro" within her mind; the silent watching of the woman dropping her dress to the floor, revealing a bosom so horrific as to be beyond words; the silence as her naked body is "taken" by Geraldine's naked body, pressing her side (is it scaley, withered, prematurely old?) against her own side; the stillness as the spell is uttered and takes effect word by word. One of the narrative voices closely watches the girl in the aftermath of this invasion. In stops and starts, hesitations and retractions, the narrator imagines what feelings may be stirring within the girl's head:

> With open eyes (ah woe is me!)
> Asleep, and dreaming fearfully,
> Fearfully dreaming, yet, I wis,
> Dreaming that alone, which is—
> O Sorrow and Shame! Can this be She,
> The Lady, who knelt at the old Oak Tree? (ll. 292–297)

Though we might see the fearfully dreaming girl as resting in satiety after finding the lost mother whom she had yearned for, we might also see this dreaming Body (ah woe is me! . . . O sorrow and shame!) as an altered being—"Can this be she?"—and in my negative reading, a broken being. For Christabel appears dazed like a prisoner stumbling from a torture chamber. So powerful is this moment of bewildered emergence that Shelley may have modeled on it his depiction of Beatrice Cenci, after the night when her father does or does not rape her, stumbling, speaking haltingly, shifting from topic to topic without her customary rhetorical elegance:

> No, I am dead! These putrefying limbs
> Shut round and sepulchre the panting soul
> Which would burst forth into the wandering air![29]

It was Geraldine's side, after all, that caused Shelley "to run shrieking from the room because he 'suddenly thought of a woman he had heard of who had eyes instead of nipples, which, taking hold of his mind, horrified him'" (quoted in Stillinger, p. 89). The aftermath of ambiguous sexual initiation in "Christabel" may have suggested to Shelley a way to imply the breaking of a vital womanly spirit without stating it.[30]

With the silencing of Christabel's will, power surges inside Geraldine; the narrator by reflection adopts a more decisive voice:

> And lo! the Worker of these Harms,
> That holds the Maiden in her Arms,
> Seems to slumber still and mild,
> As a Mother with her Child.
>
> A Star hath set, a Star hath risen,
> O Geraldine! since Arms of thine
> Have been the lovely Lady's Prison.
> O Geraldine! One hour was thine—
> Thou'st had thy Will! (ll. 298–306)

The narrator records that Geraldine is released, fulfilled, and rampant in will: "Thou'st had thy will!" echoes the phrase "The Marinere hath his will" from the "Rime," when the mariner's will overpowers the wedding guest's will and reduces him to a "three year's child" (*PW* 161 # [1798] ll. 15–16).

For Christabel, the child forced to listen to the spell and feel the sexual body, there seems to be no one left inside. The naked body, the blinking eyes, the vague smile, the leaking tears, the unquiet movements, and the baffled acquiescence suggest the draining out of selfhood from the empty shell:

> And see! the Lady Christabel
> Gathers herself from out her Trance;
> Her Limbs relax, her Countenance
> Grows sad and soft; the smooth thin Lids
> Close o'er her Eyes; and Tears she sheds—
> Large Tears that leave the Lashes bright!
> And oft the while she seems to smile
> As Infants at a sudden Light! (ll. 311–318)

These behaviors suggest that the girl's will has been obliterated. The narrator tries to reassure us—"No doubt, she hath a Vision sweet" (l. 326)—and projects upon her blankness the faith "That Saints will aid if Men will call / For the blue Sky bends over all!" (ll. 330–331). For some readers this hope for benevolence reassures, but for others it seems as ironic as the Rime's "He prayeth best who loveth best / All things both great and small" (647–648) or Tintern Abbey's "Nature never did betray the heart that loved her." The sky will still be blue whether the child suffers or not. Suspended in our judgments, we watch a girl lose inward drive and personal integrity, her boundaries broached and blurred. Only Bard Bracy will notice or care.

Coleridge's poem initially ended here in May, 1798, as the girl awakens, but the meaning of what he had composed haunted him through the next 14 months, first in Germany and then on a farm in Sockburn near Durham while falling in love with a woman not his wife. During this interlude he mused on how his poem was to unfurl. He feared it would disgust people (*CL* 1, 545), and yet he struggled to complete it, finally drinking so much wine, as he writes Josiah Wedgwood, that his "verse making faculties returned" (*CL* 1, 643). The happy result of this bibulous evening at a neighboring clergyman's house is Part II of "Christabel."

Part II may be read as answering the questions roused by part one: What is the cause of this child's neediness, susceptibility, and collapse? Why had she no will to resist, or, if she wanted and sought the seduction, to thrive in its release? Why does she cease to be an active agent or person? Once again "Christabel" pursues questions about agency that are asked hypothetically in "The Rime of the Ancient Mariner" in a different way: did the Mariner act with full intentional agency when he suddenly shot the albatross or did this "manly" act come from some unconscious impulse of perverse and unwilled cruelty? So, too, one asks if his repeated telling of his tale is willed or compulsive, and, if compulsive, what the source of compulsion is. In the case of Christabel, she can no longer speak of her present condition or her past desire, and her personal agency is more compromised than his.

In Part II, Coleridge shifts into a different voice, more assured that an evil had indeed occurred in the last section of Part I. He explains the causes of the girl's neediness by moving back a generation to imagine the formative family patterns. Christabel's mother died in childbirth. The infant has no known nurse nor female relative to substitute for the mother.[31] Christabel's father began mourning his wife from the moment of Christabel's birth with lugubrious rituals of long, slow bells tolling obsessively day in and day out. He sequestered himself in his rooms, his halls were silent, his retinue only occasionally summoned. We could suppose that he hardly knew his child. Beneath this fixated mourning for his wife was an even more intense reason for his unavailability to his child: persistent mourning for a broken friendship, passionate in its absorption, with a male friend. Here, too, the feelings were dammed up by this taboo.[32] In Part II of the poem we see Sir Leoline's feverish excitement about using Geraldine to reawaken his friendship with Sir Roland, her putative father, his determination to hunt down Geraldine's tormentors and "dislodge the reptile souls / from the bodies and forms of men" (a reminder of the interfusion of souls and bodies that has just occurred in his daughter's bedroom and will recur in a few lines), and his rage at his own daughter for her appearance, her strange facial twitches, her garbled speech, her unseemly hisses, her embarrassing lack of graciousness to his new young friend, his conduit to past happiness. We see him quickly abandon his daughter in her mute anguish, and take up her seducer and silencer as both his new daughter and his new lady. As an old man Coleridge claims that Sir Leoline's feelings are paternal and not sexual (*TT* 1, 495, note 7), though he may be forgetting the phrases his earlier wild self included in the poem:

> And now the Tears were on his Face,
> And fondly in his Arms he took

> Fair Geraldine, who met th' Embrace,
> Prolonging it with Joyous Look. (ll. 447–450)

Sir Leoline's rage, his inappropriate sexual attraction to his daughter's "companion," his fierce rejection of his motherless daughter point to his own self-absorption.

For Christabel's part this final abandonment erases her. Numerous details suggest the loss of personal identity within:

> She shrunk and shudder'd, and saw again—
> (Ah woe is me! Was it for thee,
> Thou gentle maid! such Sights to see?) (ll. 454–456)

So blank is she that in an instant her being takes the imprint of Geraldine's shrunken snake eyes (583–587):

> But Christabel in dizzy Trance
> Stumbling on the unsteady Ground
> Shudder'd aloud with a hissing sound. (ll. 589–591)

She exchanges faces and voices with her dominator:

> The Maid, alas! her thoughts are gone,
> She nothing sees—no sight but one!
> The Maid, devoid of Guile and Sin,
> I know not how, in fearful wise,
> So deeply had she drunken in
> That Look, those shrunken serpent Eyes,
> That all her Features were resign'd
> To this sole Image in her Mind:
> And passively did imitate
> That Look of dull and treacherous Hate! (ll. 597–607)

Out of her vacancy of person and in defiance of Geraldine's spell, she summons a plea, in full supplicant's posture, gripping her father's knees—"By My Mother's Soul do I intreat/That Thou this Woman send away!" (ll. 616–617). But this spark of will quickly subsides. Her changed look, taking over Geraldine's inner nature, her staggering walk, her inability to speak, explain herself, or protest, and her dazed and blank appearance attest to a childhood of terror.[33] Her father's anger is intense enough to be admonished by the narrator (ll. 634–635).

In addition to his cold, narcissistic rage Sir Leoline tyrannizes his court and creates in it a "universe of death," censoring and silencing others. He censors the Bard whose dream inspires him to help Christabel, forbidding him to travel around the countryside singing the symbolic tale that will tell the truth. This is the third and most outward layer of silencing in the poem, and one that makes Christabel a political prisoner as well as a "prisoner of childhood" (to cite Alice Miller's study of the needy offspring of narcissists[34]).

For Christabel there is no exit from her hollowed out core; there is either no one inside (consistent with children lacking nurture from birth and adopting false selves to cover this gap) or her enforced silence suffocates her. A motherless daughter with a grieving and distant father and no mentioned nurse surely sets up an experiment for any psychologist: what can happen to a girl with so little support and tenderness? Coleridge's thought experiment catches his subject at the moment of sudden sexual quest. Her impulse misfires, and she is absorbed by the (M)other she has lured to her bed.

In the midsection of the poem, then, a transfer of power seems to occur; one young woman absorbs another, eradicates her will and her speech, deprives her of the imaginary protective spirit of her mother and the fragile loyalty of her father, and fills her with the underside of her own vicious features. A negative reading of this passage—that Christabel is not purring with sexual well-being or infantile reunion with the lost mother but is emptied out by a more wide-ranging invasion of her inward fountain of agency—is reinforced by the parallels between this central section of the poem and Coleridge's continuation of Wordsworth's "The Three Graves" (*PW* #155), which he took over in the early spring of 1798 during the writing of the first part of "Christabel".

"The Three Graves," a 318 line poem in quatrains that fizzles out in mockery, explores some of the same ground as "Christabel": women's passions and jealousies, the overpowering of a younger woman by an older one, the incapacitation of one young woman by force of magic and will. Coleridge believes that the merits of "The Three Graves," "if any, are exclusively psychological." Summarizing the plot in his preface to the poem, he says that the "Mother practiced every art, both of endearment and of calumny, to transfer the affections [of her future son-in-law] from her daughter to herself." When he rejected her, she "fell on her knees, and in a loud voice that approached to a scream, she prayed for a curse both on him and on her own child." The phrases, "Away, Away!" and "a deadly leer of hate," and reactions to the spell such as silence, paralysis, and the inability to weep, link the mother's breaking of the daughter's will in "The Three Graves" with Geraldine's similar power over Christabel. As early as the 1796 "Destiny of Nations" Coleridge uses some of the phrases describing blankness and self-loss for Joan of Arc (ll. 253–277), but these phrases apply to Joan of Arc's sorrow at seeing a family in desperate poverty. "The Three Graves" is the experimental ground for the disturbing elements in "Christabel": the overpowering of another through passionate magical language[35] and through the skin-penetrating vibrations of prohibited desires. "The Three Graves" applies to women's passions Coleridge's study of Obeah witchcraft and Otaheitan Indian rites,[36] and his frequent rereadings in Greek of the powerful outcries of Electra and Antigone. "Christabel" climaxes these earlier representations of female passions and in turn prepares for later poems on jealousy and rage, such as "Alice du Clos" and "Not at Home" that explore the "smothering weight" of unbearable emotion, the "dark fluxion" of Coleridge's death bed poem "*E Coelo Descendit*," "all unfixable by thought / A phantom dim of past and future wrought" (*PW* #700).

Four years later (1804) Coleridge was still brooding about the meaning of his poem. In yet another new voice he added a coda to suggest by an elusive analogy that parental neglect and rage are not phenomena limited to the middle ages, but continue into the early nineteenth century, even among ostensibly well-meaning parents. The father of the coda speaks too much rather than too little, and this child, too, is left speechless, but at a younger age. The father's wounding words come from some inexplicable tangle of his own thwarted emotions, crashing in on his child in the midst of the child's whirling delight. A modern Sir Leoline, this father of the coda can blight a child's growth even in an enlightened time when children's psyches were known to be impressionable. In regard to the observation of child development, Coleridge was himself one of the most enlightened, and yet in this coda he obliquely confessed uncontrollable rage at his firstborn son.[37]

The disturbing power of "Christabel" may come in part from its layers of grief. This grief works on many levels: the motherless daughter desperate for any touch of kindness; the widower secluded in mourning and coldly, furiously unavailable to his child, mourning in addition a severed intimacy with a male friend, a severance that has long choked him with frustration. Coleridge puts this "*wanting*, the *craving* of Grief," this "wasting and *marasmus* of Grief" (*SWF* 2, 1451) in the character of a girl who reaches puberty without having bonded with a parent or parent substitute; he expands it into a past generation in Part 2 and applies it in the coda to a domestic personal situation in the present. The poem circles around obsessively unresolved loss that forces either inert or seething passivity. While "The Rime of the Ancient Mariner" also circles obsessively around a site of pain and guilt, "Christabel" focuses on what we now realize are difficult transitions in the personal development of young women, where what is done *to* them often feels like their own fault,[38] where they retreat from personhood into paralysis.[39] No wonder Swinburne calls Coleridge's verse "womanly rather than effeminate."[40]

"Christabel" explores a moral dimension that draws on Coleridge's horror of using other persons as things. Geraldine uses Christabel as a means to approach her father, if any such inner motivation can be ascribed to her; Sir Leoline uses Geraldine to recapture his past life and discards his daughter as now useless. Both violate Coleridge's fundamental principle: "Reverence the Individuality of your Friend" (*CN* 2, 3146), or, as expanded in *The Friend*, "the reverence which [each person] owes to the presence of Humanity in the person of his Neighbour" (*The Friend* 1809–1810, 2, 43).

In defending "Christabel" from the "rude breezes of disapprobation" stirred up by the 1816 volume, George Felton Mathew asks: "And shall it be considered unlawful for Coleridge to pay his addresses to more than one muse? or for the children of his imagination to be not only sons, but daughters?"[41] Mathew implies that the womanliness of the poem might make a difference in its reception. If seen as a study of abandonment and neglect in a girl child, and her susceptibility to being used by a dominant person, the poem might meet wider approval. It participates in the world of women that we examine in this book: the pairs of sisters, like the Evans, the Frickers, the Hutchinsons, the Brents, and the Hardings (Gillman); the women writers like Mary Robinson, Charlotte Smith, (whose sonnets he included in a 1796 consolatory volume) Dorothy Wordsworth, Mary Wollstonecraft, Mathilda Betham, Georgiana, Duchess of Devonshire, and Jane Austen, even the too somberly playing baby Mary Godwin; the younger friends he advised late in life about the necessity in marriage of not using the partner as a thing for one's own gratification. Instead of asking why Coleridge did not finish "Christabel," we should ask how he knows as much as he does about the silencing of young women, anticipating what psychologists have discovered only since 1980 about girls' desires and repressions as they approach puberty, which Coleridge called "a distinct revolutionary Epoch in the human mind & body" (*CN* 1637), when "sexual instincts begin to disquiet" the fourteen or fifteen year-old child. Just how unusual his discoveries are can be measured by the reactions of his manly critics, Hazlitt and Moore, who mock the poem's freakishness and titter nervously that Geraldine is a man in disguise. Rather, "Christabel" joins *Jane Eyre, Wuthering Heights*, and *Blythedale Romance* as studies of violent passions in women, the absorption of women's identities, and the potential collapse of their independent agency. All these girls are motherless, and Christabel's isolation is essential to Coleridge's thought experiment.

His knowledge may derive in part from his mother's degrading treatment of his sister Nancy, banished to a solitary and loveless exile and death,[42] as we have seen. His 1790–1791 sonnet "On Receiving an Account that his only Sister's Death was Inevitable" expresses his sorrow. Dorothy Wordsworth, too, may have fueled Coleridge's indignation at the uses made of young women. An orphan, Dorothy allowed herself to be absorbed into William's life, serving numerous functions for him. As she and Coleridge walked out in the moonlit nights, her emotions, what Meena Alexander describes as her "turbulence and terror," her "longing for the supportive love that she was robbed of," the "terrible void of maternal loss,"[43] touched an answering pain in her companion Coleridge. Motherless at birth in 1797, Mary Godwin playing sadly in the house of the grieving William Godwin may also have stung Coleridge, who called the house and mingled children "catacombish." In her study of the ways that girls allow themselves to be turned into objects, Jessica Benjamin describes this self-loss in a formulation that could apply to Christabel: "when the self is felt to be buried or in chaos, powerless or destructive, penetration and mastery by the powerful one serves to ward off and express self-dissolution, to overcome abandonment."[44]

Where Wordsworth in poems about mad mothers, lost daughters, and abandoned wives watched women suffer,[45] Coleridge felt from within as if it were his own this crushing of the girl child. "Christabel" is the poem that recognizes this female pain, even as its author feels a correspondent vulnerability and emptiness as a man. Coleridge's own sense of stability teetered on the edge when Wordsworth without explanation rejected "Christabel" for volume two of the *Lyrical Ballads* of 1800. Life imitated art as Wordsworth played Geraldine to Coleridge's Christabel. Coleridge, ecstatically completing his poem, strode over Helvellyn to place the beautiful object at Wordsworth's feet.[46] Dorothy Wordsworth's journal records his arrival August 29, 1800, in "the still clear moonshine in the garden," the late night reading of the poem, and the "pleasure" it gave on a later reading October 5. The entries of October 6 and 7 are as cryptic as any of the difficult gaps in "Christabel":

> Monday. A rainy day. Coleridge intending to go but did not get off. We walked after dinner to Rydale. After tea read The Pedlar. Determined not to print Christabel with the LB. Tues. Coleridge went off at 11 o'clock.[47]

The gaps between events, the absences, and silent departures mirror the suffocation of feeling within the poem itself.[48] The day after Coleridge left, Wordsworth began quickly transposing themes in "Christabel" into the poem "Michael," to fill the gap at the end of the volume left by the withdrawal of "Christabel." Susan Eilenburg perceives how "Michael" shifts motifs in "Christabel" into a different register. She notes, for instance, that in both poems "the rival child displaces the true child from his secure place in the family, and the true child, abandoned, takes on the characteristics of the rival."[49] Wordsworth materializes the themes of "Christabel" in "Michael," from spiritual possession into possession of property, from desire to inheritance, and in doing so enacts the very possession that the poems exchange, as the later poem appropriates and transforms the identity of the earlier poem.[50] In letters to friends, Coleridge tries to make light of Wordsworth's domination, reminiscent of Geraldine's: he says that his "poem grew so long & in Wordsworth's opinion so impressive, that he rejected it from his volume as disproportionate both in size & merit, & as discordant in it's [sic] character" (CL 1, 643); deep within, he felt that his career as a poet was over.

Despite Coleridge's seeming passivity to and collusion with Wordsworth's silencing of his poem (he helped copy "Michael" to send it to the press), Coleridge persisted in thinking about "Christabel" and planning to expand it. He did not give up on it and changed very few lines.[51] Coleridge wrote Poole that he planned to publish it by itself, with "two Essays annexed to it, on the Praeternatural—and on Meter" (March 16, 1801). By the time Lord Byron urged John Murray to publish it with "Kubla Khan" and "Pains of Sleep" in a twenty-three page volume of 1816, Coleridge is almost arrogant in defiance of critics, in marked contrast to the apologetic headnotes and anxious additions to "The Rime of the Ancient Mariner" and to "Kubla Khan." This poem, whatever people might think, especially after hearing Scott's metrically derivative "Lay of the Last Minstrel," came forth as a fountain, not as a leak in other men's tanks. And where the "Ancient Mariner" becomes an image of his own life as a wanderer and guilty talker, "Christabel" is an artwork apart, depicting the mysterious life of the Other. Standing in as the bewildered narrator, changing his voices, asking silly questions, gaping at human entrapment from different angles, wondering at the external evidence for the inward loss of force, he tries to enter the female world, to understand "someone the structure of whose experience is radically different from one's own."[52]

Even though the poem was banished from Wordsworth's volume, it continues to resound in the Grasmere rooms, kept alive by women readers. Dorothy Wordsworth writes Thomas DeQuincey May 1, 1809, "I was called down stairs and found Miss Hutchinson reading Coleridge's

Christabel to Johnny—she was tired, so I read the greatest part of it: he was excessively interested especially with the first part, but he asked 'why she could not say her prayers in her own room', and it was his opinion that she ought to have gone 'directly to her Father's Room to tell him that she had met with the Lady under the old oak tree and all about it' " (MY, 324). Wordsworth's little son's advice to the fictional heroine to rely on prayer and on her father's intervention points to the anxiety induced by the poem representing disintegration and self-loss. Years later, after bathing in the sea off Ramsgate, Coleridge notes, "were I free to do so I feel as if I could compose the third part of Christabel, or the song of her desolation" (Oct. 22, 1823; CN 4, 5031).

The disturbing narrative "Christabel" takes part in a conversation among Coleridge's works in other genres about the "forfeiture of Free-agency" (CL 5, 252, to Thomas Allsop, Oct. 8, 1822, about his son Hartley's disintegration). Christabel, raised from infancy in gloomy vacancy, did not make the transition from an *it* to an *I* and thus never learned to say *Thou*. She is a Phantom Soul. In her vacant passivity she anticipates the formulation that Coleridge later settles on in his *Opus Maximum*: "A will that does not contain the power of opposing itself to another will is no will at all" (*OM*, p. 172). As Coleridge thinks about this absence of will and self later in his life he finds it in people who are not technically motherless or parentless, but who have been raised in wealthy homes with costly things that reflect them, instead of among loving faces and responsive voices. To Coleridge, an increasingly mechanistic world seems to have produced more and more of these phantom souls. "Christabel" is one of his first explorations of the causes of this modern malaise.[53] The poem enunciates the silence of adolescent women, their passivity, punishment, paralysis, sense of guilt; it stands in counterpoint to its companion piece "The Rime of the Ancient Mariner" with its manly bloodthirstiness, guilty action, and loquacity. In "Christabel," Coleridge's immerses himself in the depths of female sufferings, and reveals how they exemplify the violation of his ethical principles.[54]

Chapter 6
Sara Hutchinson: Love and Reading

> or his happiest choice too late
> Shall meet, already linked and wedlock-bound
> To a fell adversary, his hate or shame:
> Which infinite calamity shall cause
> To human life, and household peace confound
> *Paradise Lost* X, 904–908

Falling in love with Sara Hutchinson crystallized Coleridge's early sensitivities to female bodies, to female warmth, and to female voices, and set the stage for his later loves including his fainter, reduplicated loves for Mrs. Morgan's sister Charlotte Brent and for Mrs. Anne Gillman. His love for Sara Hutchinson began either on Oct. 26, 1799, when he met her, or four weeks later on Nov. 24, when he held her hand and felt love's dart envenom him forever (as he wrote in his diary in Latin, to keep his wife from reading it). This love was intensified by entanglement with the Wordsworths, since Sara Hutchinson's sister Mary was to become William's wife; Coleridge in loving Wordsworth's sister-in-law attached himself all the more intimately to the Wordsworth family circle, including Dorothy, whom he loved in a more companionable way. His "passion for SH," as Dorothy called it in her letters, made him more than usually alert to other women, to their stories, songs, performances, troubles, and triumphs; it overlapped with his appreciation of literary and musical women. It followed the composition of the first part of "Christabel" and coincided with the struggle to galvanize part two of "Christabel," and to resolve the alternate possible meanings of that poem. It energized his shift from looking at women to listening to them.

Coleridge's love for Sara Hutchinson, which struck soon after his twenty-seventh birthday, filled the rest of his life. For a while this love seems to have been mutual, to judge from messages hidden in other texts. Since she herself is not a beauty, but rather short and stout, it must be her character—her vitality, warmth, and humor—(as well as her fine brown hair) that he loves. "Can see nothing extraordinary in her" begins a notebook entry (1152) proposing a poem "noting all the virtues of the mild & retiring kind," marveling at how impervious love is to external appearance. He tells Daniel Stuart that he is excited by her "Sense, Sensibility, Sweetness of Temper, perfect simplicity and unpretending Nature, joined to shrewdness and entertainingness,"[1] although he realizes that love cannot be a list of qualities but is a sudden miracle of intimate affinity. Even Southey, loyal for years to his first love Sara Fricker Coleridge, comes to dote on Sara Hutchinson, so charming and steady is her manner.[2]

The onset of Coleridge's love is recorded immediately in his poem "Love." Despite a recent claim that "Love" has nothing to do with any actual new tenderness in C's life, J. C. C. Mays declares that "the poem was inspired by C's first visit to Sockburn in Oct–Nov 1799, when he met and fell in love with SH."[3] Coleridge quickly publishes his poem in *The Morning Post* of December 21, 1799, and again in the second edition of *The Lyrical Ballads* of 1800.[4] He wants the world to know that at twenty-seven years old he has fallen in love, has experienced the ecstasy that many people never feel, has been pierced by love's arrow, and that despite the seeming passivity of that metaphor of being wounded, his love is forceful and determined. He trumpets the event despite the well-known fact that he is indissolubly married to someone else. As scandalous as this announcement might have been to the reading public (not to speak of his wife at home), the poem was one of his most popular at the time and continued throughout the nineteenth century to be his most frequently imitated poem. For reasons founded in the general neglect of Coleridge's erotic life, the poem is rarely mentioned in modern criticism and has received only one sustained analysis, one that significantly focuses on the lover's failure.[5]

1. "Love"

Despite this critical neglect, "Love" pulses with the excitement of courtship. It is one of Coleridge's many framed narratives, akin to "The Rime of the Ancient Mariner" in persuading an interlocutor to hear a story set in a distant time or place. But "Love"'s outer frame is more immediately connected with the inner story than the "Rime"'s, and its two layers advance in tandem. The outer frame depicts a male bard wooing his lady, watching her reactions, and pausing and speeding up his performance to stir her response to him and to the tale he tells.

The inner tale has a medieval theme and a violent and disturbing subject. A knight long rejected by a lady dies from wounds incurred while rescuing her from a band of brigands. He who had loved her fruitlessly dies to save her, and the lady in the tale regrets her failure to grasp at fulfillment.[6] The "old and moving story" bears some resemblance to "Christabel" with its inner tale of the "rape" of Geraldine and the "fate worse than death" of Christabel herself. It also resembles the violent material of "The Ballad of the Dark Ladie" from which the poem originally sprang. In the inner tale of "Love" the Knight is crazed by pursuing his lady in vain for ten years; he runs through a dark wood full of fiends. His haunted psyche is healed by his own sudden and unexpected act of saving the disdainful lady:

> And that unknowing what he did,
> He leap'd amid a murderous band,
> And sav'd from outrage worse than death
>   The Lady of the Land! (ll. 53–56)

The Knight's spontaneous generosity ("unknowing what he did" similar to the mariner's sudden act of blessing the water snakes "unawares") and the Lady's new gratitude cure his madness:

> And that she nursed him in a cave;
> And how his madness went away,
> When on the yellow forest-leaves
>   A dying man he lay. (ll. 61–65)

Rescuing the Lady from attack by "a murderous band," he dies from his wounds; he is the sacrificial victim, not she.

Each segment of the inner story prompts a change in the outer courtship. In swiftly alternating stanzas of telling the story and watching its effect, the narrator sings and plays the harp while he keeps his eye on the blushing face and stirring body of the woman who listens. The "woeful tale of love," the sacrifice, the cure of madness, and the dying words are enhanced by the skillful hesitations in the narrator's delivery. His voice falters, his harp pauses, his performance throbs with feeling, as he gauges her mood, watching her lose control of her emotions and succumb to their now mutual desire. The narrator of "Love" describes how the fiction and the immediate scene intertwine:

> I told her how he pined: and ah!
> The deep, the low, the pleading tone
> With which I sang another's love,
>   Interpreted my own. (ll. 33–36)

He gives the knight his own desires; the knight speaks for him.

Having heard the narrator's "old rude song," the female listener in "Love" responds from the peculiar happy warmth of her nature, for she is a woman who has few sorrows of her own and enjoys sympathizing vicariously with others. She loves him increasingly as he speaks of emotions:

> She loves me best, whene'er I sing
>   The songs that make her grieve. (ll. 19–20)

She is not "sadder and wiser," like the wedding guest in "The Rime of the Ancient Mariner" but too "disturbed" with pity to wait to hear the knight's "dying words":

> —but when I reach'd
> That tenderest strain of all the ditty,
> My faultering voice and pausing harp
> Disturbed her soul with pity! (ll. 65–68)

She is "thrilled" in "all impulses of soul and sense." The influences of the evening, the story,

> And hopes and fears that kindle hope,
> An undistinguishable throng,
> And gentle wishes long subdued,
>   Subdued and cherished long!

rouse Genevieve to tumultuous emotion:

> She half enclosed me with her arms,
> She pressed me with a meek embrace;
> And bending back her head, looked up,
>   And gazed upon my face.
>
> 'Twas partly love, and partly fear,
> And partly 'twas a bashful art,
> That I might rather feel than see,
>   The swelling of her heart. (ll. 85–92)

The woman listening in the frame heeds the intended lesson of the tale and responds to its warning by turning actively to embrace the singer in an "artful" embrace. With presence, voice, and story he rouses the lady to such a pitch that she sighs his name.

The narrator succeeds in his seduction by telling about the dire results of not loving, which include madness, desperate action, wounding, and death. He warns his lady that she will regret rejecting him, that she will spend her life expiating her scorn.

Coleridge the poet deliberately shows that the woman chooses to love on her own will: she is a full participant, eager to do what the woman in the inner tale does not have the emotional resilience to do. Where the lover/narrator had gazed upon her face involuntarily and too fondly (ll. 28 and 40), she is now the one who gazes on his face at close quarters and, the meter suggests, at length, boldly and meaningfully. Pleased with his face and his voice, she reciprocates his love. The love in "Love" is complete: it looks with the eye, listens with the ear, communicates with the soul, and torridly embraces with the body, as the woman purposely turns so that the singer can feel her breasts arched against his chest. "Love" transposes the early themes of rejection and madness to create a positive reading of the power of love.

The mutually reinforcing tale and song of "Love" build up a responsive love of watching, listening, and attending to one another. This sort of love generates creativity and power for both lovers, as the first stanza declares:

> All thoughts, all passions, all delights,
> Whatever stirs this mortal frame,
> All are but ministers of Love,
> And feed his sacred flame. (ll. 1–4)

With the overwhelming experience of love come the many energetic and joyful experiences of life; they come from love and they feed back into that fiery source, stirring this mortal frame.

It is not surprising that Wordsworth judged that "there was too much of the sensual" in Coleridge's "Love," and that Keats luxuriated in just this sensuality, and its ultimate loss, when he transposes the poem into his own "La Belle Dame Sans Merci."[7] In saying that the Knight wooed the Lady for "ten long years," Coleridge did not realize that he himself would woo Sara Hutchinson for ten years, and be abandoned by her on the cold hillside in February 1810, two months more than ten years since she first held his hand. Was she following the script provided by the inner tale of the poem to and about herself?

Far from being a poem of impotence and weakness, "Love" is a bold announcement of revived power. The narrator feels the body and breasts of his Genevieve turn assertively—by her own agency—to embrace him and thus to save him from the fate of the hero of his story, thawing the scorn that drives the knight through a tangled wilderness, deluded by fiends disguised as angels. In its doubling and mirroring narrations, moving, as J. C. C. Mays observes, at different speeds and catching up to coincide at the end, "Love" illustrates in its form one of Coleridge's definitions of Love: "Love, true human Love—i.e. two hearts, like two correspondent concave Mirrors, having a common focus, while each reflects and magnifies the other, and in the other itself, is an endless reduplication, by Sweet Thoughts and Sympathies" (cited Whalley, p. 88). The bending inward of these concave mirrors suggest shared feelings and thoughts as well as flexibility and attentiveness. It suggests a self-contained center where these lovers reduplicate and enlarge each other's best qualities. Such a magnifying focus also generates heat and can burn. Unlike its melancholy offspring, Keats's "La Belle Dame Sans Merci," where the knight is abandoned, woe begone, on the cold hillside, "Love" concludes passionately; it proclaims to the world that Coleridge has fallen in love. He is proud of it, not devious or shy. It transforms him.

2. Dante

Such an enactment of the power of storytelling is reinforced by the echoes of Dante's *Inferno* canto five, where Paolo and Francesca fall in love while reading the story of Launcelot and Guenevere. Coleridge borrowed the Reverend Henry Boyd's 1785 translation of the *Inferno* from the Bristol library on June 23, 1796, and quickly noted a plan to write a three part poem "in the manner of Dante" (CN 170). With this text in hand he did not have to wait for his 1804 trip to Malta to learn Italian or for Carey's 1814 translation to read this powerful love story inside a love story. Eric C. Brown has demonstrated that "distinct verbal and imagistic parallels exist between the *Inferno*, as translated by Boyd, and Coleridge's poem, 'The Rime of the Ancient Mariner,'" specifically in the description of Charon in canto three and in the Ulysses story in canto 23, where the tongue of flame is compelled to tell the tale of the final overweening voyage.[8] As the Boyd translation permeated the "Rime," so too it gives the form of the Paolo and Francesca story to the poem "Love," written two years later and resembling its structure. As the lovers in the outer frame of "Love" learned to love each other over storytelling, so also Coleridge and Sara Hutchinson learned to love each other from late 1799 to early 1810 as they read together. Coleridge saw their intimacy in the mirror of the love story of Paolo and Francesca, and in his "Love" he recreated their wooing.

Reading together feeds love, as Francesca boldly tells Dante. In Boyd's translation, Dante the pilgrim calls to the "wailing lovers,"

> "Afflicted pair! Descend and say
> Why thus you mourn?"

Dante bids her to tell

> "how first you saw his passion grow
> What busy demon taught thee first to know
> The secret meaning of his smother'd sighs."⁹

In a vacant hour in the quiet grove, Paolo reads to Francesca the "soft seducing story of Launcelot and fair Geneura's love" (Boyd, p. 259). Francesca sobs as she describes the stages of falling in love:

> "Too much I found th'insidious volume charm,
> And Paulo's mantling blushes rising warm;
> Still as he read the guilty secret told.
> Soon from the line his eyes began to stray;
> Soon did my yielding looks my heart betray,
> Nor needed words our wishes to unfold.
> XXVI
> Eager to realize the story'd bliss,
> Trembling he snatch'd the half-resented kiss,
> Too ill soon lesson'd by the pandar-page,
> Vile pandar-page! It smooth'd the paths of shame."
> While thus she spoke, the partner of her flame
> Tun'd his deep sorrows to the whirlwind's rage.

Francesca's narration rouses Dante the pilgrim to remember his own lost desires:

> So full the symphony of grief arose,
> My heart, responsive to the lover's woes
> With thrilling sympathy convuls'd my breast.
> Too strong at last my passion grew,
> And sick'ning at the lamentable view,
> I fell, like one by mortal pangs oppress'd.

Far from warning millions of lovers away from their desires, the story within the story arouses both fictional listeners, Virgil, whose hero Aeneas seduced and abandoned Dido, and Dante, who is so affected by Francesca's tale that he swoons at his own implication in love's excesses.

The poem "Love" is modeled on this passionate canto. It is a critical canto also for Blake in his illustrations of Dante where the framing poets Virgil and Dante are depicted as standing outside the windswept swirl of carnal sinners disapproving of this harsh placement of an all-too-natural desire. Indeed, the canto breeds seductions, either on its own or through Coleridge's "Love," generating Leigh Hunt's "The Story of Rimini" (1819) and Keats's "La Belle Dame Sans Merci." The canto illustrates "the contagion of literature." As Paolo Valesio forecasts, "Dante intuits that the very description he is writing will act through the centuries as a 'Galehot' with successive generations of readers not, of course, in the banally direct sense of making successive couples of readers fall into each other's arms, but in the subtle sense . . . to make successive generations of readers sympathize with the psychological node here invoked."[10] As Coleridge catches the contagion, the lovers in his passionate poem do seem to "fall into each other's arms," and the story becomes a "direct" (though far from "banal") pander, pimp, go-between, or Galehot, or Galleoto, joining the lovers in the frame story as well as the lovers within the tale. The phrase "Pandar-page," though awkward, may also influence Coleridge's late ballad, "Alice du Clos; or, The Forked Tongue," where the Page takes human form, as we see in chapter 9. The concatenation of stories illustrates the miraculous power of passionate words on paper or in the air to arouse living bodies, to transform reading eyes into looking eyes, reading mouths into kissing mouths, figuring what Jacqueline Pearson has called an "elision of textuality and sexuality."[11]

"Love" is the first of many poems to "Asra" that recreate a shared activity—reading, singing, story telling, writing, and revising—that unite their minds and voices as well as their bodies as they lean together: "That day we read no further," as Francesca says of their self-reflective reading aloud of Launcelot and Guenevere's almost parallel adultery. These activities bespeak the kind of radiant partnership that Coleridge had begun with Mary Ann Evans, reading and talking about *Hamlet* and seeing plays, and that he yearned for in all his connections with women. Texts pile inside texts in a complex layering that comments on the power of literary fiction while also encoding secret messages of love.

Coleridge and Sara Hutchinson, like Paolo and Francesca, read and wrote together and felt the nearness of each other among their excited words and in warm silence. He wrote in her scrap book of *Sara's Poets* to correct his own poems under her eyes. They read Bartram's "delicious" *Travels* together (*CM* 1, 226–227). He sent her the journal of his walking tour and she copied it out as if she were with him step by step. She writes in her "hand" a series of his notebook entries (1000–1008). He dictated *The Friend* to her day after day; in Dorothy Wordsworth's suggestively physical description, "he generally has dictated to Miss Hutchinson, who takes the words down from his mouth" (Whalley, p. 80). Such shared activities engage eyes, touch, movement, hands, mouths, and the warmth of proximity. The book is the go-between (or pander, or "Galleoto," to use the Italian from Dante that Boccaccio adapts for the sub-title of *The Decameron*) for the lovers. Lovers inside the tale and outside of it swoon at the tale about yielding to desire.[12] For Paolo was also the go-between for his brother's suit of Francesca, and fell in love with her in speaking words meant to convey the feelings of his brother.

3. "Love-Poems"

"Love" opens the gates of Coleridge's passion and initiates a group of other love poems, which Sara Hutchinson copied into her album, *Sara's Poets*. These poems as a group are called the Asra poems, and Mays has added new poems to the earlier group, including "After Bathing in the Sea at Scarborough in Company with T. Hutchinson, August 1801" (*CP* #275). Of Coleridge frolicking in the billows Mays writes: "the essence of his lines is their celebration of feelings of happiness and release, in the days spent at Gallow Hill in the company of SH and the others." Defying his doctor's warning Coleridge throws himself into the surge and bursts up from the waves:

> Me a thousand Loves and Pleasures
> A thousand Recollections bland,
>   Thoughts sublime and stately Measures
> Revisit on thy sounding Strand—
>
>   Dreams, the soul herself forsaking,
> Grieflike Transports, boyish Mirth,
>   Silent Adorations, making
> A blessed Shadow of this Earth!
>
>   O ye Hopes, that stir within me,
> Health comes with you from above:
>   God is with me, God is in me,
> I cannot die, if Life be Love! (ll. 13–24)

His rapture in surfing releases "boyish" energy. The poem does not mention that swimming along with her brother, Thomas Hutchinson, and Coleridge, her admirer, was Sara Hutchinson herself. This explains why the passions are those of a grown man experiencing love more deeply than ever before, with "grieflike Transports" and a fullness as if a God had entered him and he were immortal in his joy.

A shift of mood makes him tease the Hutchinson sisters in a "Verse Letter" (Aug. 1801): he advises Isabella and Joanna not to choose dukes or earls for husbands but plain men like himself:

> You may do as you like—I shall not forbid you.
> But as plain Meat is all that the healthy desire,
> Were I you, I'd put up with a simple Esquire.
> Such a one now *as me*. (*Nota bene. I'm married,*
> *And Coals to Newcastle must never be carried!!*) (*PW* #276, ll. 49–53)

He reminds two of the sisters of the woman he loves that he is already married, and thus not available to them, and also presumably not available to her: an odd reminder—humorous, teasing, withdrawing—at a time of strong passion. He writes to Sara Hutchinson with "explicit love and feeling": "Oh dear Sara how dearly I love you!" and "Bless you, my darling!" (Cited Whalley 43–45). Love invigorates him. In "Soliloquy of a Full Moon," a giddy poem that Sara Hutchinson copies into *Sara's Poets*, the poet speaks through the moon, which changes shapes and shouts for joy like the birds:

> But now Heaven be praised in contempt of the Loon,
> I am I myself I, the jolly full Moon (*PW* #290, ll. 51–52)

She also copies "The Keepsake," a poem that reveals more ardor than Coleridge is usually given credit for. "Emmeline" steals down to the bower,

> early waked
> By her full bosom's joyous restlessness[.]

Emmeline seeks assorted flowers to interweave.

> There, in that bower where first she owned her love,
> And let me kiss my own warm tear of joy
> From off her glowing cheek, she sate and stretched
> The silk upon the frame, and worked her name,
> Between the Moss-rose and Forget-me-not,
> Her own dear name, with her own auburn hair! (*PW* #299, ll. 27–30)

Emmeline creates this intricately personal and ephemeral art work, weaving her own name in the threads of flowers and hair (an early example of the hair art that became a fashion in the Victorian period[13]), so that the traveling poet/lover will not forget her smile, her look, her hair, her voice,

> Nor yet the entrancement of that maiden kiss
> With which she promised, that when spring returned,
> She would resign one half of that dear name,
> And own thenceforth no other name but mine! (ll. 37–40)

These lines hint that in those years, 1800–1802, Coleridge and Sara Hutchinson had hopes to share the same name, despite the notorious impossibility of divorce. How he expected to do this is unclear. Sara Hutchinson's full breasts, the sound of her voice, which "even in her mirthful mood" makes him weep, her kisses, and perhaps her promise to take his name suggest a period of rapture.

Mutual love returns him to the buoyant joy of childhood. In "Answer to a Child's Question," perhaps from early May, 1802, he feels like a lark "so brimful of gladness and love"; he mimics the songs of birds singing "I love and I love." In his own voice he sings "I love my Love, and my Love loves me!" One variant of the poem reiterates this glee:

> 'Tis no wonder that he's full of joy to the brim,
> When He loves his *LOVE*, and his *LOVE* loves *HIM*!
> (*PW* #291, 111–112)

With Sara Hutchinson responsive to him, he experiences happiness. He describes his emotion as an overflowing, a "brimful" gladness, a continuous song. In "The Day-Dream" this love envelops him: "A deeper Trance ne'er wrapt / A yearning spirit" (*PW* #294). These five Asra poems build on "Love" and forecast later love poems.

Writing, reading, hiding their love in books passed back and forth, they knew that they loved each other. Mays has discovered a new sonnet to Sara Hutchinson, and he describes how he found

> the only known text of a sonnet . . . in C's holograph on a piece of paper pasted into the inside cover of the transcript of *Christabel* he made for SH (ms. 2), perhaps in Nov. 1801. The sonnet is on a different paper from *Christabel*, and there is no way of knowing whether the two texts were brought together in the album by SH or, after her death, by someone else. (Mays, headnote to #295)

Both "Christabel" and this sonnet are in Coleridge's own hand, copied painstakingly for her. The sonnet is coded to tell Sara Hutchinson about his complex emotions.

> Are there two things, of all which Men possess,
> That are so like each other and so near
> As mutual Love seems like to Happiness?
> Dear Asra, Woman beyond utterance dear!
> This Love, which ever welling at my heart
> Now in it's living fount doth heave and fall,
> Now overflowing pours thro' every part
> Of all my Frame, and fills and changes all,
> Like vernal waters springing up thro' Snow—
> This Love, that seeming great beyond the power
> Of Growth, yet seemeth evermore to grow—
> Could I transmute the whole to the rich dower
> Of Happy Life, and give it all to Thee,
> Thy Lot, methinks, were Heaven, thy Age Eternity!

As in the first stanza of "Love" written for her a year earlier, in this sonnet his love for Asra fills his frame, lifts his heart, and overflows in other forms of energy and creativity. After the question posed in lines 1–3, the lines addressed to "Dear Asra" begin their uninterrupted cascade, that enjambes as it overflows "great beyond the power / Of Growth, yet seemeth evermore to grow." His love should enrich her even when he is gone.

Enlisting the vocabulary of his medieval and Renaissance predecessors, Coleridge evokes an all-encompassing love that both empowers and engulfs. He speaks of himself as pierced and wounded, adapting to his own psychology the ancient *topoi* of hearts and harts, arrows, shafts, and wounds. He expresses his falling in love in Sockburn Nov. 24, 1799, as an assault by an arrow against which he was helpless in the time-honored language of cupid's dart: "And pressed Sara's hand a long time behind her back, and then, then for the first time, love pricked me with its light arrow, poisoned alas! And hopeless" (*CN* 1, 1575 and note with translation by Coburn). If he leaves it as it is, he dies; if he tries to flee, he rips his body. In either choice, he suffers pain. These metaphors describe the struggles of love in coded figures of allegory, the distant love object, the knight's homage, the reverence for the woman's honor, the perpetuity of devotion once the arrow has pierced the heart. While this discrete language is alien to contemporary readers who think he should find someone to satisfy his hunger, it has the restrained dignity of the "l'amour lointain" of the troubadours.[14]

Coleridge uses these metaphors again in the motto to the "Love-Poems" section of *Sibylline Leaves* (1817). Quoting eleven lines from Petrarch's Latin letter to Barbato da Sulmona, he focuses on being wounded and being burned. Kathleen Coburn translates the pertinent lines thus: "You read here of tears and how the quivered boy wounded me, a boy, with piercing barb"; the lover looks back "ashamed that I myself burned. THE PEACEFUL MIND SHUDDERS AT PAST TUMULTS, AND READING AGAIN THINKS THAT SOME OTHER WROTE THOSE WORDS."[15] After these coded confessions of burning desire, the first poem in the section of "Love-Poems" is "Love."

As for Dante in his love for Beatrice, "hunger" or "desire" turns into a force that drives Coleridge's thoughts toward Platonic yearning. Right away and forever Sara Hutchinson is the "Infinitely beloved Darling" (*CN* 984). Even as she is near to slipping away from him ten years after their first meeting he still defines the love that he feels for her as "sudden": "That Love, however sudden, as affirmed of it—*fall in love*— which is perhaps *always* the case of Love in its highest sense, as defined by me elsewhere, is yet an act of the will—and that too one of the *primary* & therefore unbewusst, & ineffable Acts" (Sept. 1809; *CN* 3562). Love is unasked for and yet also willed; it is neither a fleeting affection that can evaporate without blame nor a brutalizing lust.

So ravishing is the sudden miracle of falling in love that he is not shy about announcing to his wife his right to pursue it:

> I owe duties, & solemn ones, to you, as my wife; but I owe equally solemn ones to Myself, to my Children, to my Friends, and to Society. Where Duties are at variance, dreadful as the case may be, there must be a Choice. I can neither retain my Happiness nor my Faculties, unless I move, live, & love, in perfect Freedom, limited only by my own purity & self-respect, & by my incapability of loving any person, man or woman, unless I at the same time honor & esteem them. (Nov. 23, 1802; *CL* 2, 887)

Since he wishes peace and progression in goodness to all those whom he loves, "no human Being can have a right to be jealous." He will love each person "as they appear to me to deserve my Love, & to be capable of returning it. More is not in my power." The tyrannical fiction that love should be lifelong and exclusive constricts the spirit: "That we can love but one person, is a miserable mistake, & the cause of abundant unhappiness," especially if that one person neither deserves nor returns the love. In a Godwinian vein Coleridge rages at the permanence of the marriage contract that implies "Henceforth this Woman is your only friend, your sole beloved" and everyone else "only your *acquaintance*!" He wonders what women expect and by what right they expect it.

He asks each wife to ask herself, "By what Law of God, of Man, or of general reason do I claim this Right?" He asserts his own right, as a "good & wise man," a "warm & wide hearted man" to love the many people he loves as the mother of a large brood loves all her children and not just one (*CL* 2, 887–888). He tells his wife that she should "have confidence in my honor & virtue—& suffer me to love & to be beloved without jealousy or pain" (Jan. 5, 1803; *CL* 2, 908–909). He seems to expect that she will come to welcome the woman he loves into their home and to become her friend.

Boldly, too, he visits Sara Hutchinson and stays for days, sometimes weeks, without bothering to tell his wife; with this true love nearby, the falsity of his marriage seems all the more "unendurable" (Whalley, p. 41). Because one or both of the Hutchinson brothers were at the farm, critics have always assumed these long visits were chaste, but now and then a word or two sets one wondering. A sentence like the following, for instance, takes a good bit of contortion to appear chaste: "the fuller my inner Being is of the sense, the more my outward Organs yearn & crave for it" (cited Whalley, p. 62). So, too, his translation of Stolberg's "Hymn to the Earth," from December, 1799, the month after falling in love, describe the Earth's intercourse with the Sky as a "blissful Shudder," an overt sexual allusion echoing the more covert ones in "Christabel" part 2 concurrently in progress.

He, who had opposed Godwin and other atheists for encouraging promiscuity and lasciviousness, now learns about the turmoil of the emotions. He learns that no person can be expected to love just one person all his or her life. His love for Sara Hutchinson endures, but even that love assumes new permutations in women who resemble her. Where many critics and biographers suspect that he is attached to an imaginary vision, pitifully invented to compensate for his own sexual timidity or inadequacy, Whalley argues that their love was reciprocal, so threatening to others that their correspondence was burned.

How many letters were there? A notebook entry of October 1803 (*CN,* 1601) implies that Sara Hutchinson's letters were usually "full of explicit Love & Feeling": "if I have not heard from you very recently, & if the last letter had not happened to be full of explicit Love & Feeling, then I conjure up Shadows into Substances—& am miserable." In an entry about blessing, yearning, and fear of loss, he shows how he revives his spirits after receiving a letter that is not passionate: "Misery conjures up other Forms, & binds them into Tales & Events—activity is always Pleasure—the Tale grows pleasanter—& at length you come to me / you are by my bed side, in some lonely Inn, where I lie deserted—there you have found me—there you are weeping over me!—Dear, dear Woman!" (*CN* 1601). When he tells himself this story, this Tale, does he remember or does he imagine? Surely, a jealous wife would have to burn any letters "full of explicit Love & Feeling" that burn as intensely as these remarks. When in January 1805 he mentions how "the least languor expressed in a letter from SH drives me wild" (*CN* 2398), he implies the existence not only of multiple letters but also of letters that did not show languor, that is, letters of warmth, zest, and positive delight. Another hint about the number appears in a letter of May or June 1808 from Wordsworth assuring Coleridge that he has not been censoring their letters, or even reading more than a few of them (MY 244–245).

Whalley blames Coleridge for Sara Hutchinson's despondency, because of "his own refusal ever to dissolve his marriage" (p. 52); "he refused to consider divorce" (pp. 65–66), writes Whalley. We will show that this so-called "refusal" was not his choice, but was imposed by the laws against divorce and the shame even of separation, a shame discussed in the lives and fictions of other Romantic writers such as Byron and Austen. Without the possibility of escape, what could he do: live with Sara Hutchinson in sin? Live with her as Brother and Sister? The situation is impossible, as he notes:

> A lively picture of a man, disappointed in marriage, & endeavoring to make a compensation to himself by virtuous & tender & brotherly friendship with an amiable Woman—the obstacles—the jealousies—the impossibility of it.—Best advice that he should as much as possible withdraw himself from pursuits of morals &c—& devote himself to abstract sciences— (Dec. 1801; *CN* 1065)

This advice—study more, take cold showers—sounds like a last resort borrowed from *King Lear* and anticipating Robert Graves: "Down, wanton, down!"

Nor is Coleridge the sort of man who, like Hazlitt, would go to Scotland, stage an encounter so as purposely to be caught in flagrante delicto with a prostitute, the only way in which a divorce could be granted to the wife, a "vile proceeding" that Henry Crabb Robinson and Mary Lamb found disgusting even for Hazlitt, "low, gross, and tedious and every way offensive" (*HCR*, pp. 72–76). Coleridge's wife had given no cause for him to divorce her, the only acceptable reason for divorce being the wife's adultery.

The "Letter to ...," originally addressed to Sara Hutchinson and then variously disguised, demonstrates the bind he was in. This verse letter is often described as shameful for its self-pity, and many passages seem undignified. But other sections reveal the nature of his intimacy with Sara Hutchinson; he acknowledges his weakness of character, but also his involvement with her as they both express their emotions. Throughout the verse letter he refers to her understanding of his fears (ll. 21–23), his knowledge of where she stands to gaze at the same moon he gazes at (ll. 54–57) and of her preference for robin song and his for beehives (ll. 88–90), and his certainty of her love for him:

> O Sister! O Beloved!
> Those dear mild Eyes, that see
>   Even now the Heaven, *I* see—
> There is a Prayer in them! It is for *me*—
> And I, dear Sara—*I* am blessing *thee*! (*PW* #289, ll. 94–98)

He recalls moments of happiness so intense as to have "trance-like Depth" (l. 110). He regrets that

>   On the fretting Hour
> Then when I wrote thee that complaining Scroll
> Which even to bodily Sickness bruis'd thy soul!
> And yet thou blam'st thyself alone! And yet
>   Forbidd'st me all Regret!
>
> And must I not regret, that I distress'd
> Thee, best belov'd! Who lovest me the best? (ll. 114–120)

He chides himself for sending her sorrow instead of blessing, and thanks her for her letter to him:

> I read thy guileless Letter o'er again—
> I hear thee of thy blameless Self complain—
> And only this I learn—& this, alas! I know—
> That thou art weak & pale with Sickness, Grief, & Pain—
> And I—I made thee so! (ll. 125–129)

Imbedded in "A Letter to—" are thus two inner letters, his to her, hers back to him blaming herself for his suffering (both letters now lost or destroyed). He hopes that she and the Wordsworth family will be happy; if he knows that she is happy, he can be content, even without seeing, feeling, or hearing her. But if he thinks she is unwell and he is not there to soothe her, then he cannot bear even to finish his thought:

> To know that thou are weak & worn with pain,
> And not to hear thee, Sara! not to view thee—

> Not sit beside thy Bed,
> Not press thy aching Head,
> Not bring thee Health again—
>   At least to hope, to try—
> By this Voice, which thou lov'st, & by this earnest Eye—
> Nay, wherefore did I let it haunt my Mind
>   The dark distressful dream! (ll. 177–185)

These references to their intimacy, where he sat beside her bed and comforted her, mingle with despair about his marriage and alienation from the happier Wordsworth/ Hutchinson group, but nevertheless tell us that the love was shared. She knows that she is his dearest one, married or not:

> But thou, dear Sara! (dear indeed thou art,
>   My comforter! A Heart within my Heart!) (ll. 249–250)

and that he is "the Poet's Philomel": "I sing / My Love-song, with my breast against a Thorn" (ll. 284–285).

By most critical accounts this verse letter deals with the loss of imagination, with poetic rivalry, with depression, and with other abstract troubles always excluding his feelings for the woman to whom the letter is addressed.[16] When he writes the famous lines,

> For not to think of what I needs must feel,
> But to be still & patient all I can:
> And haply by abstruse Research to steal
> From my own Nature all the Natural Man—
>   This was my sole Resource, my wisest plan! (ll. 265–269),

readers read opium, depression, and failure of poetic power, but not that he must suppress his feelings for the woman he loves because he is already married; that he must keep his mind occupied so he does not express his natural man, his nature, his passion.

With such intimacy to remember, notebook entries of several years later seems less like hapless fantasies. "Why then should I fear or blush to say, I *love* you—love you always, and if I sometimes feel desire at the same time, yet Love endures when no such feeling blends with it—yet I desire because I love, & not Imagine that I love because I desire" (*CN* 3, 3284; 1808–1809). Do these desires, which he seems to be apologizing for by integrating them into his higher love, force him ultimately to renounce her because he cannot legally act on them? He recalls how her smile animated her face as she acknowledges his devotion:

> O that suppressed Gladness & attempted Calmness, when the Smile Passed off from the Lips moves to the Eyes or perhaps to the Nose, with which the fond Lover tells his success—& the broad sweet tumult of Joy with wch the Beloved hears him! (Oct.–Dec. 1812; *CN* 4172)

This "sweet tumult of Joy" recalls the lady's enthusiasm at the culmination of the poem "Love," and suggests that he himself has received such a response.

What love poet including Shakespeare or Donne so anticipates, honors, and integrates the responses of the loved one into his own expressions of love? The loved one's responses are implied within the "Letter"'s dialogue, an ongoing undertone of her voice, that sometimes rises to overtone. Coleridge acknowledges Sara Hutchinson's complex feelings because he knows and hears them. Only if we realize how well they know each other and how much they talk together will we understand that this Letter is an attempt to untangle the feelings of two people. The work of revising this poem into "Dejection: An Ode" will show an even closer intertwining of voices that approach the harmony of the duet, as we see in the next chapter on singing.

The poem "Love" begins the sequence of love poems truly sapphic, (*CN* 1064) and it is based on Dante's canto 5. Petrarch provides the headnote for the group of "Love Poems" in *Sibylline Leaves*; and Boccaccio will be the model for his later relations with groups of lovelorn young women. Even before he went there, Italy was the land that told him about his own passions.

4. Books

As between Paolo and Francesca, books are emblems of their love and sites of desire and anguish. As Michael Camille explains, books were part of the discipline of secrecy in courtly love: "another important medium for creating an imaginary space of love was the book, whose unfolding images were often bedecked with flower borders and lush vines." The borders contained naked male and female figures, "sprightly rabbits," and other reminders of "the amatory joys of spring." The book was the place of love as well as its sign; it roused absent lovers as well as present ones."[17] So on his way to Malta on March 10, 1804, Coleridge annotated and gave one of his favorite books to Sara Hutchinson, his *Works* of Thomas Browne. The book follows a trail of generosity from Charles

Lamb, who bought it for Coleridge March 9, 1804, and gave it to him while "dining and punching" the next day, to Coleridge, to Sara Hutchinson, who writes in her own hand below Lamb's inscription, "Given by STC to S. Hutchinson March 1804." The book contains a letter to Sara Hutchinson that is "the sole survivor of the correspondence" between them; "Mrs. Wordworth, so her granddaughter Mrs. Jane Kennedy told me, burnt all the rest of S.T. C.'s letters to Sara H.," after Sara Hutchinson's death in 1835, as his nephew Ernest Hartley Coleridge records. This single extant complete letter from Coleridge to Sara Hutchinson follows an unknown but "heart-wringing Letter" from her, on Feb. 21, 1804. He writes in his notebook that her letter "put Despair into my Heart, and not merely as a Lodger, I fear, but as a Tenant for Life" (*CN* 2, 1912). Her words are lost in the ashes of burnt letters.

Sara Hutchinson seems to have suffered, too, both when he left for Malta on the verge of death and when he returned to her at the end of 1806. They worked together on and off until 1810, but she grew harassed meeting the demands to transcribe for him and for Wordsworth, feeling a sharp pain in her side, worn out by Coleridge's need, her own, the stresses of the household, and their inability to complete and continue their love. Wordsworth admits that the women in his family told Sara Hutchinson often that Coleridge's "passion" for her was "a source to [C] of much misery" and that his choice of her was chance; she was the "innocent occasion of this unhappiness" since he might have applied these passions to another object. The Wordsworth clan believed that love was easily changed, and randomly assigned, so "that it was a gross error to appropriate this to herself" (*MY*, 245). In dismissing the intense particularity of Coleridge's love for her, Wordsworth sounds very much like Polonius warning Ophelia that Hamlet's love could be easily changed, and therefore was not to be trusted.

However hopeless her expectations of him, passionate her frustrations in not being able to marry him, or timid in her feelings for him (a doubtful point), his letter in the end papers of Thomas Browne's *Works* carries on their dialogue, for he continues to enjoy her imagined presence thinking beside him as he writes, and she, in turn, may imagine him chatting to her as she reads. This annotated copy of Thomas Browne's *Works* is itself as a whole a love poem, its offertory letter, its marginalia, its erasures, its respectful clarifications, and its allusions to other works they have read together breathe the depth of their intimacy. The copy, with its easy companionship, suggests that in his heart at least they will always be communing, whatever she might have said in her "heart-wringing" letter.

The love between them glows along the margins. As she reads the book, Coleridge journeys over a rough ocean to Malta, but a line, an X, and a few words—"the difficulty of recollecting the images of those we most dearly love"—draw her attention to his devotion to her echoed in the words of Thomas Browne. The text tells her "there are wonders in true affection. . . . wherein two so become one, as they both become two; I love my friend before my selfe, and yet me thinkes I doe not love him enough; some few months hence my multiplied affection will make me beleive I have not loved him at all; when I am from him, I am dead till I be with him; when I am with him, I am not satisfied, but would still be nearer him: united soules are not satisfied with embraces, but desire to be truely each other, which being impossible, their desires are infinite, & must proceed with a possibility of satisfaction" (*CM* 1, 788–789, note 44 [2]). Accustomed to reading beside him, she can absorb these yearning words and know that he means them for her, and that they describe their "united soules" even as he relinquishes her actual presence. The line in the margin recreates from a distance the passionate glance that would have passed between them in reading aloud together these words about united souls.

These words about infinitely unsatisfied desire adumbrate his thoughts about the incompleteness of love that he will define years later, placing love as the core of human aspiration. In addition to references to the nature of true love, other bits of marginal comment remind her of his enthusiasm for stirring phrases—" 'The Huntsmen are up in America' / what Life, what Fancy!"; his gentle way of explaining contexts (how Heraclitus made mistakes but not Herodotus, how magnetism and crystals work); his humor (about aphrodisiacs and powdered hemp leaves); and his tact (in crossing out how beavers bite off their own testicles). She can hear him speaking as she reads, so she does not read alone.

In his letter to Sara Hutchinson on the frontispiece, Coleridge makes the case for his own peculiar nature by analogy with Browne's. His praise of Browne's oddity is an indirect way of reminding her to admire his own oddity as well. Browne is "rich in various knowledge; exuberant in conceptions and conceits, contemplative, imaginative, often truly great and magnificent in his style and diction"; he is "the Humourist constantly mingling with & flashing across the Philosopher, as the darting colours in shot silk play upon the main dye!" Browne's thinking is "always the result of a feeling heart conjoined with a mind of active curiosity (the natural & becoming egotism of a man) who loving other men as himself, gains the habit & the privilege of talking about himself as familiarly as about other men." Browne was "fond of the Curious, and a Hunter of

Oddities & Strangenesses"; like Coleridge in his best state, Browne is original: "So compleatly does he see every thing in a light of his own, reading Nature neither by Sun, Moon, or Candle-Light, but by the Light of the faery Glory around his own Head, that you might say, that Nature had granted to him in perpetuity a Patent and Monopoly for all his Thoughts" (*CM* 1, 763). Reading Browne with Coleridge's pointers may lead Sara Hutchinson to see Coleridge in a warm light, to see the "*little Twist* in the Brains" as a "faery Glory" (p. 762).

Throughout, the letter breathes his love for her as a dialogue over the years: "in the words of Sir Thomas, which will serve you, my darling Sara!" and "Think you, my dear Sara!" The words written at midnight send him to bed in Holborn awaiting his trip to Plymouth for embarkation into dangerous seas; the words imagine her up north already "quietly asleep":

> And all the Stars hang bright above your Dwelling,
> Silent as tho' they watch'd the sleeping Earth!— (p. 765)

As with the intimate letters to Mary Ann Evans eleven years before, this one summons the physical realities of their sleeping under the same stars, far away from each other but close in spirit. The book stands in for him, and he reminds her in the quotation from his "Dejection: An Ode," with its final starlit blessing, that two years earlier he had also been thinking about her over the hills from Greta Hall, while he lay awake underneath the same stars composing his famous poem to her. The whole book, with its mingled texts, is a gift of love to her, pledging his loyalty as he departs.

Another copy of Sir Thomas Browne also exists, one that Sara Hutchinson may not have seen or may have read after their parting in 1810. The editors of the marginalia have ingeniously poured over the handwritings of this text, the *Religio Medici*, to see when and where the layers of notes were added in the margins at times varying from 1802 to after 1806. If she in fact read this text and still loved him, she must have struggled to endure the strong feelings in these margins. To Browne's admission that he has "never yet cast a true affection on a woman," Coleridge responds defiantly:

> So I have loved one Woman; & believe that such a love of such a Woman is the highest Friendship—for we cannot love a Friend as a Woman, but we can love a woman as a Friend.[18]

Love with friendship—"concord and unity betwixt all parts of our nature"—constitutes that rare oneness of being that all but the most independent people long for. It is embodied in that even rarer situation, a "happy marriage," which is the symbol of more spiritual unions as well:

> Friendship satisfies the highest parts of our nature; but a wife, who is capable of friendship, satisfies *all*. The great business of real unostentatious Virtue is—not to eradicate any real genuine instinct or appetite of human nature; but—to establish a concord and unity betwixt all parts of our nature, to give a Life and a Feeling & a Passion to our purer Intellect, and to intellectualize our feelings & passions. This a happy marriage, blessed with children, effectuates, in the highest degree, of which our nature is capable, & is therefore chosen by St. Paul, as the symbol of the Union of the Church with Christ . . . (*CM* 1, p. 751)

In happy marriages there is not only a union but an integrity in each partner where the old happily married man can "scarcely distinguish . . . the wife of my old age from the wife of my youth; for when we were both young, & she was beautiful, for *once* that I caressed her with a meaner passion I caressed her a thousand times with *Love*—& *these* caresses still remain to us!" (*CM* 1, 751–752). In most marriages however there is some fluctuation in the exclusiveness of love, so that reciprocity is almost never perfect. The one who loves the most feels that his or her love is incomplete, and thus this idolizing love is "accompanied with a *craving* after something that is *not*, & yet *might be* . . ." (752). Such a craving is the core of his later proof of immortality.

Knowing that she is the blessed recipient of such sure and constant love, hearing his own words in the margins and imagining his voice reading aloud the marked passages, Sara Hutchinson reads Browne's *Works*. We are ignorant of her responses to these passionate texts, because she must be discreet and because her letters have been destroyed. Similar to his early letters to Mary Evans where he imagines her physical presence and shifts his perspective to accommodate her, Coleridge reads with Sara Hutchinson's imagined warm presence beside him, anticipates her distaste and rushes to remove such offending passages.

Depending on the dates of the marginal notes, Sara Hutchinson either did or did not see the balanced view of sex and love that her "dear one" gave in response to Browne's strange wish that human beings could copulate like trees "without the trivial and vulgar way of coition." Coleridge responds with wit and wisdom: "He says, he is a Batchelor, but he talks as if he had been a married man, & married to a Woman who did not love him, & whom he did not love. Taken by itself, no doubt, the act is both foolish, & debasing. But what a misery is contained in those words, 'taken by itself'? Are there not thoughts, & affections, &

Hopes, & a *Religion* of the Heart,—that lift & sanctify all our bodily Actions where the union of the Bodies is but a language & *conversation* of united Souls?" (754). Only in loveless unions is sex "taken by itself" and thus ridiculous; in loving ones it forms part of the many-layered conversation of united souls. Whether Coleridge has experienced at any time such a union of bodies and souls is unknown; as he writes, he suffers "the painful craving Void of Solitude!" There is no one for whom he is "the *very* dearest to that Being!" (754) Does Sara Hutchinson see this cry at the time it was written, long after, or not at all? If she sees it, does she feel regret, or love, or indifference?

Squirreled away in his copy of Chapman's *Homer* is yet another stash of secret communications to her. This volume opens "S.T. Coleridge— (given by him to his friend S. Hutchinson)" with the parenthesis in her hand. This book she begs Joseph Henry Green to find and return: the letter in it will prove that "Chapman's *Homer* was a gift of our dear Friend to me—& therefore will not wonder that I am desirous of re-possessing it" (*SHL*, 439; *CM* 2, p. 1117). The words "our dear friend" may sound remote, but may also be a discreet reference to their special closeness written to a friend who knew of it. The letter was mutilated so brutally at the words "O dearest" and "So dearest do forgive" that readers may wonder at the long enduring indignation of the censor. Despite these gashes the tenderness still stirs between them in the explanations of Homeric epithets and the sweetness of the verse. The letter tells her a funny story about the poet Laura Sophia Temple of Bristol, who had written Coleridge a "blush-compelling" fan letter about his poem "Love," aroused indirectly by the poem that had signaled the mutuality of Coleridge's and Sara Hutchinson's feelings for each other. Their love had inspired another's love for him, in a chain of love stories inspiring further love. Even as he tells her she looks like Charlotte Brent (a resemblance which Mary Lamb seconds but Charles Lamb later insists is not true[19]) he carries on his courtship by describing Laura Sophia Temple's rhapsody over the poem that marks the beginning of their love, and reminding her that a single woman resembling herself now lives once more under his roof. As with his letters to Mary Ann Evans, he keeps the feelings simmering with his physicality and attentiveness.

Although they could not marry and may never have had sex (though his knowledge of how a complete union feels suggests that they did), their loving friendship is mediated by books, poems, chatter, laughter, and ideas. His giving her a copy of "Christabel," his sexiest poem, with a love poem to her pressed inside it, indicates real and imaginary desires. Her copying his poems to herself suggests her delight at being loved.

The annotations in Homer and Sir Thomas Browne radiate communicative love. Their association may seem arid to some, but to others full of wit, quick responsiveness, and a creativity that makes its own music. Their loving relationship fulfils Milton's definition that "a meet and happy conversation is the chiefest and noblest end of mariage" ("Doctrine and Discipline of Divorce," p. 245).

From June 1809 to March 1810 Coleridge and Sarah Hutchinson worked hard together on *The Friend* in Coleridge's study, sometimes late at night, whenever after much reading his ideas cohered. The complex emotions inside that silent room with the high windows were so intense that on March 5, 1810 Sara Hutchinson bolted to her brothers' farm in Wales, leaving Coleridge to complete one final issue alone, to write his despair in his notebooks, to wait in vain for a letter from his infinitely beloved darling, to irritate even Dorothy Wordsworth, who called him "hopeless" and wrote Catherine Clarkson that he had frazzled Sara Hutchinson's nerves. When Richard Holmes narrates this breakup, we are reminded once again of the mysteries of the passions—did she want him to be her lover? was she tired of his desires? did she now love William Wordsworth more than Coleridge?—mysteries already opaque but more so in the absence of documents.[20] Coleridge's biographers, especially Holmes, penetrate the cycle of addiction and exhilaration during months of suicidal withdrawal after the "heart-griping" losses of both treacherous manly friend, Wordsworth, and beloved woman, Sara Hutchinson, and the additional frenzy to rescue his protector John Morgan's finances. Guarded by doctors, he was still stirred by the blushes of women, excited by flirting with Charlotte Brent, and inspired to compose a delicate love poem centered on the willow, emblem of unrequited love, an echo of Desdemona's song, while he waited in vain to hear from his loved one:

> Once again, sweet Willow, wave thee!
>   Why stays my Love?
> Bend and in yon streamlet—lave thee
>   Why stays my Love?
> Oft have I at evening straying,
> Stood, thy Branches long surveying
> Graceful in the light Breeze playing,—
> Why stays my Love? (Cited Holmes, p. 297)

In sorrow, he keeps the music tapping in notebooks imitating Sapphic meter, filling the rhythms with feelings, expressing the feelings in sound.

Coleridge's cogent denunciations of the bondage of marriage—the smoking torch of Juno, extinguishing the butterfly of true feeling—begin a long series of thoughts about duty and inclination, renunciation and rapture, that lead him twice and forever to exile himself from Sara Hutchinson, to allow her to find someone who is free to marry her, and to develop by default a recognition that unsatisfied yearning is the core of love. Despite her silence, her siding with Wordsworth in the quarrel of 1810–1812, and her participation in the Wordsworth family accusations that he had abandoned them, she remains an image of perfection in Coleridge's mind, an image that shimmers behind Charlotte Brent, John Morgan's sister-in-law, whom she uncannily resembled, and, later, behind Anne Gillman. Henry Crabb Robinson mentions both Sara Hutchinson and Coleridge as present at dinners in 1817 and 1823; she visited Coleridge at Ramsgate and at Highgate several times during his last illness. As late as 1828 in "A Day-Dream" he writes, "I dream thee with mine eyes, and at my heart I feel thee!" (*PW* #630, l.30). She never married, but remained for Coleridge the "Soother of Absence," the love object as the Other, the example of personal integrity, the soul of music.

Chapter 7
Hearkening to the Voices of Women

> When the Soul seeks to hear; when all is hush'd
> And the Heart listens!
> *PW* #129, ll. 25–26

> "The trick of that voice I do remember well"
> *King Lear* 4, 6, 105

In his aesthetic criticism, Coleridge divides the art of language into "poetry of the ear, or music; and poetry of the eye." This distinction between eye and ear also involves the location of personhood in other people: the eye sees the face, which could be blank or angry and therefore unreliable or repugnant, and the ear hears the voice, which comes from within the other person and reverberates with breath and heart beat. Throughout Coleridge's writings, gazing and listening—faces and voices—alternate. Particularly in his efforts to understand women as persons, Coleridge makes a significant aesthetic and ethical transition when he shifts from seeing women to hearing them.[1] He consciously learns to listen when he tells Thelwall, "I am an immense favorite, for I pun, conundrumize, *listen* and dance" (Feb. 6, 1797; *CL* 1, 308). By underlining the word "*listen*" he points to the peculiarity of his doing so and to his deliberate intention to cultivate that skill. He listens to women's voices in their poems and in their singing, and comes to associate music with women.

The change from watching to listening releases his poetry into the dimension of music. In early poems Coleridge reveals a fascination with women in the act of making music, but he focuses on the arms, throats, and bodices that are bared in movement. The listening poet in the sonnet "Genevieve" (1794) praises the woman's sweet "Seraph's song," but pays most attention to recalling how he has "seen your breast with pity heave" (pp. 50, l. 13). In the 1795 "To the Nightingale" the lady's harp vibrates with love, and love "heaves her breast of snow" (pp. 55, l. 22). When he begins to listen to the voices this voyeurism abates.

Suddenly his poems fill with voices. Voices resound through the famous poems: the choruses of voices in the "Rime of the Ancient Mariner"; the many intonations and modes of song in "Kubla Khan," from a woman's wailing to the damsel's "symphony and song"; the many voices that Geraldine simulates in "Christabel," her muttering asides, groans, complaints, and rebukes. Coleridge hears music in the air and recreates its syncopations in printed verse.

His passion for voices corresponds to a realization that voices may be a more reliable gauge of personhood than faces, because utterance brings the inner life to the surface, and "outers" it. The twentieth-century philosopher Jonathan Ree credits late eighteenth century philosophers with the discovery that "the human voice was the most perfect instrument for giving expression to the inwardness of the soul" and "that your voice comes straight from your self, from deep inside you, from your soul." Ree asks, "Where else should it come from, indeed? And perhaps the converse is equally true: how else could we imagine the soul, except as the source or the seat of the voice?"[2] Also locating the source of human society in listening and speaking, Coleridge asks his notebook, "What makes society differ from a *Herd*? The human EAR. A person born deaf is dumb, too" (*CN* 1739). When Coleridge described his love as a "vibratory pain" trembling through the fibers of his being (*CN* 3370), he reveals that his emotional life is intensely auditory. His emotions, ethics, and art deepen with his increased attention to voice.

While some of the voices he recreates are male, such as the disembodied spirits in "The Rime of the Ancient Mariner" who chorus over the swooning mariner as "Two voices in the air" (1. 397), and the real William Linley Esq., who sang a song to Purcell's music that made Coleridge swoon as if he were entering heaven (*CP* #157), most of the voices he records are female. In "Kubla Khan," for instance, the decree that establishes the pleasure dome is unheard and patriarchal, but the song that the poet yearns to imitate is the woman's song, "Singing of Mount Abora." The poet wishes that he could recreate "her symphony and song," but his conditional syntax indicates that he might never be able to:

> Could I revive within me
> Her symphony and song,
> To such a deep delight 'twould win me,
>
> That with music loud and long,
> I would build that dome in air,
> That sunny dome! Those caves of ice! (*PW* #178, ll. 41–47)

If he were able to hear her song again, or recreate it in his own song, he might himself build that dome using her language filtered through his own. The "damsel with a dulcimer" is the original musician while the poet is the copyist, yearning to reconstitute her art in a different voice. Hers is epic and orchestral music; his the Romantic mini-epic derivative and individual. The damsel with a dulcimer sings the wildly chanted epic that has the acoustic force of a symphony; the male singer takes a humble stance, and hopes to recall or translate her archaic grandeur in his own secondary form. If he could, he would narrow her massive "symphony" of strings, brass, percussion, and winds into his single male voice, a poignant echo of her performance.[3]

Coleridge thought Sara Hutchinson had a beautiful speaking and singing voice, not the usual "piano-fortery" tinkling from the upper stories, and in writing to or about her he often mentioned her voice coming to him across the hills or reading aloud to him. With these reverberations in his head, his poems swirl all the more with women's voices. He associates love with music because of the heightening of passions and senses: "Love to all the Passions & Faculties, as Music to all the varieties of Sound/" (Aug.–Sept. 1802; *CN* 1229). In a proposed "Ode to Music" he hopes to recapture "the thought I lost . . . that perhaps Music bringing me back to primary Feelings did really make moral regeneration" (Sept. 1803; *CN* 1505).

Just after meeting Sara Hutchinson, Coleridge shows his admiration for women in poems to the grand ladies of his day, Mary Robinson, Georgiana, Duchess of Devonshire, and Mathilda Betham. He fills his tribute to Mary Robinson with references to her voice. Writing in November 1800, he hears her voice singing on Mount Skiddaw:

> And by this laugh, and by this tear,
> I would, old Skiddaw! SHE were here!
> A Lady of sweet song is she,
> Her soft blue eye was made for thee! (*PW* #271, ll. 22–26)

Her songs are powerful enough for the Mountain to praise her music:

> But many a stranger in my height
>   Hath sung to me her magic song,
>   Sending forth his extacy
>   In her divinest melody;
> And hence I know, her soul is free,
> She is, where'er she wills to be,
>   Unfetter'd by mortality! (ll. 47–54)

Mount Skiddaw wishes that his own music were as mighty as Mary Robinson's:

> To me too might belong
> The honour of her song, and witching melody,
>   Which most resembles me,
>   Soft, various, and sublime,
>   Exempt from wrongs of Time! (ll. 63–68)

When a great mountain sings praises to a poet, she must be sublime indeed.[4]

By allusion and quotation, Coleridge pays tribute also to the dashing literary and political lady, Georgiana, the Duchess of Devonshire. A month after meeting Sara Hutchinson he read the Duchess's long ode to William Tell, "The Passage of the Mountain of Saint Gothard" in *The Morning Post* and immediately responded with an ode in praise of her art, her politics, and her courage. Published in the *Morning Post* December 24, 1799, the "Ode to Georgiana" reveals a Coleridge who recorded parliamentary debates without going to bed for days, knew the details of the Prince's misbehavior and of Pitt's conniving; knew that these men were intimates of Georgiana Cavendish, on the other edge of a London buzzing with gossip and politics. Coleridge knew that the Duchess was not as sheltered in her wealth as his ode suggests, she who was the subject of daily notices about her routs, her towering hairdos with ships in them, her serious work in attempting to unify a fragmented opposition, her lovers and pregnancies, and her addictive gambling.[5] Sharply at variance with the caricatures by Rowlandson and others that mock her vivacious participation in the public scene,[6] Coleridge praises her success in politics, literature, and family life.

Although he wished that his ode had been better (*CL* 1, 552), it is nevertheless a complex tribute to her achievements. Coleridge's ode shows how a wealthy and titled woman came to transcend the impressions of her upbringing; how her essential self remained natural in a culture of artifice; how a miraculous genius touched her to understand the sufferings of the poor who had labored to give her family useless luxuries; how this sympathy for others increased when she became a mother, not just in the pains of childbirth, but also in the continuing nurture of her children, giving birth to their souls by nursing them and gazing at their faces so that they would come to know the reality of the Other:

> You were a Mother! at your bosom fed
>   The Babes that lov'd you. You, with laughing eye,

> Each twilight-thought, each nascent feeling read,
>   Which you yourself created. Oh! delight!
> A second time to be a Mother,
>   Without the Mother's bitter groans:
> Another thought, and yet another,
>   By touch, or taste, by looks or tones,
> O'er the growing Sense to roll,
>   The Mother of your Infant's Soul! (*PW* #254, ll. 58–67)

By caring for, gazing at, and feeling with her children, as many aristocratic women did not (they dropped them to grow in solitude like the "poor caterpillar"), Georgiana is twice a mother because she creates the soul as well as the body of the child. By a miraculous parallel she herself is mothered by an "Angel of the Earth" who gazes on her and shelters her, while she is gazing at her babies.

Georgiana in writing reveals who she is under her glossy silks and notoriously bared bosom, a bosom both *dulce et utile*, as Coleridge is pleased to note and as cartoons by Aitken and Rowlandson from Spring, 1784, affirm, showing her accessible bosom swelling over the front of her dress (Foreman, p. 150). Georgiana's poem adds a potent voice to her face, body, dress, and deeds. Coleridge marvels at the twenty-fourth stanza of her poem, "The Passage of the Mountain of St. Gothard, A Poem, to my children" (1802):

> And hail the Chapel! hail the Platform wild!
>   Where Tell directed the avenging dart,
> With well-strung arm, that first preserv'd his child,
>   Then aim'd the arrow at the tyrant's heart.[7]

With his antennae for rhythm, Coleridge locates the best stanza in her otherwise desultory travelogue. He quotes its rousing meters as his ode begins and again as each of his own stanzas rounds to a close, introducing the quotation each time with a slightly varied salute to the Duchess's natural self:

> And yet, free Nature's uncorrupted child,
> You hailed the Chapel and the Platform wild,
>   Where once the Austrian fell
>   Beneath the shaft of Tell!
> O Lady, nurs'd in pomp and pleasure!
> Whence learnt you that heroic measure? (ll. 19–24)

The fourth repetition exalts her:

> O beautiful! O Nature's child!
> 'Twas thence you hail'd the Platform wild. (ll. 78–79)

The frequency of the repetitions may verge on mockery, as Foreman believes, but the mockery is negated by respectful amazement that a woman so coddled—"Splendour's fondly-fostered child!"—whose early days had brightly circled "Far, far removed" "From all that teaches brotherhood to Man," could have learned to care for heroism among the poor republicans of the Swiss mountains fighting against the tyranny of aristocrats like herself, defying by her own feeling and will what Coleridge elsewhere calls "the anti-human Influences of Riches" (*CL* 2, 711). Not only her sympathy for freedom but her metrical mastery of the "heroic measure" moves his admiration. Her quoted words vouch for the authenticity of her person as a deep and resonant being, when her authentic feeling circulates from one reader to another.[8] Although she was "nursed in pomp and pleasure," amid "Emblazonments and old ancestral crests," "Rich viands and the pleasurable wine" (a Madeline in a proleptic Keatsian castle) and although these luxuries had come to the Spencer country seat at Althorp Park, Northamptonshire, "unearned by toil" and far from the sight of "The unenjoying toiler's misery," she preserves her core self, "Nature's uncorrupted child." She has a voice that sounds out her person, what Eric Griffiths calls the "irreducibly individual existence of the voice."[9] Her class, her education, her self-assurance and joie de vivre encourage her to speak.

When Coleridge reads Georgiana's poem, he hears her voice, and it leads him to forget her lush appearances that so amuse the cartoonists. He moves from seeing the generic body to listening to the individual voice, with its recognizable voiceprint, its "trick," the word King Lear uses to identify the unique sound of his friend Gloucester in the epigraph to this chapter. When he hears and quotes women's voices he acknowledges them as free agents whose written voices are acts, or in the words of Mathew Campbell, "rhythms for representing agency in crisis . . . central to the identify of the self."[10]

In praising the Duchess, Coleridge ignores her reputation for having many lovers and sharing her husband with her best friend Bess. He focuses instead on her mind and her liberation from the constrictions of class, looks, and propriety. Just as he had praised the actress, fellow poet, and celebrity Mary Robinson, also ten years older than himself, he similarly admires the Duchess of Devonshire's craft and independence. In both cases Coleridge defends these older women, both intelligent and glamorous celebrities, from the prudery of small-minded gossips. An unpublished translation of an epigram from Lessing supports this liberal view of experienced women:

> We still call Bet a maid—perchance, from this,
> That a fallen Angel still an Angel is. (*PW* #229)

This is high praise from a fallen archangel.

Where Mary Robinson and Georgiana Cavendish were bold, Mathilda Betham needs to be roused from her timidity. In "To Matilda Betham, From a Stranger" (Sept. 1802) Coleridge addresses her as a fellow poet. He has seen her *Elegies, and Other Smaller Poems* (1797) and cannot refrain from telling her that she has a fine ear—"a sweet Tune play'd / On a sweet Instrument"—, "subtle Tones of TASTE," lively imagination producing "fair wild Offspring of thy Genius," but that she needs to read and think in order to enlarge her poetic voice. As he had similarly advised Wordsworth to abandon little poems and write an epic, here he tells Betham she is a natural musician:

> And 'tis my faith, that there's a natural Bond
> Between the female Mind, and measur'd Sounds—
> Nor do I know a sweeter Hope than this,
> Than this sweet Hope, by Judgment unreprov'd
> That our own Britain, our dear Mother Isle,
> May boast one Maid, a Poetess *indeed*,
> Great, as th'impassion'd Lesbian, in sweet song
> And O! Of holier Mind and happier Fate. (*PW* #304, ll. 18–28)

Betham has the genius to become a Christian and British Sappho, but she must work at it as Milton did, as Coleridge himself studied every subject he could get his hands on to prepare for his great work:

> But thou
> Be wise! Be bold! fulfill my Auspices!
> Tho' sweet thy Measures, stern must be thy Thought,
> Patient thy Study, watchful thy mild Eye! (*PW* #304, ll. 30–33)

"Be bold, meek Woman! But be wisely bold!" Such adjuration, far from condescending, respects her power, urging her to aim high, to make up in solitary study what she must have lost by the absence of formal education for women and by the lack of stern encouragement from the kind of barking schoolmasters who disciplined Coleridge's own diction. He cries out to her: "Look round thee! Look within thee! Think & feel!" He has hopes that she will win the "nobler meed" (ll. 46–47). Though six years later Betham will paint a miniature of Coleridge, he begs her here to eschew the miniature, the small, pretty, and meekly feminine, and become an "oak." These three poems to literary women encourage their genius. Influenced perhaps by talking with Sara Hutchinson about the writings of women, they may reflect Coleridge's sharpened sensitivity to poor young women, lace-making women, dashing literary women, ruined women, theatrical women, and operatic women.

Much has been written in the last ten years about the remarkable efflorescence of women in the theater, working as writers like Joanna Baillie and Elizabeth Inchbald and as actresses like Mrs. Jordan and Mrs. Siddons. Marilyn Gaull described the excitement generated by Mrs. Siddons's work when "her audiences not only shrieked, groaned, wept, and collapsed in fits but also made crude and inappropriate comments."[11] Judith Pascoe also noticed the spectacular performances of Mrs. Siddons, a model "of female creative power," inspiring women poets, fiction writers, and actresses to dare to display themselves.[12] When Mrs. Siddons wore lace given to her by Queen Marie Antoinette, she did more than act; she presented an evocation of the "body politic."[13] Coleridge himself heard and watched Siddons. In his sonnet to her—the only one to a woman in his series on "eminent characters"—he recreates his sense of being transported by her voice and movements:

> Ev'n such the shiv'ring joys thy tones impart,
> Ev'n so thou, SIDDONS! meltest my sad heart! (*PW* #96, ll. 13–14)

Powerful actresses generated powerful new roles for women.

Coleridge himself provided opportunities for displaying passion in Theresa in *Remorse* and Glycine in *Zapolya*. These women characters revenge their men and orate with rhetorical force. Julie Carlson examines the ways that Coleridge "showcas[ed] the commanding activity of female characters," who rescue their male lovers, assert "the feminine subject's autonomous agency," and reject "domesticity." In his plays, writes Carlson, "far more than in his other writings, Coleridge debates the role of women in England. In his accounts of his experiences with theatre, he makes the 'woman problem' his own."[14] Coleridge's passionate women characters "act like men and are never at home" (Carlson, 122). These heroines further stimulate the already eroticized aura of play-going; seeing and being seen in boxes; getting close to other bodies in the pit; eating and drinking before and after; feeling vicarious passions.

While the Romantic culture of theatrical women has engaged recent critics, few Romantic era critics have noted the parallel culture of choral singing, oratorios, operas, and popular songs. Women singers came to prominence in the mid and late eighteenth century, and offered their elegant bodies, movements, voices, and reputations for public consumption, with the word consumption meaning not only delectation but also absorption and devouring.[15] These were not meek provincial ladies crushed by exigencies and fears. Many of them learned to manage their fame and their money on their own; many used their sexuality to get their wishes instead of being used by others. Susan Levin gives the example of Harriet Abrams to examine how shrewdly some of these singers managed all aspects of their public appearances. Despite Abrams's short stature, she invented a large reputation for gorgeous singing, efficient performance, sharp finances, and vigorous sexual adventure.[16]

Coleridge's enthusiasm for singing women began in his youth. As we saw in looking at his early flirtations, he addressed his attentions to the Brunton girls, Ann and Eliza, in Bristol, and played Cyrano by translating Wrangham's Latin verses to Eliza Brunton and conveying them in his stead. He and his friends participated in the passion for opera, attending concerts, talking about singers with dubious reputations, gazing at their beautiful bodies and gowns. This era saw an outpouring of oratorios, operas, and symphonic music by such visiting luminaries as Handel, Michael Haydn, and J. C. Bach, as well as the frequent performance of popular ballads, glees and comic songs in pleasure gardens and clubs.[17] Coleridge was in the thick of these performances, even in years when he is reputed to be deeply depressed. In 1808, for instance, he attended the impresario Thomas Dibdin's musical lectures and he visited "a sort of Glee or Catch Club, composed wholly of professional Singers [who] were, or were polite enough all to appear to be, marvellously delighted with me; & all the musical Entertainments of the Town are open to me without expence" (Jan. 14, 1808; *CL* 3, 45).

Within this flourishing instrumental and choral scene women sopranos stood out as flamboyant novelties. Trained by the maestros J. C. Bach or Michael Haydn, or by their own musician fathers, they sported the new bel canto techniques perfected in Italian opera houses.[18] Virtuosi like Mrs. Billington and Angelica Catalani drew raves in salons as their reputations for profligacy added to the excitement.[19] These early divas, sumptuously dressed, surrounded by admirers, lovers, and claques, engaged not only the ears but also the eyes. Combed-up ringlets, rich fabrics, perfumes, glances, jewels, and cleavage magnetized listeners in the pit, on balconies, or in concert rooms. Sara Hutchinson, a connoisseur of books, art, nature, and music, recommends Angelica Catalani to her friend Mary Monkhouse:

> I would not have you spend your money at the Theatre—for as you have already seen Mrs Jordan & the House, I am sure there is nothing else worth looking at—& though you may not be so much delighted with Madame Catalani's *singing* as those who understand it, or pretend to do

so, yet *she* is worth going to see for her beauty's sake; & for the grace & elegance of her motions—and the contrast between her & all the rest of the "*objects*" upon the stage, at the Opera, is amusing—besides the *hatefulness* of the dancing is worth seeing if it were but to know *what* it is the folks made such a rout about! (Oct. 1808; *SHL*, p. 10)

In her raucous language referring mannishly to theatrical women as "objects," Sara Hutchinson shows how glamor, gossip, and intrigue contributed to the sensuous shimmer of these venues. Sara's rival, Sara Fricker Coleridge, also raves about Madame Catalani after a concert in Liverpool, but true to form gives less lively information: "she is handsome, and her manner is exceedingly lively and engaging" (*Minnow*, p. 8).

Coleridge not only heard the local Bristol stars, but at Cambridge wiled away his days and evenings listening to concerts, gazing at gorgeous females like Elizabeth Billington, Gertrude Elisabeth Mara, and Anna Maria Crouch, and partying afterwards. As he had written Mary Evans in 1792, he heard Billington herself, and he recreates her florid and exquisite soprano voice: "I went the other evening to the concert, and spent the time there much to my heart's content in cursing Mr. Hague, who played on the Violin most piggishly, and a Miss (I forget her name) Miss Humstrum, who sung most sowishly! O the Billington! That I should be absent during the Oratorios!—The Prince unable to conceal his pain—Oh! Oh! Oh! Oh! Oh! Oh! Oh! Oh! Oh!—To which House is Mrs. B. engaged this Season?—" (*CL* 1, 31). The nine Oh's must reproduce the bel canto embellishments of the queen of opera, and the prince's pain may be desire, since he snatched up many of these singers to become his mistresses. Ten years later (Feb. 22, 1802), still a passionate Billington fan, Coleridge goes to her benefit and sits in the box of Sir William Rush: "it was *perfection*! I seem to have acquired a new sense by hearing her!"(*CL* 2, 789). As late as 1818, in an anecdote about misunderstandings, Coleridge recounts a conversation about his inhaling nitrous oxide:

> a gentleman came from the other side of the theatre and said to me,—"Was it not ravishingly delightful, Sir?"—"It was highly pleasurable, no doubt."—"Was it not very like sweet music?"—"I cannot say I perceived any analogy to it."—"Did you not say it was very like Mrs. Billington singing by your ear?"—"No, Sir, I said that while I was breathing the gas, there was a singing in my ears."[20]

Hearing Elizabeth Billington was like taking laughing gas, and the gentleman associates Coleridge with his harping on Billington.

In a culture abuzz with music and aglow with sexually adventurous female singers, Coleridge seems to have been more active in the music world than readers have previously imagined. He describes himself to his wife as being in demand at musical parties. Wittily he mocks himself as "the very *tonish* Poet & Jemmy Jessamy fine Talker in Town," judging music and painting, passing "criticisms on furniture & chandeliers," paying "handsome Compliments to all Women of Fashion," receiving "fine *Cards*" and "tender Smiles." Attending salons and concerts, he writes home about his associations with fashionable singers to stir his wife's jealousy, promising that he is a "faithful Hus.," though he adds in a scribble, "notwithstanding the Honorable Mrs. D[amer] & Lady Charlotte." The influence of opera on Coleridge's own artistry emerges when he describes the meter of "Christabel" as "Short Airs to a recitative" (*SWF* 1, 442), indicating that the intensities of opera have informed the music of this narrative.

As much as he chuckles about his intimacy with the music world, he may have felt threatened by the rhythmic words and visible, tangible, and thermal flesh of the divas. Unlike musical women in paintings like Vermeer's, holding lutes, sitting at harpsichords, and staying inside their own spaces, singing women come alive in their voices, alerting the senses of the observer, often against the observer's will. Steeped in these performances and acutely susceptible to sound, Coleridge had strong opinions about singers that he outlined in his poem of September 1799, "Lines Composed in a Concert Room" (*PW* #248). This little-noted poem is an ambitious study of Coleridge's responses to different kinds of music and different kinds of women making that music. It was published only two months before his meeting with Sara Hutchinson, significantly suggesting Coleridge's readiness to be overwhelmed.

"Lines" reflects the two dangers of being overwhelmed by physical presence and being forced to listen to excessively passionate sounds. Coleridge has been described as "having no ear" but being "all ear" (*TT* 1, 564), especially when bombarded by the sustained vocal technique perfected and prized at the end of the eighteenth century. Unable to shut his ears, he is captive to the voice which may please and thereby subdue. The first part of "Lines" describes the kind of singing that enthralls the ear and enforces submission by relentlessly depriving the listener of his or her will. The song is so powerful that he lashes himself to the mast or stuffs wax in his ears for fear of being broken against the rocks by the siren's song. Coleridge the poet presents himself trapped in a hall dominated by the trilling of a large-breasted opera singer. As we have seen in previous poems and notebook entries, large breasts would not usually be a problem for him, but here he is uncomfortable.

In examining his own titillated discomfort, he anticipates a number of twentieth-century writers who have tried to capture the experience of listening to operatic divas. Gary Schmidgall describes the "splendidly excessive acrobatic aural feats" and "relishes, shakes, mordants, and accacciaturas" of the diva; he notes how the sounds invade the listener's space and engage the passions by multiplying and expanding the listener's senses.[21] For some opera fans, this invasive power is addictively desired. Wayne Koestenbaum analyzes the submission to these "aural feats" as a form of osmosis: "the singer, through osmosis, passes through the self's porous membrane, and discredits the fiction that bodies are separate boundaried packages"; "she becomes part of my brain." The listener is liquefied, melted, and effeminized, his reason suspended.[22] These theorists of opera find this broaching of boundaries pleasing.

But the 27 year-old Coleridge seems not to want his porous membrane crossed. He does not want the diva's scent or voice invading his brain. He "detest[s]" the social conformity and hypocrisy that vibrate through the concert. At the focus of these "scented Rooms," ringed by "a gaudy crowd," looms the diva:

> Heaves the proud Harlot her distended breast,
> In intricacies of laborious song. (ll. 3–4)

With harsh censoriousness (perhaps justified by the open promiscuity of many of the singers), the poet impugns the singer's morals, her excessive bodice, her unnatural exertions of voice.[23] Now the delicious heaving of the earlier poems has become dangerous. Indeed, the poet seems to be fighting off the diva's power to engulf him, fearing "the volume, height, depth, lushness, and excess of operatic utterance" that reminds the listener "how small [his] gestures have been until now, how impoverished [his] physicality" (Koestenbaum, p. 44). Coleridge's "long-breathed" spondees and overflowing enjambement mimic the diva's sound:

> But when the long-breathed singer's uptrilled strain
> Bursts in a squall—they gape for wonderment. (ll. 7–8)

The metrical reenactment of her bel canto aria—straining, sustaining, trilling, and bursting—rouses the poet to exclaim against the excess that spills over to the musical consumers and infects them with falseness and snobbery:

> Hark! the deep buzz of Vanity and Hate!
>   Scornful, yet envious, with self-torturing sneer
> My lady eyes some maid of humbler state;
>   While the pert Captain, or the primmer Priest,
> Prattles accordant scandal in her ear. (ll. 9–13)

He is enraged by the self-display, obsequiousness, and entitlement that surround the new commodity of the diva.[24] This prattling, "pert" world resembles the "vain, speech-mouthing, speech-reporting Guild" that Coleridge had decried the year before in "Fears in Solitude" (*PW* #175, l. 57). Here he feels suffocated by the diva's extravagantly swollen presence, her absorption of the air otherwise free to all, and her corruption of others.[25] He who had echoed the "Oh Oh Oh Oh Oh Oh" of Billington longs to escape, to run away from the insistent sounds of the arias, and wishes for a genuine music and a genuine human being. An epigram from this period translated from German—

> Swans sing before they die—'twere no bad thing
> Should certain persons die before they sing (*PW* #241)—

suggests his frustration at voices too loud for his sensitive hearing to bear. He seems to feel his ears sprouting from his head like the large ears of the music critic who sits in front of him (*PW* #166, l. 6).

The "lines" of the title are both written lines and drawn sketches, suggesting the poet scribbling on his program, his pen and the metrical flow of his lines creating an outlet for authentic self-expression and ongoing reflection in the midst of the din. The lines are also his musical staff, for noting the varied notes and rhythms that he hears, remembers, and imagines in the "acoustic world" of concert-going London.[26] These lines are far from sketchy: they trace the process of his musings. The poem is closely structured into four unequal parts, representing four kinds of music, four kinds of stanza, and four different places. As the stanzas proceed, they loosen up and lengthen; they recreate the sequence from oppression to expansion: the three opening stanzas describing the concert room are tightly rhyming and satirical (with a fifth line added to the third stanza); the second part lengthens into a seven line stanza in which the poet praises the folk musician from his boyhood who provided music for country dancing; the third part, an eight line stanza, recreates the "sad airs, so wild and slow" of the flute player on the glossy lake whose music is as spontaneous as tears. The fourth part begins in exultant liberation with a direct address—"But O, dear Anne!"—as the poet cries out and then is released into a twelve line stanza, a free flow of song created by and voiced by a different kind of singing woman.

Anne's singing constitutes the fourth and best way of making music. Ranging through the sounds of nature and ballads of woe, Anne's voice

> remeasures
> Whatever tones and melancholy pleasures
> The things of Nature utter. (ll. 35–37)

She humanizes natural noises by the artifice of measure, the coinage "remeasure" indicating that her voice imitates or represents in a new medium the sounds of nature. Anne could be one of the many "Annes" addressed in poems throughout his life; his recently dead (1791) and adored sister Anne, called Nancy by her brothers; or Anna Cruikshanks, his Nether Stowey neighbor; or some other natural and spontaneous precursor of the Sara Hutchinson of the end of the Dejection Ode. Her loose, natural, and variable style of music provides a contrast and a release from the hot jostling competition of the concert room, and yet is more original than the Ottery fiddler's tunes and more social than the solitary flautist Edward's, so maudlin as to recall Wordsworth's dying Boy of Winander.

Most remarkably, Anne's music is disembodied. The poet listens to the many varied voices she can create, undistracted by any fleshly heaving. An epigram from a few months after the writing of this poem indicates the desire to listen to a woman's music without the distractions of her seen beauty:

> Wherefore, wherefore, most unwise,
> Did you bring the candles here?
> Why remind us we have eyes,
> When we wished to be *all ear*? (*PW* #261)

This respectful listening reappears in stanzas seven and eight of "Dejection: An Ode."

The skillful organization of this poem extends to its auditory effects.[27] The four segments also recreate four kinds of musical sounds, the flamboyantly brassy aria angering the poet; the jaunty folk song perhaps with hurdy gurdy waking nostalgia for the "tedded hay"; the wistful flute wafting over the still and lonely water; and then the multiple quick changes of pace in Anne's remeasure of "midnight wind," "the gust pelting on the out-house shed," the "ballad full of woe,"

> Ballad of ship-wreck'd sailor floating dead,
> Whom his own true-love buried in the sands! (ll. 33–34)

Dropping from this crescendo that imitates the female imitator of natural sounds, Coleridge softens his conclusion. Anne's voice renders "melancholy pleasures" and Coleridge reproduces these pleasures in onomatopoeic diminuendo:

> birds or trees,
> Or moan of ocean-gale in weedy caves,
> Or where the stiff grass mid the heath-plant waves,
> Murmur and music thin of sudden breeze. (ll. 37–40)

These muted sounds of winds through weedy caves and stiff grass conclude the poem in a "thin music" that Coleridge, a skilled reciter, might have chanted as a hush or a moan.[28] As the poem comes to a close, the demonic, demonstrative, vast-breasted diva gives way to a calm self-contained woman expressing her emotions musically in a natural setting, her music rendered by the now calmly expansive poet.

But Coleridge's detestation for and attraction to divas did not end in the oppressive heat of this provincial concert room. In Malta and Sicily he often attended the opera and became a connoisseur of bel canto singing. In Malta in 1805, in even more intense heat, he was once again accosted by an operatic dominatrix, exuding lust and theatricality. As Graham Davidson reveals in "Coleridge in Malta: Figures in a Landscape,"[29] Coleridge finds himself "at the bedside of the too fascinating Siren against whose witcheries Ulysses's wax would have proved but half-protection—poor Cecilia Bertozzoli! Yet neither her beauty, with all her power of employing it, neither heavenly song, were as dangerous as her sincere vehemence of attachment to me—vehemence, for I trust it was not depth, and attachment, for it was not mere passion, and yet, Heaven forbid that I should call it love." "The outworks of my nature" were "already carried by the sweetness of her temper" and by "the very great relief to my depression and to the deathy weighing-down of my heart from her singing and playing so that I had begun to crave after her society." Almost seduced by opera, by beauty, and by desire, the luscious and physical Coleridge trembles "to think what I was at that moment on the very brink of being surprised into by the prejudices of the shame of sex as much as by the force of its ordinary impulses." He was saved from this lapse by a vision of Sara Hutchinson as a Guardian Angel, who brings to his "self-dissatisfied spirit" "one spot of cloudless and fixed sunshine in the memory of conscience" (*CN* 3, 3404). He imagines the blurring of these female faces frightening him on his deathbed. As in "Lines Composed in a Concert Room," the self-contained Anne figure rescues the poet from the threats of the diva sweating with loudly insistent emotion and a sexuality divided from the wholeness of being.

Why does he need to resist this powerful vehemence and beauty? Why does he need rescuing from his desires, if he is separated from his wife and on his own on a steamy Mediterranean island? Godwinians may well wonder, wishing him freedom. But it was not the thought of his wife that stopped him in mid swoon. It was Sara Hutchinson, and loyalty to her spirit. He is not a lascivious man, nor a beast with no will, but a devoted lover of one woman, as he writes in the marginalia to Thomas Browne, even if English law prevents him from having her. Coleridge's late letters on marriage may give us insight into his resistance in our final chapter.

"Lines Written in a Concert Room" serves as a model for soothing the inward turmoil lurking beneath "The Letter to Sara——" and leads to the revision of that verse letter in "Dejection: An Ode" in 1804. "Lines" and "Dejection: An Ode" are closely related poems, both published in *The Morning Post*. They show how Coleridge gradually steadies his strong passions by an ethical repositioning. The resolution of "Lines" helps Coleridge resolve the artistic and psychological struggle represented in the gap between "The Letter to Sara Hutchinson" (1802) and "Dejection: An Ode" (1804). This gap can be imagined as a "chasm, with ceaseless turmoil seething" ("Kubla Khan," l. 17). Coleridge crosses this gap by choosing to return to his earlier "Lines" and specifically by adapting its last twelve lines rendering Anne's music. Anne sings ballads; she is a gentle woman whose voice gives musical structure to nature.

More obliquely, the Lady of "Dejection: An Ode" makes the despairing poet realize that

> from the soul itself must there be sent
> A sweet and potent voice of its own birth,
> Of all sweet sounds the life and element! (ll. 56–58)

Because of her pure heart she radiates joy: this joy in turn modulates into the "sweet voice"; and the voice fills nature: "all melodies the echoes of that voice." Stanza seven of the ode, like the last segment of "Lines," describes a shifting weather in shifting tempos:

> 'Tis of the Rushing of an Host in rout,
> With groans of trampled men, with smarting wounds—
> At once they groan with pain, and shudder with the cold!
> But hush! There is a pause of deepest silence!
>   And all that noise, as of a rushing crowd;
> With groans, and tremulous shudderings—all is over—
>   It tells another tale, with sounds less deep and loud!
>   A tale of less affright,
>   And temper'd with delight,
> As Otway's self had fram'd the tender lay,—
>   'Tis of a little child
>   Upon a lonesome wild,
> Not far from home, but she hath lost her way:
> And now moans low in bitter grief and fear,
> And now screams loud, and hopes to make her mother hear.
> (ll. 110–125)

Although the wind is the mad lutanist making these variations, the sweet voice of the Lady informs it, and the model of Anne's varying songs affirms the femaleness of melody. It is "*her* potent voice" as it is "*her* symphony and song" in "Kubla Khan."

While both of these poems demonstrate a process of learning a peaceful music and an appreciation of women who produce music out of a naturally self-generating personal integrity, the "Letter to Sara——" that intervenes roils with passion. The differences between the letter and the ode, often discussed, are so great as to make them alien poems, written from different sides of the poet's brain. The first is raw, rambling, and confessional (openly wishing, for example, that his children had never been born). It is the voice of a demon wailing for his woman lover. In it, the poet is the vehement diva demanding attention and forcing the loved one to shrink away. In a tumult of uncontrolled words, and sometimes guttering meter (e.g. ll. 68–71) it screeches "I want, I suffer." It wishes to be glad that Sara Hutchinson is content, but cannot feel this gladness.

In the two year interval between the letter and the ode, changes occur, not just in style and omission, but in wisdom. The mode, key, and tune modulate because the voice changes, as if the speaker has taken a deep breath and called to mind personal dignity (which includes attention to his metrical craft) and respect for the Other. Robert Barth declares that "Dejection: An Ode" is a love poem rather than a poem about the sources of the imagination, even though the word love appears only negatively in the phrase "the loveless ever anxious crowd." Although the "Letter to SH" uses the word "love" 22 times, Barth calls it a poem of self-love; by contrast, "Dejection: An Ode" redirects the passion to a loved person.[30] As the focus turns from Self to Other, the screech softens into the blessing, the wail steadies into melody. Instructed and transformed by the Lady's sweet voice, he can now pray for her continued creativity: "Joy lift her spirit, joy attune her voice" (l. 134). The last long stanza of "Lines" breathes release; so Coleridge returns to this kind of fluent medley at the end of "Dejection: An Ode" as a way of overcoming his sufferings. Both Anne's creative song in "Lines in a Concert Room" and the Lady's singing in "Dejection: An Ode" free the poet from suffocation and allow him to roam across spaces represented by different rhythms and speeds.

Coleridge's reading of Schiller helped him to value the graceful self-coherent moral action that Schiller associates with women. As Michael John Kooy argues, Schiller's poems, plays, and thought have a pervasive influence on Coleridge's thought, craftsmanship, idea of genius, and practice of drama. Schiller's speculations about the aesthetic state are specifically related to Coleridge's plans for a clerisy and the role of women in it. Schiller disagrees with Kant's praise of heroic struggle to perform one's duty and prefers "a state of affairs where duty is performed unconsciously, out of habit rather than deliberation—in his word, 'gracefully'. Such a state is achieved by what he calls the *schone Seele*, or 'beautiful soul'. " It is easier for women than for men to integrate their inclination with their duty: "Having in effect internalized the moral law, and thus done away with the need for reflection and struggle, Schiller's female moral agent inherits the moral prize that the male can earn only by an effort of self-mastery. She embodies the goal for which the male must fight."[31] As with ease of moral action, so with singing: for women there is no gap between the content and the performance, but the melody and the voice meld gracefully.

But who is actually singing: the poet, the lady, or the wind? Paul Fry believes that the counterturn at "I turn from you, and listen to the wind," is the moment when the poet realizes that "he has nothing more to say in his own person" and in losing his voice inside that of the child in Wordsworth's Lucy poems he "concedes" the " 'femininity' of his own character, the helpless passivity and lack of sexually polar magnetism that makes it impossible for him to woo nature in a great spousal verse of his own. His inability to make Nature hear increases the louder he screams."[32] While Fry associates personal emptiness in a man with femininity, we could view this "turn" in another light, that the poet defers to the woman and allows her to sing her song. Where in "Lines Composed in a Concert Room" Anne's section is decisively her own, in Dejection 7 the lady's voice blends with the poet's, ventriloquized through his voice, since he has written her lines for her. This incorporation is not as egocentric as it might seem. Rather, the example of "Lines" suggests an alternative musical interpretation: blended voices where the male poet ends by adapting the womanly inclusiveness that he praises. Is it a woman's voice imagined or his own voice speaking through hers? Is it a duet of intertwining melodies? Do the poet and the lady alternate or sing in counterpoint?

A note of September 1808, more beautiful than most people's poems, associates this blending with music:

> Some philosophers have affirmed, that two bodies may be supposed to fill one space, each the whole, without a contradiction in reason. Whether this be true of matter I am as ignorant as whether matter has a being at all—but in the things of Soul and Spirit I am sure it is true. For Love, passionate in its deepest tranquillity, Love unutterable fills my whole Spirit, so that every fibre of my Heart, nay, of my whole frame seems to tremble under its perpetual touch and sweet pressure, like the string of a Lute—with a sense of vibratory Pain distinct from all other sensations, a Joy, that cannot be entered into while I am embodied—a pain of yearning which all the Pleasure on earth could not induce me to relinquish, even were it in my power—and yet it *is* a pain, an aking that spreads even into the eyes, that have a look as if they were asking . . . even of Vacancy—yea, and asking for her very Self within or even beyond her apparent Form—And yet full as my Being is of this Love, a sense of Gratitude seems to penetrate and permeate that omnipresent affection / O well may I be grateful—She loves me—*me*, who—O noble dear generous [Asra]!—Herein my Love, which in *degree* cannot be surpassed, is yet in kind inferior to yours! (Sept. 9, 1808; *CN* 3370)

His emotion is musical throughout the fibers of his frame, which vibrate and tremble with aching joy. He yearns more completely to love her, and knows that he is loved in return.

"Dejection: an Ode" ends in harmony.[33] The transformation occurs when the harmonizing center of the poem becomes female, a "*Schone Seele*," and this female is a fountain of music, rather than an overwhelming body tantalizing or engulfing the poet who listens. In *Revision and Romantic Authorship*, Zachary Leader situates the profound changes from "a whining, childish" "Letter to Sara" to a mature meditation on self-making in "Dejection: An Ode." Disputing views that multiple versions of poems reveal their meaninglessness, Leader argues that poetic revision and composition "is no mere 'activity' or play of signifiers to Coleridge: it remains, for all Coleridge's sense of belatedness and of the impossibility of authorial autonomy, a way of making not only things or poems, but a self, it is an expression of 'logocentric belief'."[34] Along with omitting confessional indiscretions, Coleridge is also, and more centrally, working on his own character: in Leader's words, "Personal identity . . . is conceived of by Coleridge as something one makes or creates," as in "the act of revision."[34] Poetic revision is a decision as ethical as thinking about the other person, as imagining how the other person feels, as listening to another person's very different song. The revisions follow a specifically ethical line toward a recognition of the inner life of the other, which involves a shift in positioning of the subject and a move away from looking at flesh to listening to what other people sing. Looking at flesh sees surface; listening to voice hears soul. Coleridge, writing and revising, learns to listen.

Both "Lines Composed in a Concert Room" and "Dejection: An Ode" stanzas five and seven support Coleridge's faith in the natural connection between the female mind and measured sounds. He made this connection in his praise of Matilda Betham's "sweet tune":

> The Almighty, having first composed a Man,
> Set him to music, framing Woman for him,
> And fitted each to each, and made them one!
> And 'tis my faith, that there's a natural bond
> Between the female mind and measured sounds. ("To Matilda Betham from a Stranger", *PW* #304, ll. 18–22)

The woman whose grace is an enacted morality is associated with music in Schiller, as Michael John Kooy has shown. Echoing Schiller, Coleridge writes in "*Ad Vilmum Axiologum*" "Love is the Spirit of Life, and Music the Life of the Spirit" (*PW* #392), and discovers, "Love to all passions as Music to all varieties of sound" (*CN* 1229).

Inspired by real actresses, real women poets and political figures, and real women opera singers, Coleridge glorifies woman as the spirit of music. The Damsel of "Kubla Khan" is an early expression of woman as source of the beauty and power of voice. The Damsel and the Lady singing in "Dejection: An Ode" both allow creativity to flow, but "Kubla Khan" precedes his meeting with Sara Hutchinson by a year. "Kubla Khan" tuned his strings for love, readying him to feel how "every fibre of my Heart, nay, of my whole frame seems to tremble under its perpetual touch and sweet pressure, like the string of a Lute" (*CN* 3370).

A similar evolution occurs 110 years later in James Joyce's musically complex story "The Dead." Amid talk about divas and tenors, Gabriel Conroy first sees his wife as a painting, a surface with salmon colored panels, which he presumes to entitle "Distant Music." For his wife, however, this music is not distant, but internally alive with old emotion. Preoccupied with his own clownish lusts, Gabriel tries to understand why her face is troubled; he tries to achieve "mastery" over her mood; he questions her about the past, but does not listen, caught up in the clever ironies of his own questions. Finally the truth penetrates. He learns that the song "The Lass of Aughrim" carries within it the lost mutual love with Michael Furey. He sees himself as an outcast from life's feast, cast down for his superficiality and arrogance. He learns to hear the song that his wife heard resonating with a love that he does not know how to feel. He starts by imagining music as a posture to be looked at and admired from a distance; he ends by knowing it to be a feeling to be sung and heard inside the body. Joyce and Coleridge both show the limitations of the male eye. Their men, fictional or poetic, look at surfaces until they are surprised by voices coming from beneath the surfaces. All of a sudden, they are forced to listen. Listening opens up a tumult of emotion; women, music, and emotion surge over the boundaries of their egos. They become human beings when they participate in the "conversation of united souls."

Chapter 8
Divorce and the Law

The English law forbidding divorce prevented Coleridge from achieving the completion to which the songs of women summoned him. Unique in Protestant Europe, this English law was a far more oppressive element in Romantic culture than critics have yet observed. It cast a pall over many unhappily married men and women, demanded the expense of two establishments for separated couples, and gave unusual power to husbands over their wives. At this time of Romantic rebellion against the forces that constricted individual liberty, under the very eyes of reformers, the lives of women worsened, and the shouts of men swelled, "Hear, Hear!" In 1800 the House of Lords held a debate lasting two months, March 21 to May 19, to establish increasingly harsh punishments for aristocratic wives who violated their marriage vows.[1] Just a few months after falling in love with a woman not his wife, Coleridge attended the first two weeks of these debates. This chapter shows what the debates revealed about lordly British attitudes toward women, how Coleridge responded in print to these legal realities in the midst of his own emotional turmoil, and how these laws prevented Coleridge and Sara Hutchinson from legalizing their love for each other. It was not his choice to "refuse to divorce his wife," as even his admirers have suggested, but the law of the land.

The debates started with a particular proposal and widened to include a range of issues related to women and the prevention of adultery in marriage. William Wilberforce believed these issues were the most important for the culture as a whole, and he who had championed the liberation of slaves did not rise to the liberation of wives. Wilberforce said that he "considered this subject of much more importance than any question about peace or war or any constitutional question, for the question then before the House went to the inmost recesses of domestic happiness; to the very foundations of civil society, and could destroy the whole fabric of society" (vol. 35, col. 322).

The Lords began by addressing the specific problem of Standing Order 142, because in the long process of court appearances it unnecessarily aggravated the humiliation of cuckolds. Standing Order 142 demands that the husband suing for divorce in the House of Lords give evidence against the persons supposed to be guilty of adultery not only to the ecclesiastical court (which had permitted him separation from bed and board) and the civil court (which had awarded him damages for loss of property) but also again to the committee of the House of Lords.[2] He must thus repeat the lurid details of his betrayal in front of his peers. Lord Mulgrave begins the debate by asking to rescind this standing order on the grounds that the husband would have to incriminate himself, suffer double jeopardy in being tried a second time, and thereby cast suspicion on the efficacy of the previous courts. He asks the lords to "consider how painful it must be for a man of honour to have his feelings additionally wounded, by being . . . made the fixed figure for 'the slow unmoving finger of scorn to point at' for the rest of his days" (cols. 1552–1553). In addition to this humiliation, the assumption that the husband has colluded with the wife's lover to take her for some payment "does flagrant injustice to the morals of the gentry of this country." Instead of calling him once again to rehearse his sufferings, "Why not examine the lady? or let the seducer be brought to the bar to be questioned?" (1554). Lord Mulgrave pities only the poor husband, and wonders if the Abyssinians were correct in believing that "when the husband failed in conjugal fidelity, the wife was punished for neglect of duty, [because] if a woman was as full of attentions as her duty required, the husband would not have gone astray" (vol. 35, col. 1556). Lord Mulgrave must have known that it would have been impossible to "examine the lady" who, not being a separate person, could not testify in court or swear an oath.

But the move to rescind Standing Order 142 is rebuffed right away. The Bishop of Rochester opposes all easing of divorce because he sees collusion between husband, wife, and adulterer; even "the innocent, virtuous, and deeply injured husband . . . must yield to the paramount duty of preserving the morals of the people" (vol. 34, col. 1558). Subtly shifting the ground, Lord Auckland proposes "that no bill of divorce shall be admissible without a clause to make it unlawful for the offending parties to intermarry." A "general cry of Hear, Hear," greets this new and much fiercer plan, one that avoids any taint of French revolutionary immorality from that "system of legalized prostitution and profligacy, now prevalent in a neighbouring country" (cols. 1559–1560). Lord Mulgrave's original plan has not only failed but has roused up the lords to harsher and more imaginative punishments and turned attention from collusive males to the wife at the center of the collusion.

After ten days, April 2, 1800, Lord Auckland has revised his bill to forbid "intermarrying with the person with whom the adultery shall have been committed" (vol. 35, cols. 225–226). His aim was to avoid benefitting the criminals and ultimately to warn potential adulteresses that they could never get what they want. On April 4, the Duke of Clarence, later William IV, who himself had ten illegitimate children with the actress Mrs. Jordan,[3] rises to oppose the bill and to defend those "persons who from the amiableness of their sex, were best entitled to compassion and liberality" (col. 228). The bill deprived the adulteress of her only hope of "salving her reputation by a marriage with the man whose arts had beguiled her of her virtue, deprived her of her husband's affections, and destroyed her domestic happiness" (col. 228). The wives of wealthy noblemen "could not work as menial servants; they were not instructed in any line of business; they could not beg. And what other line of providing the means of life was left open to them, but abandoning themselves to prostitution?" The Duke asks his fellow Lords to imagine the case as their own: would they wish their own ladies to suffer such "misery and wretchedness"?

The bishops of London and Durham oppose him. The adulterous wife need not become a prostitute; in the course of time she might marry some person other than her criminal lover who might support her, though they do not suggest how she would survive in the intervening years. The bishops remind the other lords that before the Restoration adultery was a capital offense. Lord Eldon points out that simple and silly women might believe the promises of their seducers (col. 234); Lord Grenville retorts that the Lords were not gathered here to favor a guilty party, and must defy "the force of the amiable private feelings of the human breast." Parliament pauses until May 16 while Lord Auckland revises his bill, making it still more punitive by adding fines and imprisonment (col. 236).

Coleridge attended a few days of these debates, which must have brought home to him the difficulties of his personal situation. He himself throbbed at the center of a triangle very like those lambasted in Parliament or narrated in Lawrence Stone's case histories, except that he was poor, the would-be seducer, his wife the abandoned victim, and he himself whirled sobbing in the carnal winds of Dante's first circle. Coleridge's own marriage was undermined by adulterous desires and domestic rages at this time, as we have seen. On Nov. 27, 1799, he moved into rooms at number 21 Buckingham Street, The Strand; on Dec. 17, 1799, Sara Fricker Coleridge and their firstborn Hartley joined him. Despite this apparently cozy domestic setup, it should be noted that two weeks prior to arriving in London Coleridge had gone missing, his whereabouts unknown to his wife, who thought he had gone in search of his book boxes. He had, in fact, been holed up in Sockburn with Sara Hutchinson and her brothers since October 26, writing letters to no one (*CL* 1, 542), to his wife's fury, but experiencing closeness with "the infinitely beloved darling."

Driven perhaps by such a multiplicity of passions, Coleridge threw himself into a new phase of London life, attending debates in Parliament and writing for Daniel Stuart. He delighted in tracing "a happy phrase, good image, or new argument running thro' the Town, & sliding into all the papers"; he enjoyed hearing his own arguments repeated in the House of Commons, and chuckled over "the plagiarism" "in the silent self-complacence of [his] own Heart"; he was thrilled that "few Wine merchants can boast of creating more sensation" than his printed words (*CL* 1, 569). Letters and notes (e.g. *CN* 619 and note to 619) record several engagements with Godwin and his children for the three months Sara and Hartley stayed in London, but no mention of how Sara liked her husband's absences when sessions went through the night, his frenzied absorption in writing the long reports on Pitt, Napoleon, and the Irish Union that date from these months, the no doubt irregular meals.[4] Two physical facts stand out: Sara left with her four year old to stay with the Roskillys near Bristol on March 2; and she must have become pregnant soon after she arrived in London, for five weeks later Coleridge writes Southey in that coy, passive voice that he used for such surprises in which he seemingly has no part, "a circumstance has taken place, which will render a Sea-voyage utterly unfit for Sara—Indeed, it is a pretty clear case" (Jan. 25, 1800; *CL* 1, 563). (Derwent was born Sept. 14, 1800.) These facts suggest that as irritating as it was to live in close quarters together in London, and as passionately as he loved another woman, he and his wife still had sexual relations. The evening his family departed Coleridge careened out to Pentonville to Lamb's rooms for a binge.

Two weeks later, March 21, 1800, the lords began their debate on "the Standing Order respecting Divorce Bills." Despite two Latin paragraphs complaining about his wife in letters to friends,[5] Coleridge returned north to her, and to Sara Hutchinson, on April 2, allowing himself just two weeks to attend these debates. He goes to Grasmere, takes a walk with his wife and son, and throughout the summer of 1801 (*CN* 970–979) slips off to Sockburn to visit Sara Hutchinson.

When Coleridge came to London to write for *The Morning Post*, he anticipated that he would be covering, among many other topics, the debates on divorce law. He made a note to himself already in

February, 1800, to write "An Essay on the Adultery Bill."[6] Although this essay as a whole has not been found or was not written, before Coleridge returned north he contributed to *The Morning Post* a page assessing his views—"Parliament X: the Adultery Bill and the Rights of Women"— published April 16, 1800. This page is full of those ironies that confound readers whenever Coleridge talks about women's rights.[7] After listening to the debates described above, Coleridge realizes that the books written in the 1790's about the rights of women—which he had previously believed "were too absurd to require any answer"—suddenly make sense: "With more reason might a book on that subject be written when women are run down with severity by the new Divorce Bill, now before the House of Lords" (*EOT* 1, 239). Hearing how fiercely women are "run down" like hunted animals, Coleridge sees that Mary Wollstonecraft and other feminists were describing real situations in their "fictions" and that the power of husbands to incarcerate their wives in Bedlam might have more truth than he had previously imagined.[8] In his page Coleridge presents a revolutionary way of looking at these debates. That is: men can be adulterers, too, and deserve to be punished equally with the adulterous women:

> All good men abhor the crime of adultery, and good women too abhor it; but is it equal justice to make the whole weight of punishment fall upon the weaker sex? Is not every guilty woman punished throughout life in her reception by society? But what punishment is inflicted upon the man beyond that which the courts of common law, or his own conscience, may inflict? Why is the man, the superior being, the protector of the other sex; why is he to escape when he uses his great endowments for wicked purposes, and betrays his trust? We shall not object to further punishment for the crime, even in the persons of women; but before we consent, a very severe punishment, indeed, must be decreed against the male seducer. (*EOT* 1, 239–240)

Of course, many people will ruffle their feathers over the phrases about the superior being and the protector, but Coleridge may be speaking sarcastically about these hypocritical nabobs who have forgotten the carelessly seductive goals of their fellow superior beings. He is making a point—consistent with his view that rights entail responsibilities—that privileged, educated, land-owning, monied rulers of the universe should use their rights responsibly.[9] His words assume that both wife and seducer are agents, that there are good women as well as good men, and both are capable of choosing the good.

When the debates begin again on May 16 the Earl of Moira immediately attacks the revised bill, first on the grounds that it criminalizes a civil offence, second on grounds similar to and verbally echoing those that Coleridge had argued in the *Morning Post* one month earlier, that is, that under the bill the seducer was left unshackled, the husband was also left unshackled, and "the whole penalty fell upon the unfortunate victim of seduction. . . . it was false to say that no punishment already attached to the crime. Every woman who violated her conjugal vows lost her reputation, the esteem of her friends, and of the world, and never could raise herself to the rank from which she had fallen. The severity with which it was now proposed to pursue her, was contrary to the spirit of our laws. . . . Was then no allowance to be made for female weakness, blinded by passion, and assailed by all the arts of seduction?" (vol. 35, col. 236–237). Coleridge may thus have had a real influence exceeding that of wine merchants, as he had hoped, when his happy phrases and new arguments slide into the "plagiarisms" of Lord Moira.

In *Road to Divorce*, Lawrence Stone describes this dramatic shift from punishing the seducer to punishing the wife. The original plan was to sniff out "crim.con.," or criminal conversation, "to punish the seducers of married women and to compensate the latter's cuckolded husbands." Most lords turned quickly to punish the wife because it was easier. She lacked a legal personality and "was therefore unable to testify, either in person or through her counsel, or even to produce witnesses in her defence, in a civil suit or damages brought by her husband against her alleged lover."[10] For these reasons, when the fault lay with a promiscuous, violent, and drunken husband, who may have encouraged adultery to gain exorbitant damages (Earl of Carlisle, col. 279) evidence for his culpability could not be "produced in court" (Stone, *Road*, 31). Even the few lords sympathetic to the plight of women forced to sell their bodies on the street cannot conceive that these women might actually have emotions, might love their lovers and risk all to be near them.[11] The debaters agree on one thing: adultery is a female offense; men may move as they choose from blossom to blossom; the phrase "female adultery" is a tautology, since "adultery" is not a term or activity applied to men.[12]

These debates reveal manly rage at females throughout the land. Lawrence Stone calls wives slaves, and his list of what they lose by marrying proves that this is not a metaphor:

> All the income from her real estate was retained by her husband, as well as all future legacies which might come to her. All her personal property, including her future earnings from a trade and her business stock and tools, were liable to seizure by her husband at any moment. She was unable to enter into a legal contract, to use credit to borrow money, or to buy or sell property. All her savings belonged to her husband. And finally

all her children were controlled entirely by their father, who was free to dispose of them as he wished, and to deprive their mother of any opportunity ever to speak to them again. (Stone, *Road*, 3–4, 13)

Like slaves, wives are property, breeders of future property, their work and future work the property of others; and like slaves, they are not legal persons and have no right to dispose of their own persons or to own objects, paper, money, or a public voice. If a slave is "a human being who is owned by and absolutely subject to another human being, as by capture, purchase, or birth," how is a wife in this period not a slave? And why, in the context of debates on abolition in this period, is the similarity between the two kinds of non-persons ignored?[13]

Women belonged with their property and offspring to their husbands: as possessions, they stood in some intermediate status between persons and objects of use; as bodies, they were vessels for the presumably authentic continuity of lineage and counters for exchange of property, reduced to the status of things. The thingness of women is an underlying assumption in the vivid rhetoric of the Parliamentary debates.

By an additional twist of the screw, however, the wife is less than a slave because she is not a person at all. Her person is merged into her husband's and does not exist. William Blackstone describes the obliteration of her being as an extension of the Biblical phrase "flesh of my flesh," prompting the question, which is worse: to be a thing possessed or not to be at all?[14] William Godwin was correct in calling marriage "an affair of property, and the worst of all properties,"[15] the ownership of other persons and their obliteration.

While these suits for divorce applied only to the richest men in the land, among the lower classes, wife-sale was an alternative method of releasing the cuckold from liability. This solution to marital incompatibility seems to have been common through the fifteenth and eighteenth centuries, and not only in Thomas Hardy's fictional Casterbridge. It took place at markets where wives roped by the neck were handed over to more compatible males, who often had already tested that compatibility.[16] Wives were put up for sale at auctions, announced by town criers, posted on notices in pubs, or described on broadsheets like livestock, as in this newspaper advertisement from 1796: "To be sold for *five shillings*, my wife, Jane Hebland. She is stout built, stands firm on her posterns, and is sound wind and limb. She can sow and reap, hold a plough, and drive a team, and would answer any stout able men, that can hold a *tight rein*, for she is damned *hard mouthed* and headstrong; but, if properly managed would either lead or drive as tame as a rabbit.

She now and then, if not watched, will make a *false step*. Her husband parts with her because she is too much for him" (Menefee, 75). From the purchaser's point of view, wife-sale, "by securing proof of the husband's acquiescence in a new relationship, could insure against an action for crim.con" (Menefee, 66). We learn something about our culture today when even many women find these details hilarious, while similar bills of auction, sales, posters, and roped transfers of human flesh in the trade in African slaves rouse rage. Here, the language is similarly animalistic, turning a human into a horse, then devolving that horse down into a rabbit.

The debates in the House of Lords, with the shouts of "Hear! Hear!" resounding, show that attitudes toward women had hardened in the eighteenth century from a more generous treatment of daughters and wives in earlier centuries. Researching documents from the fifteenth and sixteenth centuries, Amy Louise Erickson finds wills made by fathers specifically including their daughters by giving them the movables of the estate; wills made by unmarried women without brothers for their nieces; suits in courts of law by women, usually with fathers or brothers, to regain their portions in cases of failed marriages and separations. Erickson's statistics, graphs, and legal documents from varied regions of Great Britain show that women had some legal rights as persons even though the country as a whole forbade divorces.[17] Also writing about this earlier period of tolerance, Barbara J. Harris finds among aristocrats a benign insouciance toward adulterous wives and their obscurely fathered offspring.[18]

Over the course of the eighteenth century women lost the right to exercise wills, suits, and other legal activities that they had enjoyed in the fifteenth century, as the whole country moved toward larger estates, less flexible primogeniture, and the incorporation of inheritances and portions to fund the empire.[19] Even remaining single became a difficult option in the eighteenth century. Whether they wanted to marry or not, their family's economic interests dictated that young women's properties be joined with neighboring ones through marriage. These were not love matches but alliances between exceedingly wealthy landed families or between landed gentry and plutocratic commercial families. Erickson suggests that girls were forced to marry earlier, giving them a shorter period of independence and more children: "by the eighteenth century the number of women never marrying had dropped to less than half its previous level, so more women fell under the shadow of an even harsher coverture" (p. 229). The pressure on women to submit to this system intensified as never-married women became increasingly stigmatized.

At the same time, the language describing the unions of man and woman became more absolute in obliterating the woman's own identity and legal status as a separate individual within the union. *She* was now *He* in a more than emotional sense.

Erickson summarizes the debasement of women that had occurred by the end of the eighteenth century:

> Many men would have liked to regard women as property in and of themselves; but while married women's legal disabilities put them in the same category with idiots, convicted criminals and infants, they were never legally classed with chattels. Nonetheless, there are ways in which women were treated as a form of property.... Widows and women abandoned by their husbands in England were among the least protected anywhere in the world, let alone in Europe, where a restitution of dowry was legally required. (pp. 232–233)

Primogeniture and coverture were the English institutions that obliterated the separate personhood of married women. By the middle of the eighteenth century, as April London shows, the "debate concerning the relationship of property (the ownership of things) to propriety (the possession of one's own person)" has been resolved in favor of land-owning males.[20] Coleridge notes, "Property, Propriety—curious instance of Desynonimization" (Jan. 1803; *CN* 1, 1336). He plays with the meaning of *propre*, one's own and owning things. Owning property gives the property-owner a proper self. In the case of women, their propriety, in the sense of chaste behavior, makes them eligible to marry, so that then their father's property is given away in a marriage settlement. In a curious paradox, the woman's propriety deprives her of property and even of self-possession, since she must give up her property and own nothing (London, p. 30).

When Coleridge mentions in his *Morning Post* page the fictions by women that now made sense, he may be referring to Mary Wollstonecraft's terrifying novel *Maria* (1795). Readers today roll their eyes at the extremes of poor Maria's victimization. Maria's husband can be disgusting, drunk, violent, abusive, unfaithful in her own house; he can offer her body to his cronies for cash and as proof of her degraded nature; and then he can incarcerate her in a madhouse for complaining. And this is just the beginning. He can rip her suckling infant from her while she floods with tears and wasted milk, and she has no legal recourse to argue her way out of a prison full of abusive guards. Her money and land are her husband's. If she were not in prison, she would be begging or prostituting herself on the street. To judge by the parliamentary debates, however, Mary Wollstonecraft is in fact describing the legal reality of eighteenth century marriage. By a series of encroaching laws and customs that even Erickson cannot quite locate, women had by this time lost their rights to property and funds, except in the rare cases of high ranking unmarried women or widows (like Austen's Lady Catherine de Bourgh), of tradeswomen whose husbands did not insist upon claiming their earnings, and of daughters who clung to benevolent often widowed fathers and served them as secretaries and hostesses.

The debates of 1799–1801 must be seen in the context of England's prohibition of divorce, the layering of courts, and the publicity involved in creating a separate bill of divorce with the public watching the proceedings and the stories filling the press with tales of adultery.[21] Although there was no way to get rid of a husband, there were three levels for expelling a wife perceived as adulterous, as Allen Horstman outlines. The sequence went from a church court to plead for "a divorce *a mensa et thoro*, a divorce from bed and board," forbidding both parties from remarrying, to the common law court where the husband sued his wife's lover for "trespass, assault, and criminal conversation." Here he demanded payment for loss of services, payment which he sometimes returned to the lover as part of their "crim.con." collusion to pass the wife along. "The wife, not directly a party to a crim.con. suit, saw her actions paraded before a 'grinning jury' and her reputation ruined. After a crim.con. suit, few men, other than the lover, would ever consider marriage to her." The third stage required the husband to repeat the humiliating details in front of the House of Lords, in order to be granted a private bill of divorce, "a divorce *a vinculo matrimonii*," and be allowed to remarry.

This long procedure daunted many unhappily married men, so that they turned a blind eye to their wives' affairs and even to the arrival of illegitimate offspring in their households. Wives, since they had no legal rights, could not sue for divorce under any circumstances. "With all these considerations governing couples, the complicated three-step procedure yielded, by 1800, 128 divorces, including three dukes, one marquess, one earl, five barons, five baronets, and numerous sons, daughters, and relations of the peerage.... Countless other couples quietly separated or simply waited for the release of death."[22] These 128 divorces constitute the "wave" of divorces that prompted parliament in 1799 to try to punish adulterous wives more harshly and thus to stop the epidemic of divorce at its source.

But Coleridge's responses were not entirely outraged. He may also have been amused at the range of possibilities that opened up when the punitive bill passed the House of Lords, but was stayed in Commons.

Ten months later, while debating George Taylor's suit against his wife Catherine, Lord Kenyon tries again to attach the clause forbidding the marriage of adulterous lovers.[23] It is this debate, reiterating many of the arguments that Coleridge had heard earlier, that inspired the poem "Philosophical Apology for the Ladies, An Ode, addressed to Lord Kenyon," which was published in *The Morning Post*, 22 June 1801, and reprinted in the *Courier* the same day. David Erdman believes that this satirical ode was by Coleridge (Erdman, note 1, *EOT* 3, p. 302). J. C. C. Mays has averred that "the case is not convincing" (*PW*, 2, p. 840). Perhaps Coleridge's interest in the divorce debates will provide a context for reconsidering the possibility that Coleridge was indeed the author of this satirical ode.

The ode satirizes a giddy world of sex and power, where old men try to regulate young desire, husbands whip themselves up into a froth to control their wives even after they have ejected them and been paid off for them, and wives, influenced by revolutionary French morals, follow their bliss as they defy their men. Sanctioned by Ovid's *Amores*, by David Hume, and by the new sciences of pullulating nature, riotously described by Tim Fulford,[24] this new high society is a free-for-all.

The ode asks a number of comical questions with Swiftian irony: why should husbands care about activities that they need not notice? Only country bumpkins object to frolicking wives; urbane and clever men use these opportunities to make new friends and business partners, smilingly sharing the same women. Instead of suspicious harangues about collusion, husbands should let their wives buzz about in loose cyprian robes.

> Ah! Kenyon, let Minerva's lyre
> Attune thy passions, sooth thy ire,
>   Thy ardent genius rule;
> If plants and flow'rs with sexual charms,
> Fondly entwine their sentient arms,
>   Can flesh and blood be cool? (*EOT* 3, 302)

Should women be free to choose love where they find it? The institution of marriage may be a spirit-constricting law, as William Godwin, echoing John Milton, warned clearly, but even so, women, let loose, seem worse than animals, verging on insects, creatures that in Coleridge's later parlance earn a place of scorn as "the Symbol of Appetite, Desire—Lust hard by hate" (*SWF*, 1455). What should be done with female desires?

> Each fragrant plant, and blooming flow'r,
> In am'rous bliss enjoy the hour,

> And various pleasures taste;
> So beauties sport away frail life,
> And scorn the dull domestic wife,
> Unpolish'd, dull, and chaste. (p. 303)

Should girls be forbidden knowledge of botany, if anthers and pistils are stimulating and looking into the centers of tulips conduces to rapture? Curling up like tentacles, notes to lustful botanists provide the context of Lucretian naturalism for these divorce debates. Nature inspires freely expressed ardor:

> Then why impede the soft caress,
> Cry 'Vive l'amour, and la jeunesse,'
> Wing Cupid's vivid darts;
> By nature's law, the roving spouse
> Breaks her first tie, and maiden vows,
> To join congenial hearts. (p. 305)

Citing the flighty Anacreon, the ode turns to its target:

> Dear Kenyon, move a moral bill,
> Founded on woman's claims—FREE WILL,
> That sympathetic dames
> On genial rights their thoughts may turn,
> And throbbing hearts no longer mourn,
> But melt in mutual flames. (p. 306)

The ironies that Coleridge piled up in his page on the divorce bill suggest to me that he is also the author of this ode, which accommodates many points of view, skeptical of holy matrimony and at the same time skeptical about women who are skeptical about it, like Mary Wollstonecraft or the Duchess of Devonshire, admirable women who nevertheless present the possibility of uncontrolled desires terrifying to men. But since the ode is addressed to Lord Kenyon whose purpose was to forbid women from marrying their adulterous lovers, does the ode agree with Kenyon that they should not be allowed to settle down with the man with whom they originally violated their marriage vows? Or does it speculate on what will happen to women who are not allowed to marry these original lovers and are thus released into society as free agents without attachments or overseers, free agents also desperate for food and shelter? Holding in suspension such diverse alternatives, the ode presents a true Coleridgean muddle.

This jeu d'esprit turns attention on what to do with human beings who cannot legally speak in their own defense or explain their motivations, who have no legal existence as persons, and who nevertheless have desires for the uses of their bodies. They must be pummeled, disgraced, and ruined; as William Wilberforce declares, forgetting in this case his work to humanize the treatment of people of other races, this issue is more important than any issue of foreign affairs, because it goes to the root of the national life, because it leads to chaos in the manner of the French Revolution, because it calls into question legitimate succession of property.[25]

Between lordly collusions by means of large and secret payments and village trades of womenfolk in market places, the middling sorts were stuck, unable to muster the vast sums for a parliamentary act, on the one hand, and too abstemious to hawk their wives like farm animals, on the other. They were forced to stay in incompatible marriages in cramped spaces of shared residence maintaining an air of respectability over their snarling daily interactions.

Where does he stand? Between "Parliament X" and "Apology for the Ladies" lies the muddle, since both alternatives are viable—the beginnings of sympathy for women hounded by men "and yet" the recognition of the potential for anarchy if they are released—, one ironical, the other satirical. Coleridge's speculative prose and the mocking ode that I believe is his are conjectural responses to the severity with which women are "run down." They suggest a curiosity about women's individuality, how it is negated by social forces and how it disappears in the hive of desire. Having heard the debates and read Milton, Godwin, and Wollstonecraft, having suffered what he suffers—loving one women and impregnating another—Coleridge might well wonder with Stephen Blackpool of *Hard Times* why divorce is forbidden to the poor and not to the Bounderbys of the world: "it's aw a muddle."[26]

These writings suggest a complicated tug of war between ethics and delight in absurdity. Coleridge's ambiguous expression of sympathy with injustice, on the one hand, and, on the other hand, irony about the consequences of its correction are further complicated by his sporadic separations from his wife and adulterous yearnings. His outrage at the public trial of Queen Caroline in 1820 reveals that his earlier disgust with the system has intensified. He fulminates at how "Sorrows and Losses fell fast and heavy on her head." As the king continued to revel in his own adultery with the Countess of Hertford, he launched an attack on his queen for her adventures in Europe during their long separation, adventures which Coleridge admits were "Levities the most unbecoming and the grossest improprieties." The public was outraged at the king's attempt to divorce her in the House of Lords. At the king's coronation as George IV, she nevertheless arrived to claim her rightful role as queen, but was turned away at the door. Sympathizing with the *"persecuted"* Woman and seeing how "Matronage" was hounded by the heavy excesses of masculine power, Coleridge roars: "What now when the Queen of England has had announced to her the direful Alternative, attaint of High Treason with the collected might, talent, and influence of the Executive to conduct and carry it into effect, or self-avowed Infamy and with perpetual Exile? And the latter is to be turned into a Bribe! . . . All this *may* be just. But it *is* hard! Hard and heavy, almost beyond Record!" (*EOT* 3, 258–259).[27] Though James Gillman convinced him not to publish this outcry, Coleridge seems to have felt that the punishment outweighed the crime and that the king's own adulteries should have been considered as a cause of hers.

Having heard some of the debates about divorce in the spring of 1800, and no doubt having followed the subsequent proceedings in the papers, Coleridge knows that the only way out for him, as it would be for Stephen Blackpool, is the death of his wife. A note from July–August 1803 seems through its euphemisms to renounce any such evil thought:

> There is one thing wholly out of my Power. I cannot look forward even with the faintest pleasure of Hope, to the Death of any human Being, tho' it were, as it seems to be, the only condition of the greatest imaginable Happiness to me, and the emancipation of all my noblest faculties that must remain fettered during that Being's Life.—I dare not, for I can not: I cannot, for I dare not. The very effort to look onward to it with a stedfast wish would be a suicide, far beyond what the dagger or pistol could realize—absolutely suicide, coelicide, not mere viticide.— (*CN* 1421)

To hope for his wife's death would be to kill the self in himself and to poison his nature. But the note turns now to a proposal to the woman he loves to live somehow within these impossible circumstances under a law of their own beyond the outward forms of law:

> But if I could secure you full Independence, if I could give too all my original Self healed & renovated from all infirm Habits; & if by all the forms in my power I could bind myself more effectively even in relation to Law, than the Form out of my power would effect—then, *then*, would you be the remover of my Loneliness, my perpetual Companion? (*CN* 1421)

Here is the tragic bind. What independence can he offer the woman he loves, Sara Hutchinson? How can he be a healed and renovated self magically nine years younger and unbruised? How can they live together as perpetual companions in their own little universe?

He yearns, staggers on, goes off for two years to Malta and slowly, reluctantly, returns "determined to break off his marriage." In mid-April 1807, Southey writes John Rickman that "C is about to separate from his wife, and as he chuses to do every thing in a way different from the rest of the world, is first going with her to visit his relations where however she has long since been introduced. The separation is a good thing—his habits are so murderous of all domestic comfort that I am only surprized Mrs. C. is not rejoiced at being rid of him. He besots himself with opium, or with spirits, till his eyes look like a Turks who is half reduced to idiotcy by the practice" (*RSL* 1, 448). After arguing that the Wordsworths have selfishly instigated Coleridge's dislike of his wife so as to monopolize his services for themselves, Southey writes: "I myself, as I have told Coleridge, think it highly fit that the separation should take place, but by no means so that it should ever have been necessary" (p. 449). Rickman's response is full of interest: "I have your Letter, and very well agree with you in thinking it better that Coleridge should part from his Wife. It will hinder perhaps all his public declamations about the propriety of easy Divorces, and such like stuff: You know that I love him not" (p. 448, note 2). This ambiguous phrasing is clarified in Southey's next letter, to Charles Danvers:

> This affair is not in consequence of any new disagreement. C. has been brooding over it during his absence, and for the three months that he went visiting about before he came home—and this was the purpose with which he returned to his family. For her it is a very happy thing, for not only his habits are destructive of all comfort, but—what I should once never have thought possible, his temper has become so too: and as the thing is done with systematic civility, and they are to continue the best friends in the world, I think it the wisest thing they can do, things being as they are, tho that they are as they are, I consider, as I have told him, as his own fault. I hope it will prevent him from declaiming every where in favour of easy divorces in the mischievous way he does, which has grievously provoked Rickman. When men of such mighty powers always shape their systems to suit their own individual inclinations the mischief they do is very great, and perhaps C. will be sensible when he has openly divorced himself, that every person must feel this to be his case. (May 24, 1807; *RSL* 1, 451)

Southey willfully misrepresents Coleridge, in order to continue his contemptuous satirizing of him. Coleridge's widespread advocacy of easy divorces was not mischievous but of long standing, originating in his early reading of Godwin's *Political Justice*, which denounces marriage as an affair of property and the worst of property, and of Mary Wollstonecraft, whose many pronouncements speak of marriage as a cause of the destruction of personal development on both sides. He says as much in letters to his wife explaining his need to love freely where he loves. His attendance at the parliamentary debates of Spring, 1800, suggests a theoretical interest that is not necessarily personal. Southey's mockery of the visit to the Ottery Coleridges inverts its purpose, which was to allow Sara to save face by presenting an appearance of congeniality to the world, her main interest. Coleridge was willing to accommodate her wish, though in the event his brother George asks him not to come because of the many sickly and neurotic family members, including their old mother, under his roof. Coleridge's personal desire for divorce does not shape his system (as it would for a prudential man) but rather falls under the principles of an already existing system. Southey strangely supposes that Coleridge will be able to "openly divorce[ ] himself."

In addition, Coleridge does not divorce Sara, but separates from her, and continues to try to send funds to support her and other members of her family including her mother. The salutations of letters to his wife long after his separation are "My dear love." Dorothy Wordsworth writes, "Mr. Coleridge and his wife are separated, and I hope they will both be the happier for it. They are on friendly terms, and occasionally see each other." A few days later she writes again, "C is chearful"; "Sara [H] and he are sitting together in his parlour" (Dec. 4 and 8, 1808; *MY*, 280, 282). Coleridge seems not to have used the word "divorce" in connection with his separation. He speaks only of "separation," knowing that "divorce" is financially and socially out of his range, would require a preposterous charge of adultery on his wife's part, or a degrading arrangement for himself like Hazlitt's in Scotland, and would subject his wife to humiliation and ostracism, which she would not deserve. Separation was humiliating enough. In December, 1807, Dorothy Wordsworth describes Sara Fricker Coleridge's horror at hearing even the word "separation," her pretenses to others that all is well in her family, and Coleridge's inability to be firm in telling her he is separating from her, letting himself be caught over again in the maelstrom of her rage.[28]

Sharing many of Mary Wollstonecraft's views and concerns, Coleridge at the end of his life became interested in the issue of women's property. Surrounded, as we will see by women friends, he came to believe that women with property had the same rights as men with property, and he urged his women friends to preserve their property by remaining single, if necessary. In *Table Talk* on August 16, 1833, he declares that "there can be no reason why women should not choose their representatives to legislate." He anticipates the objection that wives "are merged in their husbands," and he grants that this objection does apply "where the wife has no separate property," and therefore no separate identity or will. But he argues that if the wife does have her own property, she alone should be allowed to decide the legislator who will best serve her interests. Coleridge asks: "where she has a distinct taxable estate, in which her husband has no interest, what right can her husband have to choose for her the person whose vote may affect her separate interest?" Coleridge's words imply that there are rare cases of wives who manage to keep some parts of their portions out of their husbands' hands. His argument is all the stronger when he turns to unmarried women of age who have inherited money. These clever strategists preserve their money and their independence, and thus, have "surely as good a moral right to vote, if taxation without representation is tyranny, as any ten-pounder in the kingdom" (*TT* 1, 250). Though he does not believe in direct votes for the people, he believes that if men are voting then women of independent means should vote as well (*Friend* 1, 195–196; *TT* 1, 420).[29] He recommends the French and German custom of hyphenated names to prevent the "disruption of the married Daughter from her parent Stock, and absorption into the name and family of the Husband." Keeping the maiden name prevents "the *discontinuity* in descents—and a Nothingizing of the Female" (*CM* 5, 97).[30]

Questions of marriage, separation, and divorce form an uncharted undercurrent of Romanticism in England. In a cultural movement initiated by demands for liberty in all areas it is not surprising that theorists and individual sufferers should cry out for an escape from unwanted life-long bondage to an incompatible person. The parents of Romantic libertarianism, William Godwin and Mary Wollstonecraft, who wrote against marriage as "an affair of property" and marriage as a degrading tyranny, and held on to their principles of not marrying almost until the birth of their daughter, initiated profound skepticism about the institution. Along with Coleridge, Hazlitt, Byron, Austen, and Blake wonder why individuals who do not suit each other should be forced to continue their intimacies forever. Though we think of Lord Byron as divorced when he goes off into exile in scandal and ostracism, he, like Coleridge, is only separated, a scandal in itself, papers which Byron resists signing for three months. Lady Byron is Lady Byron to the end, asked to be in charge of her husband's burial arrangements but demurring. Even this Lord does not use his lordly rights to sue for parliamentary divorce, especially since he was garishly at fault, and his wife pure to excess. Though at the birth of their daughter in 1816 Byron sent Lady Byron home to her parents, rumors swirled about his incest and possibly about his homosexuality, and many lords would not shake his hand, the couple corresponded warmly up to his exile. William Galperin has recently argued that Byron admired Annabella Millbank, and believed that she was his equal.[31] Arrangements for the separation were conducted by lawyers. Byron's lawyer Hanson and Lady Byron's lawyers agreed that Byron, despite his wicked ways, would get 500 pounds (half) her dowry, plus "on Lady Noel's death, an arbitrator would divide between husband and wife the incomes accruing from the Wentworth inheritance. So Byron kept his personal income, plus five hundred pounds a year and large expectations. Hanson had not played his cards badly."[32] If he had lived, his investment in his property (which included her person and her property) would have paid off. Landor also separated from his wife, and Crabb Robinson details the decision-making and hard financial arrangements (*HCR*, pp. 156 and 172) that supported his beautiful wife and children in Italy in separate lodgings.

During these years when Coleridge's personal anguish was being debated among his friends, Jane Austen was publishing her attack on British divorce laws in *Sense and Sensibility*. She may have been drafting it as early as 1797, but the novel appeared in 1811. In the context of the increased punishment of wives, whether truly or allegedly adulterous, as discussed in the press, Austen's usually neglected story of the two Elizas startles the reader with new meaning. Colonel Brandon's story within the story is a dark intrusion into the novel and it explains his mournful silences at the margins of the action. The Colonel tells Elinor how his father interrupted his elopement with his orphan cousin Eliza, and forced her to marry his older brother so that her inheritance could be used to pay the debts on the family estate. As he, the younger brother, lost the love of his life, his brother took charge of a woman whom he did not love. He betrayed and brutalized her. The Colonel confesses to Elinor,

> "My brother had no regard for her; his pleasures were not what they ought to have been, and from the first he treated her unkindly. . . . But can we wonder that with such a husband to provoke inconstancy, and without a friend to advise or restrain her, (for my father lived only a few months after their marriage, and I was with my regiment in the East Indies) she should fall?. . . . The shock which her marriage had given me," he continued, in a voice of great agitation, "was of trifling weight—was nothing—to what I felt when I heard, about two years afterwards, of her divorce. It was that which threw this gloom,—even now the recollection of what I suffered—"

At the word "divorce" Colonel Brandon can speak no more. Because the divorce signifies Eliza's public sin and disgrace, it is far more devastating than the news of her forced marriage and his loss of her. He returns to England to seek her, for Eliza is cast out, impregnated by her first lover, abandoned, and forced to sink "deeper in a life of sin" and further down into debtor's prison, profligacy, and death by consumption. Colonel Brandon becomes the guardian of her baby Eliza and places her in a school. While on a visit to Bath with a school friend, she is kidnapped, ravaged, and left penniless by the very same Willoughby who is making his assaults on Elinor's sister Marianne. Austen has Brandon speak frankly about solitary childbirth, illegitimacy, and homes for unwed mothers: "as soon as she recovered from her lying-in, for I found her near her delivery, I removed her and her child into the country and there she remains" (p. 211). This sequence of vulnerability, predation, and injustice over two generations would have been averted if the lovers Colonel Brandon and Eliza could have eloped to Scotland as they originally planned, but their plot was revealed by a treacherous maid, and the father was eager to use her dowry to pay his older son's debts. Throughout Austen's novels predatory males threaten not just respectability but even survival. In this story Brandon warns Elinor and through Elinor her sister Marianne; through Brandon Austen can describe one of the great evils of her time: the concatenation of forced marriage, unhappiness, seduction, discovery, divorce, ejection, and a short life on the streets. She comes close to sounding out Blake's rage at the end of "London":

> But most thro' midnight streets I hear
> How the youthful Harlots curse
> Blasts the new-born Infants tear
> And blights with plagues the Marriage hearse. (ll. 13–16)

How critics can exonerate the charmingly petulant Willoughby after this tale of his participation in layers of manly villainy and womanly ruin is hard to fathom, but even the justly judging Elinor says "Poor, poor Willoughby."[33]

Austen encounters divorce again head-on in *Mansfield Park*, where a series of causes—careless upbringing, frivolous vanity, and idle seduction—combine to ruin Maria Bertram, who runs away with Henry Crawford, leaving her rich cuckolded husband Mr. Rushworth in despair. Fanny Price's father reads of this scandal in his newspaper and exclaims, "by G—if she belonged to me, I'd give her the rope's end as long as I could stand over her" (*MP*, p. 440). For this "sin of the first magnitude"

(p. 441), she is condemned to live in seclusion with her Aunt Norris in a foreign country, a hellish *huis clos.* (p. 465). Austen defies the euphemisms of the day; she blames women's folly as well as men's, but notes in a sly aside that the seducers get off scot free:

> That punishment, the public punishment of disgrace, should in a just measure attend *his* share of the offence, is, we know, not one of the barriers, which society gives to virtue. In this world, the penalty is less equal than could be wished. . . . (*MP*, 468)

Arguing like Coleridge that adulterous wives should not be the only ones to pay, she blames the frequency of adulterous scandals on an absence of principles.

Coleridge, who once thought "domestic happiness is the greatest of all things sublunary" (*CL* 1, 158, 160–161), found that he was incapable "of loving any person, man or woman, unless I at the same time honor & esteem them" *CL* 2, 887). On his slow return from Malta he "recoil[ed] so much from the thought of domesticating with Mrs. Coleridge," as Wordsworth explained it to Sir George Beaumont, that he did not dare to bring up the subject to her or go north to see her, inventing one excuse after another to explain his absence (*CL* 2, 1181 note). Arranging his finances he hoped that his widow would marry "a second time, happily" (*CL* 2, 926). Like Jane Austen herself, Sara Hutchinson remained single. Lamb, celibate himself and therefore forgetful of his friend's robust physicality, told Crabb Robinson that Coleridge "ought not to have a wife or children; he should have a sort of diocesan care of the world, no parish duty" (1823; *HCR*, p. 73). Meanwhile Hazlitt unloaded his wife Sarah Stoddart in the time-honored way of setting up an unseemly tryst in Scotland, where he was caught, as planned, *in flagrante.*

Chapter 9
"A Kite's Dinner"

Coleridge's passions flair and subside, are encouraged and crushed, soothed by drugs and brandy, or roused by them. The man of politics, theology, and poetry ebbs and flows with the acceptance or rejection of a stocky good-humored woman. Her "heart-wringing" letter of Feb. 21, 1804 sends him to Malta two months later to recover from wounds of body and spirit. He wrestles away from the embraces of the violently adoring diva, Cecilia Bertolossi, as we saw in the chapter on singing, because Asra's spirit intrudes at the end of the bed. Returning reluctantly and most slowly to England in 1806, bloated and drugged, "determined to separate from his wife" with her "endless *heart-wasting*," he is ripe for suffering. Wrung or wasted, his heart yearns for love; he is thirty-four years old and alone.

Like his first teacher on the ways of women, Mary Wollstonecraft, he knows with the understanding that no one can love just one person (*CL* 2, 887) and that it is not realistic to expect exclusive possession for life. As Wollstonecraft's friend William Blake shows, using the butterfly image that Coleridge also favors for love as it flies—

> He who bends to himself a Joy
> Does the winged life destroy;
> But he who kisses the Joy as it flies
> Lives in Eternity's sunrise—

each lover must leave the loved one free to fly. But as Mary Wollstonecraft tried to kill herself twice when twice she found Gilbert Imlay in the arms of actresses (at least they were different actresses), Coleridge too is eaten up by jealousy when it is his turn to play second fiddle.

The torments of Coleridge's desire increase between October and December 1806, and rage throughout the following year. Richard Holmes tells the kind of erotic story that Dr. James Gillman steered completely away from to protect his friend from detractors who conflated his opium addiction with sensuality. Holmes has found that after the reunion with the Wordsworths at an inn at Kendal, William stayed behind to talk to Coleridge on the night of Oct. 29, 1806, and so did Sara Hutchinson, "unchaperoned," "with some risk of scandal" (Holmes, p. 75). Holmes writes that on this momentous night Coleridge felt from looks and touches that his love was reciprocated, and excitedly recorded in his notebook, "I know, you love me!—My reason knows it, my heart feels it; yet still let your eyes, your hands tell me; still say, O often & often say, 'My Beloved! I love you'; indeed I love you: for why should not my ears, and all my outward Being share in the Joy—the fuller my inward Being is of the sense, the more my outward organs yearn & crave for it. O bring my whole nature into balance and harmony" (CN 2938). (One marvels here, once again, at how Desmond McCarthy, quoted approvingly by J. C. C. Mays, could decisively assert that "Coleridge was never passionate.") Holmes speculates about the mysteries in this meeting. Was Wordsworth, friend and confidant, also a "go-between with Asra"? "Was Wordsworth prepared for Sara to become Coleridge's mistress under his own roof at Coleorton? Or did he believe that Sara herself really wished this? It is very hard to tell" (Holmes, p. 76). Holmes shines a dazzling light on the possibilities in these obscure consultations.

Seemingly encouraged by this reciprocated love, Coleridge goes boldly to break the news to his wife that he will separate from her. For almost two months he endures her rages and the heart-wrenching joys of his children at seeing him, and then returns with Hartley to the community of Wordsworths and Hutchinsons living together in Lord and Lady Beaumont's borrowed farm at Coleorton. In less than a week the bottom falls out of his expectations.

On a Saturday morning after Christmas 1806 Coleridge, drunk and desperate, in huge letters writes: "**THE EPOCH**. Saturday, 27 December, 1806—Queen's Head, Stringston, 1/2 a mile from Coleorton Church, 50 minutes after 10/" (*CN* 2975). Three times again he returns in anguish to write about this moment. In Sept. 1807 "O agony! O the vision of that Saturday morning—of the Bed—O cruel! Is he not beloved, adored by two—& two such Beings.—And must I not be beloved *near* him except as a Satellite?—But O mercy, mercy! Is he not better, greater, more *manly*, & altogether more attractive to any but the purest Woman? And yet . . . he does not pretend, he does not wish to love you as I love you, Sara!" (*CN* 3148). He yearns to have her love him as intensely as he loves her: "even to make her already loving me love me to that unutterableness, that impatience at the not enoughness of dependence, with which I love her! . . . I want, I yearn to make her Love of me delightful to her own mind" (*CN* 3148). A few months later, the vision gnaws at him again: "But a minute and a half with ME and all the time evidently *restless &* going—An hour and more with Wordsworth—[in Greek code] *in bed*—O agony!" (*CN* 3328). This vision of the treacherous, manly, self-confident Wordsworth and the woman he loves in bed, her "beautiful breasts uncovered" (*CN* 4537), is riveted into his brain, a physical, emotional, psychic wound. Richard Holmes narrates this anguish as taking place at the house in Coleorton, with Coleridge then running to the inn to drink strong ale and write in his notebook. He wonders if Coleridge imagined it. Stephen Gill, Wordsworth's biographer, suspects that Wordsworth and Sara Hutchinson did actually become lovers in the Queen's Head inn near Coleorton at the hour STC specified.[1] It is a startling possibility.

Did Coleridge imagine the whole encounter? Is it enough that he thought he saw it? Did he see a glimpse of tenderness and magnify it? If it is true, how could he have borne the clarity of the physical details circling in his mind, the turmoil of desire and jealousy? If it did happen, had an affair been going on while he was in Malta? Did it start at the inn in Kendal when they three stayed together? And after the revelation, how could he have gone on living in this tight community and working on Wordsworth's edition of poems as if nothing had happened? How could he have worked with Sara Hutchinson night after night on the *Friend* knowing that she was one of Wordsworth's "three wives" in a real sense, that she had experienced sexual relations with William Wordsworth and not with him who had loved her entirely? How could he sob and revile Wordsworth three years later during their quarrel without mentioning this mighty betrayal along with the betrayal of telling Basil Montagu that he had no hope of him and found him a nuisance? Was having sex with Sara Hutchinson less of a betrayal than speaking demeaningly of him? Was this use of Sara Hutchinson another aspect of Wordsworth's using others as things, as couches or coats, particularly the women who copied and recopied his poems? Or was he arrogantly displaying his power in order to crush Coleridge's will under his as he had done many times before, especially with the rejection of "Christabel"? Or was he acting on his wife's behalf to keep her sister in her family and protect her from her lover? What would his wife Mary Hutchinson, whom he had married just four years earlier, think of this infidelity? Kathleen Coburn cites a late meditation where Coleridge ascribes his fancies to the "Strange Self-power in the Imagination" that simulates "*place & Substance & living energy*" and rouses evil suspicions. "That dreadful Saturday Morning, at

[Coleorton] did I *believe* it? Did I not even *know*, that it *was* not so, *could* not be so? . . . Yes! Yes! I *knew* the horrid phantasm to be a mere phantasm: and yet what anguish, what gnawings of despair, what throbbings and lancinations of positive Jealousy!" (*CN* 2975 note). At the time of these jealousies he thinks by contrast of his own near capitulation in Sicily and of his determination to forego the pleasure that was almost forced upon him:

> Could I feel for a moment the supremacy of Love suspended in my nature, by accidents of temporary Desire; were I conscious for a moment of an Interregnum in the Heart, were the Rebel to sit on the *Throne* of my Being, even tho' it were only that the rightful Lord of my Bosom were sleeping, soon to awake & expel the Usurper, I should feel myself as much fallen & as unworthy of her Love in any such tumult of Body indulged toward her, as if I had roamed, like a Hog in the rankest Lanes of a city, battening on the loathsome offals of Harlotry. (*CN* 2984)

He dwells on how bestial he might have been if he had betrayed Sara Hutchinson, and continues to describe lust and love in terms of gnawings, throbbings, and roilings:

> But when Love, like a Volcano beneath a sea always burning, tho' in silence, flames up in his strength at some new accession, o how can the waters but heave & roll in billows—driven by no wind on the mere Surface, save that which their own tumult creates, but the mass is agitated from the depths, & the waves tower up as if to make room for the stormy Swelling. (*CN* 2984)

Ten years after the first roarings in "Kubla Khan" of

> this Chasm with hideous Turmoil seething
> As if this Earth in fast thick Pants were breathing
> A mighty Fountain momently was forc'd,
> Amid whose swift half-intermitted Burst
> Huge Fragments vaulted. (ll. 17–21),

Coleridge uses this vocabulary of tumult to describe the powerful physical effect of his own passions: desire, love, and jealousy.

In notebooks and scraps of verse Coleridge explores the implications of this devastating discovery or hallucination. Coming to terms with the death of this all-consuming love, Coleridge mocks his earlier joy seven years before when he had cried out,

> God is *with* me! God is *in* me!
> I *cannot* die: for Life is Love!

Now this exaltation vanishes: "the echo of my own voice in an empty vault," rather than "the substantial voice of its indwelling Spirit" (*CN* 3231):

> And now, that I am alone, & utterly hopeless for myself—yet still I *love*—& more strongly than ever feel that Conscience, or the Duty of Love, is the Proof of continuing, as it is the Cause & Condition of existing, Consciousness. How beautiful the Harmony! Whence could the Proof come, so appropriately—so conformly with all nature, in which the cause & condition of each Thing is its revealing & infallible Prophecy! (*CN* 3231)

The continuance of his love as a consciousness and as a duty against all odds is one of his many efforts to prove that passion outlasts the body in immortality.

As for Wordsworth, great and ambitious poet, he had undermined Coleridge's universe long before the quarrel of 1810 by centering himself in Sara Hutchinson's attentions. Wordsworth may deny an affair with Sara Hutchinson, or urge reason, or denigrate Coleridge's passion, but Coleridge continues to suffer:

> Nor all his virtues, great tho' they be,
> Nor all his Genius can free
> His friend's Soul from this agony! (*PW* #420; Sept. 1807)

In the hidden Latin version of "Ad Vilmum Axiologum" (*CP* #430), Coleridge rebukes Wordsworth in a voice like Goethe's Werther, arguing like Werther that love cannot be willed away:

> Do you command me to endure Asra's forgetting me? and to be able to look at my Asra's averted eyes? and to know that she is false and cruel who was and always will be dear to me? And to endure the daylight ... when I love an empty woman and the whole of Nature ... shakes and totters? ... But I have seen the last rites of faith and I am dying! Do you think that I shall be overcome by facile reasoning/ by *Reason*? The Devil take the man who can apply reasonings in Love! The Devil take him who can love without total abandon! Let those whose hearts are whole see what is right and proper, and what is not. My life is over! Asra lives on, forgetting me.[2]

Like Werther's, Coleridge's love is beyond reason, it exists only in "total abandon," and it leads to personal and universal death; Wordsworth, like Goethe's pragmatic, prudential, and finally successful Albert, calculates love as the sum of friendship and lust, and counsels good sense and discretion—move on to someone else, as he explained to STC in a letter in 1808—a counsel that might as well rip his guts with a knife.

This sorrow inspires a series of laments, which form a second wave of "Asra Poems." Finding solace in translating the lovelorn sorrows of Italian madrigals, in recalling past moments of bliss, and in coming face to face with emptiness—the ache of the lost limb and the lost half—, Coleridge struggles, like John Donne looking into absence, with the fact that he is alone. These laments from 1808 to 1810 make up the poetry that critics call "Nightmare" poems, but many of them are love poems as well. These laments include poems #441 "After Marino," #442 "Happy Husband," #461 "Separation, after Cotton," #466 "Written in Dejection," #467 "Visionary Hope," and #468 "Fragment in Blank Verse." Other poems also may skirt his loss in occasional lines; the notebooks are full of confessions of his sorrow. These laments appear in the context first of a real love that turns to loss; second, of a lifetime of experiencing kinds and levels of love; and third, as the foundation of what comes later, meditations on how to go on living when love fails. These laments are raw, and readers respond variously to them, embarrassed, sympathetic, disapproving the "unmanly" emotion, surprised at Coleridge's modernity in revealing it.

"The Blossoming of the Solitary Date-Tree" laments that his passions meet with no answering love, and like a lone date tree he thus remains infertile or unproductive. From this physical fact of dual fertilization characteristic also of the holly and the ginko tree, Coleridge develops the Socratic image of the yearning human soul always seeking but rarely finding its counterpart. Without a response from the "best belov'd" the love is no longer "buoyed . . . aloft." The excess of love turns backward onto the lover to torment him.

> It is Joy's greatness and it's overflow
> Which, being incompleat, disquieteth me so!
> (*PW* #396, ll. 6–7)

The more joyful the lover is, "the more heavily will he feel the ache of solitariness," the more will he overflow with love:

> I am not a God, that I should stand alone,
> And having all, but Love, I want the Whole. (ll. 9–10)

The speaker boasts "a Heart attun'd alike to Joy or Mirth!" and yet no voice answers him in his "lonesome Tent." He is "incompleat"; he suffers "want." Like a mother listening for a child's sweet echo of her voice even when she knows that the child is dead, the poet hears no echo and feels that his songs avail nothing:

> —Sweet Friend! no Prattler at a Mother's Knee
> Was e'er so deeply priz'd, as I prize Thee:
> Why was I made for Love, yet Love denied to Me! (ll. 33–35)

The two halves of the original human being from Plato's *Symposium* haunt him, for he sees himself as for ever craving, yearning, and waiting to be fulfilled by the physical and spiritual other half. Searching for the other half, he is doomed to live in but half his being. Although he began his natural being full of joy and mirth, he is now a half-person, heart-bitten by "the secret pang that eats away the Heart" (#426).

Glimpses of this half being, and of visitations of potential completeness, appear in the fragments and cries written during this period when he returns from Malta (1806–1810).

> You lie in all my many thoughts, like Light;
> Like the fair Light of Dawn, or summer Eve
> On rippling Stream, or cloud-reflecting Lake. (#406; b, ll. 3–5)

In confusingly dated notes he suffers aloud:

> Yet the deep Yearning will not die! . . .
> . . . . . .
> O ask not for my Heart! My Heart is but
> The darksome Vault where Hope lies dead & buried.
> (cited #412, p. 826)

A translation from Marino compares the lovers to Pyramus and Thisbe, wedded hearts separated by their Wall, this time a wall of law and custom:

> O Joy with thy own Joy at Strife,
> That yearning for the Realm above
> Would'st die into intenser Life
> And union absolute of Love. (#441, p. 853)

Yearning to "die into intenser life," a phrase from unpublished notes used five years later in *Hyperion* by Keats, these lovers "cling, and try in vain to touch!"

Two poems never before noted seem to speak directly of negotiations between Coleridge and Sara Hutchinson to resolve their lives either together or apart. The first, "The Happy Husband: A Fragment" (#442) suggests intervals of comfort together:

> Oft, oft methinks, the while with Thee
>   I breathe, as from the heart, thy dear
>   And dedicated name, I hear
> A promise and a mystery,
>   A pledge of more than passing life,
>   Yea, in that very name of Wife! (ll. 1–6)

This comfort rises to rapture:

> A pulse of love, that ne'er can sleep!
>   A feeling that upbraids the heart
>   With happiness beyond desert,
> That gladness half requests to weep! (ll. 7–10)

But the "pulse of love" alternates with a sorrow worse than death; the second poem, "Separation: After Charles Cotton" (#461) addresses this sorrow directly:

> O! Asra, Asra! couldst thou see
>   Into the bottom of my heart,
> There's such a mine of Love for thee,
>   As almost might supply desert!
>
> (This separation is, alas!
>   Too great a punishment to bear;
> O! Take my life, or let me pass
>   That life, that happy life, with her!)
>
> The perils, erst with steadfast eye
>   Encounter'd, now I shrink to see—
> Oh! I have heart enough to die—
>   Not half enough to part from Thee! (ll. 13–24)

Anguish flashes through many of the poems of this period when he realizes that separation is their only choice:

> For neither death, nor absence, nor demerit
> Can free the love-enchanted spirit.
>   ("Written in Dejection," #466, ll. 1–2)

He describes himself as "the love-stricken visionary" who "wishes and *can* wish for this alone!" ("The Visionary Hope," #467, ll. 24 and 22).

Responding obsessively to her departure, he fills the margins of his notebook with her name and wonders how he can live: "Why then live on?/ . . . That Hope of Her, say rather, that pure Faith / In her fix'd Love, which held me to keep truce / With the Tyranny of Life—is gone ah whither?" ("Fragment in Blank Verse," #468, ll. 8, 11–13).

Worse was to come. The disaster occurred in February, 1810, when Basil Montagu told him that Wordsworth found him a nuisance, that he had no hope of him, and that he was rotting out his entrails with intemperance. Worse yet, Sara Hutchinson cast her lot with the Wordsworths and wrote to him only rarely. 1812 found him near suicide, dosing himself with laudanum and brandy, answering no letters. Loss of hope for their love plunges Coleridge into a despair where the world has lost meaning, where creatures writhe in "the mere Horror of blank Naught at all" ("Limbo: A Fragment," #478, l. 23), and where individual human life seems a "vessel purposeless, unmeant/ Yet drone-hive strange of phantom purposes!" ("Human Life, or the Denial of Immortality" #482, ll. 8–9). Loveless, he is nobody and does not wish to live. He did not ask to be born. But Nature answers his plea with a disturbing question: is your life "return'd as 'twas sent? Is't no worse for the Wear?" Does he dare give back a ruined life? ("The Suicide's Argument, With Nature's Answer," #490, ll. 5 and 11). His response seems to be no.

Living among women teaches Coleridge about women's power, and allows him to reimagine his betrayals at the hand of Wordsworth. In a late poem, "Alice du Clos or, The Forked Tongue: A Ballad" (1828–1829), an unfinished narrative, Coleridge gathers the tangled themes of jealousy that he experienced in 1806, the moment of the EPOCH, and in 1810, when he was torn to pieces by the break with the Wordsworths and Sara Hutchinson. Here he dares to put the jealousies in vaguely disguised personal terms, where he seems to be Lord Julian, Sara Hutchinson his betrothed Alice whom he cannot marry, and William Wordsworth the ubiquitous and also imaginary Page who occupies the lady's daily attentions. The tangled plot includes a vassal knight Sir Hugh who bears false witness against the bookish Alice; Alice herself who sits "loosely wrapt in Maiden White," (l. 21) with a book on her knee (l. 26)—

> O! Alice could read passing well,
>   And she was conning then
> Dan Ovid's mazy tale of Loves,
>   And Gods and Beasts and Men (ll. 35–38)

and rebukes both Sir Hugh for "his taunting Vein" and Lord Julian for sending this venomous emissary "against my earnest suit" (ll. 39–50).

Since Alice refuses to raise her head from her book of Ovid's love stories, Sir Hugh informs the impatient Lord Julian that she is not going to join him in the hunt because her eyes are otherwise engaged:

> "I saw them fix'd with steadfast gaze
>   Full on her wanton Page." (ll. 168–169)

Misinterpreting this page/ Page pun, Lord Julian believes that his lady is unfaithful to him as she lingers in "the lattic'd Bower" (l. 148) with her page. As she rides up, he hurls his shaft at her:

> Dark as a dream Lord Julian stood,
>
> Swift as a dream, from forth the wood,
>   Sprang on the plighted Maid!
> With fatal aim, and frantic force,
> The shaft was hurl'd—a lifeless corse,
> Fair Alice from her vaunting horse,
>   Lies bleeding on the glade (ll. 187–193)

Submerged bitterness rises to the surface in this strange poem about women's power to choose, about women who read, about romantic triangles, misunderstandings, and imagined treachery, and finally about violence, when the STC character shoots the woman he loves because she lingers at home with her "Page." I suspect that the pun on Page may derive from Henry Boyd's translation of *Inferno* 5, where Francesca rails against "the Pandar-Page" that indirectly seduced and murdered her.

Is Coleridge admitting his own folly in misinterpreting the feelings between Sara Hutchinson and William, reading and hearing "Page" for "page," fact for fiction, body for book, failing to desynonymize the forked word of the pun? The commanding males cannot understand the woman consumed by her book and not obeying. Whose fault is this murder—hers for being stubborn, Sir Hugh's for toying with treacherously "forked" messages, or Lord Julian's for demanding compliance and enacting his frustrated rage? Women can have agency, and use it to drive men mad.

The experience of jealousy in "Alice du Clos" is even more pointed in "Not at Home," three quatrains, which Mays conjecturally dates from 1830. The first quatrain is blunt:

> That jealousy may rule a mind
>   Where Love could never be
> I know: but ne'er expect to find
>   Love without Jealousy. (*PW* #666, ll. 1–4)

Jealousy is the "twin-sister" and "house-mate" of Love (ll. 7 and 8). Coleridge returns to dwell on erotic treachery in 1828–1830: does he revile himself for his misinterpretations and exaggerations of 1806, his betrayal in 1810, or some new triangle of passion in the Gillman menage? He tries in vain to free himself "from feeble Yearnings," to damp down his passions and to expect less from people he loves—

> Love them for what they *are*: nor love them less,
> Because to *thee* they are not what they *were* (*PW* #627, ll. 13–4)—

but his yearnings and desires refuse to subside.

The heart is for Coleridge a physical organ. When he says to Thomas Allsop that "the heart in its physical sense is not sufficient for a kite's dinner; yet the whole world is not sufficient for it," he imagines the human heart being plucked or gnawed. He jots down a fragment,

> And sudden Thoughts that riv'd his heart asunder
> By the road-side, the while he gaz'd at flowers. (*PW* #332, ll. 4–5; 1803)

He records that his physical heart is "riv'd," "grasped," "griped," wrung in a fist, or cut open to reveal words "written at the core," as Queen Mary claimed the word "Calais!" would be inscribed on hers (*CL* 6, 797–798). He can joke that his heart is an incinerated cricket, still chirping in its ashes (*CN* 3, 3379). When he enumerates on Oct. 8, 1822, his "four griping and grasping Sorrows, each of which seemed to have my very heart in it's hands, compressing or wringing," he lists the failure of his marriage, the loss of Wordsworth's friendship along with "Wordsworth's last total Transfiguration into Baseness," a third sorrow "in some sort included in the second—what the former was to Friendship, the latter was to a yet more inward Bond," and the fourth, the charge of sottishness against his son Hartley. Some commentators have interpreted the third sorrow as his own opium-addiction, and this is possible in view of the phrase "a darkness deeper within myself." But the phrases "in some sort included in the second" and "a yet more inward Bond" seem to me to point to the loss of Sara Hutchinson congruent with the loss of Wordsworth's friendship (*CL* 5, 249–251), and to some extent the loss of her and the addiction may be connected.

Coleridge works to resolve the crisis of lovelessness over the next seventeen years, from age 37 to 54, trying to find more moderate forms of love. He is rescued by the generous John Morgan, with his wife Mary and her sister Charlotte, who keep him in their home, laugh at his poems to them (e.g. #s 431, 432 and 433), and struggle to monitor his opium intake, sometimes tracking him down in abject hiding places.[3] When Morgan suffers bankruptcy (and Coleridge tries to rescue him with the proceeds from his successful play *Remorse*), the generous Dr. James Gillman, with his wife Anne and her sister Lucy, forms a parallel rescue system in Highgate that lasts until Coleridge's death in 1834. In the care of these families, and visiting young men and women whom he advises about love's difficulties, he retains a sense of humor and a resilient musical note:

> And thus he sang: Adieu! Adieu!
> Love's dreams prove seldom true. ("Glycine's Song," #517, ll. 9–10)

Chapter 10
Communities of Women: Developing as Persons

In the midst of sorrow the buoyant Coleridge develops new flirtations, makes new jokes, and learns to go on living in the absence of the one beloved person. His recuperation is astonishing, as he turns his attentive eyes and ears to new pairs of sisters and to new young friends who are choosing partners to love. Coleridge enjoyed the resemblances and differences of living with pairs of women who illustrated his aesthetic principles of sameness in difference and stirred his desire with their piquant similarities to each other. Women who resemble Sara Hutchinson make him dizzy. In Malta 1804 breakfasting with Sir Alexander Ball, he "saw a Lady with Hair, Complexion, and a certain cast of Countenance that on the first glance of her troubled me inconceivably—after a while I perceived the likeness to S. H. & was near fainting—O what an inconceivable faintness with fondness" (*CN* 2, 2137). In four intermittent years living with the Morgans (1811–1813, 1814–1816), he came to love Mary Morgan and her younger unmarried sister Charlotte Brent, who also resembled Sara Hutchinson, and even to behave tempestuously with them, frightening them with his passions and his addictions. Recovering on their couch in Bristol, Coleridge publishes "The Two Sisters" in *The Courier* of December 10, 1807, a poem about their kindness to him and their resemblances to Mary and Sara Hutchinson, broadcasting his tangled emotions to the world.

> Even thus did you call up before mine eyes
> Two dear, dear Sisters, prized all price above,
> Sisters, like you, with more than Sisters' love;
> *So* like you *they*, and so in *you* were seen
> Their relative statures, tempers, looks, and mien,
> That oft, dear Ladies! You have been to me,
> At once a vision and reality (*PW* #423, ll. 21–27)

Seeing that Mary and Charlotte replicate Mary and Sara Hutchinson, he wonders, "Are you for *their* sakes dear, or for your own?" (l. 38). Even as he laments that "In Grief I love you, yet I love you well!," he can turn to make fun of Mary Morgan:

> All these hast thou! Of Teeth what jetty rows!
> Thy lips, how white! How very blue thy Nose!
> Thy Hair so red resembles, charming Friend!
> The fibres from a tough old Carrot's End,
> Thine Eyes (the light how modestly they shun!)
> Red as the Gravy from Beef underdone. (*PW* #431, ll. 5–10)

The Morgans' couch continues to inspire Coleridge to witticism: "Charlotte. At full length on a sofa thee, Coleridge! an Oaf I call. S.T. Coleridge. Yet you'll allow my dear Charlotte! 'Twas quite *fill-a-sopha-Col*" (*PW* #433). Holmes quotes Coleridge imitating Charlotte's speech: "O La! No! Write to a man, tho old enough to be my father—!—my neck-and-breast kerchief is downright scorched & iron-moulded with the intensity of my expansive Blush" (Holmes, p. 347). A humorous poem from 1815 when he stayed with the Morgans at Calne, "Lines On Aurelia Coates" (*PW* #523), toys with the story of a local butcher who lives with two women:

> The Butcher Davis, then a lusty Gallant,
> Lived as an House-mate with two gentle Damsels,
> Both their fair forms pleas'd *him*—and his fair form
> Both *them* did please! Ah then! Had swell'd their Hearts!
> Their waists too swell'd. What could the Lover do?
> One only could he wed, and one did wed,
> His present Spouse—and time enough to save
> If not her Honor, yet the Child's. (ll. 1–8)

Basing his poem on a real incident, he refers to the two damsels whom the resident butcher impregnated. The one he did not marry had a daughter who caused her lover's suicide and then turned to drinking British gin. Coleridge may fancy himself this house-mate, this lusty butcher satisfying two women.

Still he feels the absence in the Brent sisters of "the flush, the overflow, the rapture . . . the Sympathy of Joy" apparent in lips, eyes, and nose, that he remembers experiencing with Sara Hutchinson. He notes that the Brent sisters are

> Beautiful, feminine, attractive, without affectation—add to this amusing and (female foibles out of the question which we scarcely wish away) of

excellent Good Sense—yet with all this not permanently lovely (or loveable.) How can this be? They are loveless—if any trait of the Lover appear, it is to each other. To each other I have noticed a soft, soothing, and caressing character. But to men, however intimate, they uniformly bear the semblance of persons to be attended to . . . They will *look* nothing, *say* nothing. (Oct.–Dec. 1812; *CN* 4172)

Like the deliberately or fearfully blank faces he had noted in early poems about young women (discussed in chapter 3), Coleridge watches the masks of the Brent sisters block out male admirers, while they turn their excessively intense attachment toward each other in a narcissistic mirroring. Indeed, a number of brief late poems sport with the ideas of love between women, even punning in Latin on a lesbian love that "will not succeed or suck seed" (*PW* # 503). Watching women together he speculates that they are more passionately intertwined with each other than men are: "Female friendship borders more on Love than men's—The latter affect each other in the Reflection of noble or friendly Acts—While the Female asks less proofs and more (signs &) expressions of Attachment" (1815–1816; *CN* 4297). Because they live in constricted social arrangements of visits and returned visits and gifts and corresponding gifts, they are more eager than men to repay obligations and cannot rest peacefully in the knowledge of another person's generosity. Coleridge watched women so closely that he considered writing a novel to prove their social differences from men (Dec. 1815; *CN* 4272).

When Coleridge, forty-four years old and at the end of his rope once again, moved in as a resident patient with Dr. James Gillman and Anne Gillman in 1816, the couple had been married eight years, with two sons, James Jr. and Henry, whom Coleridge tutored and advised. Gradually, through talking, sharing the amusements and worry about the boys, watching each other, listening to each other, and swimming together, Coleridge seems to have fallen in love with his protector's wife, whose looks and character also reminded him of Sara Hutchinson. He called himself the Jacob to her Rachel (*CN* 4, 5184). A rumor circulated that Coleridge "was living in a state of open a--------y with Mrs. ******* at Highgate." Charles Lamb passed the rumor to Sara Hutchinson, of all people, adding in his mock-prudish voice, "Such it is if Ladies will go gadding about with other people's husbands at watering places. How careful we should be to avoid the appearance of evil" (quoted in note to *CL* 5, 512–513). Lamb oddly emphasizes Coleridge's married status rather than Mrs. Gillman's.

Coleridge observed Anne Gillman's physical state, her plumpness, the circles around her eyes, her flushed cheeks, her vigor in walking and swimming, and kept her husband the doctor informed about the changes in her appearance and mood, usually telling him that she was improving daily with the sea air and would profit from more time diving into the waves with him, if her husband could stand their remaining away a bit longer. After a "swimlet bath, the sea just stirring," he worries that "her Flow of Strength, the tiny Spring at the bottom of the natural Fountain, requires careful *husbanding*" (Oct. 15, 1823; *CN* 5025), a curious word to describe his care. His attention to her physicality recalls his attention to Mary Ann Evans's thirty years before. When Anne Gillman screams falling downstairs, his description of how she slipped and landed shows the solicitude of love (Feb. 18, 1824; *CL* 5, 335; letter 1376). Like her predecessor, Sara Hutchinson, she, too, comes to embody music; he praises her voice: "As oratory is Passion in the Service of Reason, so should vocal music be Passion connective in the service of Passion. If there were as much Spirit and Liberty, as Feeling and Sweetness in her singing, Mrs. Gillman would excel to my judgment all the singers I have ever heard" (Dec. 1824; *CL* 5, 402; letter 1422).

From 1807 to his death in 1834 Coleridge lived in communities of women, first with Mary Morgan and Charlotte Brent, then from April 1816 in Highgate, centering on Anne Gillman, and surrounded by her sister Lucy, her neighbors, her neighbors' daughters, Susan Steel and Eliza Nixon, and assorted lady visitors like the vigorous conversationalist Mrs. Elizabeth Aders (see poem #613) and the philosopher Lady Mary Shepherd (see poems #696 and #697). Anne's two sons replaced Coleridge's two sons, especially as Hartley sank into alcoholic disgrace. Her husband, Dr. James Gillman, was a busy surgeon who often stayed late at work and could not get away for vacations at Ramsgate with the rest of the group, but worried about the health of STC and his wife, and worked on medical essays with Coleridge when he was home. Coleridge's many visitors were usually but not always male, their voices preserved in *Table Talk* and *Coleridge the Talker*; some of his male visitors, like Thomas Allsop, became intimate friends with Anne Gillman as well, learning about good women from her own strength and grace and from her outspoken advice. This pattern of attendant sisters with a busy husband duplicates earlier groupings with Wordsworths, Hutchinsons, Southeys, and Morgans, with Coleridge's passions often stirred by one sister or several, as Dr. Morgan's unmarried sister-in-law Charlotte Brent's resemblance to Sara Hutchinson also stirred Coleridge's passions.

In the Gillman household of intelligent women, with women of several ages visiting and staying, young men coming in and out, Coleridge plays the role of advisor on the sufferings of the heart because he knew those sufferings first hand. He was amazed, for instance, that women must mask their own pain while caring for other people. To his neighbor Mrs. Elizabeth Aders, "a beautiful and accomplished lady, of much conversational power, able to hold her own with the gifted men who were in the habit of frequenting her house" (headnote to *PW* #613), he writes the long poem "The Two Founts: Stanzas Addressed to a Lady on her Recovery with Unblemished Looks, from a Severe Attack of Pain" (1826–1827). He is not in fact concerned with Eliza Aders's looks, unblemished or not, but with the banked up anguish beneath the facade of sweetness. He begs her:

> O sweet, sweet sufferer! If the case be so,
> I pray thee, be *less* good, *less* sweet, *less* wise!
>
> In every look a barbed arrow send,
> On those soft lips let scorn and anger live!
> Do *any* thing, rather than thus, sweet friend!
> Hoard for thyself the pain, thou wilt not give! (*PW* #618, ll. 41–48)

Begging Eliza to release the inward pain in outwardly directed aggression, he seems to perceive that the stress of appearing to be an angel in the house takes a toll on women's physical health.

In this atmosphere of neighborly sympathy, of flowery gifts, and of visiting babies, Coleridge's study of love matures to include many kinds and intensities of love. The atmosphere of talking and listening in this household glimmers in the shifting metrical and prose sections of the poem "The *Improvisatore*" of 1826. The mini-drama recreates the discussions of poems and plays, of metrical skill and songs, the *badinage*, and the easy, non-pedantic education going on in these homes despite the girls' lack of university education, a far more sophisticated evening than the one Austen satirizes at Netherfield in *Pride and Prejudice*, where the Bingley girls stroll around the salon and jingle their bracelets.

Coleridge's poetic mini-drama demonstrates the influence of real Italian street poets (women like Madame de Stael's fictional Corinne or L. E. L.'s "*Improvisatrice*" who could improvise freely for hours), of operatic recitative, and of conversation in large and affectionate family groupings where speakers allude to poems by Burns and Moore and to plays by Beaumont and Fletcher, and debate the "questions of love"— who loves more, who suffers more—common in medieval love poems and in Boccaccio's fictional gatherings. The popular poems by women in the Romantic period, by Charlotte Smith, and especially by Letitia Elizabeth Landon, further spur such contests about love and suffering.

Landon's "*Improvisatrice*" of 1824 is a 100 page frame narrative containing many tales of sorrowful love from around the globe, a poem frequently republished, and disturbing to any young person hoping to find love before it is too late. Obviously echoing L. E. L.'s famous narrative poem in his title, Coleridge's poem tries to console the women in his extended group by suggesting that some lives can be happy even without love. The loose flow of the conversation in Coleridge's long poem indicates his ease in this household, though the poem ends with him standing alone, speaking of the difficulty of finding and keeping true love.[1]

These difficulties arise from personality clashes but more universally from the unattainable, always receding distance of the perfect love each person imagines. In this poem, the narrator, the old Boccaccio/Coleridge/Plato, defines this rare occurrence, this miraculous concatenation of "a peculiar sensibility and tenderness of nature; a constitutional communicativeness and *utterancy* of heart and soul; a delight in the detail of sympathy, in the outward and visible signs of the sacrament within." These unusual qualities unite into love, and love also "supposes a soul" in the lover and the loved one. As often as the young women Eliza and Katherine ask him about his own experience of love, the old Coleridge cannot explain why his love vanished and how much was his own fault; he cannot find the words to convey his experience of love and loss to the young women. Eliza says: "There is something *here* (*pointing to her heart*) that *seems* to understand you, but wants the *word* that would make it understand itself." His explanation is rooted in Plato's Diotima when he calls love a yearning; he believes it is a process of reaching beyond oneself in expanding circles:

> Love is that *willing* sense of the insufficingness of the *self* for itself, which predisposes a generous nature to see, in the total being of another, the supplement and completion of its own;—that quiet perpetual *seeking* which the presence of the beloved object modulates, not suspends, where the heart momently finds, and finding, again seeks on: Love recognizes humbly its own self-insufficingness, for the human being instinctively seeks what may fill the emptiness, the gap within.

Love is a *want*, that is, a desire and an absence. Love is an impossible yearning, a "hunger," that cannot be satisfied in this world and therefore leads the human being to yearn beyond this world to a supernatural rest where the yearning for love might be resolved.

Referring proudly to his own poem "The Improvisatore: or John Anderson my Jo, John," Coleridge refines the definition of love in his essay "On The Passions," written at about this time (1826): the sense of "incompleteness.... forms that peculiar State & Affection which we understand by *Storge* in the widest sense of the word—and in the human Being as the grounding Sensation of LOVE" (*SWF* 2, 1441). His coinage "insufficingness" sometimes changes to other forms like "unsatisfyingness." He struggles to capture the sense that love is never "enough," is always incomplete, is always yearning beyond its actual moment. As Milton did, he learns from Plato's Diotima that "*Love* was the Sonne of *Penury*" (*Doctrine and Discipline of Divorce*, p. 252), arising from absence rather than presence, from lack or want rather than from fullness. Coleridge notes "the unsatisfyingness, the felt insufficiency, of all Finites in themselves, and the necessity which the Understanding feels of seeking their solution elsewhere—i.e. in an x that is not finite" (*CN* 5294). Although the perfection that human beings desire is rare, Coleridge comes to terms with loneliness and accepts "craving" as essential to human nature. This craving, yearning, wanting, and needing is so deeply embedded that it may justify belief in a future life to satisfy the need, or why would God have implanted this hunger in human hearts?

Later poems, like the long narrative poem "The Garden of Boccaccio" (1828), find amusement in moments of social happiness. Like "The *Improvisatore*" it, too, is Italian in mood, theme, and *sprezzatura*, but it reverses the moods in "The *Improvisatore*": it begins in solitude and moves toward the affirmation of friendship, art, and artists like Boccaccio. Anne Gillman's hand touches the sad poet in his "Vacancy," and "dull continuous Ache" (*PW* #652; ll. 8 and 9). She gives him an illustration by Thomas Stothard from *The Keepsake for 1829* that depicts Boccaccio surrounded by suffering lovers.[2] Her gesture suggests her sympathy with his mood; it suggests, too, as Graham Davidson perceives, the possibility that she sat by his side in silent communion, and recognized her role as "Rachel ministering to her Jacob."[3] The picture rouses the poet and summons in his mind the great writers in the history of literature and the gods and lively goddesses, all produced by human creativity. Susan Luther suggests that the poem celebrates the picture, and by extension all human artistry, further refuting Wordsworth's claim that we are consoled only by nature.[4] In addition, the poem offers advice about happiness to women.

Although Coleridge had disparaged Boccaccio in the *Biographia Literaria* for mocking the women in Dante's life (1, 229), he realizes now that he himself resembles Boccaccio. Where he had begun his love poems in the voice of Dante's Francesca, and introduced his *Sybilline*

Leaves of 1816 with an epigraph from Petrarch, so now he adapts the avuncular role of Boccaccio's narrators in his collections of stories, the *Filocolo* and the *Decameron*. Coleridge sees his position on the outskirts of London in Highgate, among yearning young women, talking about love, as parallel to Boccaccio's on the outskirts of Naples in the *Filocolo* or of plague stricken Florence in the *Decameron*. He, too, studies "The Holy Book of Love," his version of Ovid's "Art of Love," the book that absorbed Alice du Clos as she sat in her bower. He has become by 1821 the Prince Galleoto of the *Decameron*, a man who has lost love but preserves the delight of still feeling it in his memory. Prince Galleoto confesses that from his suffering of "a most exalted and noble love," he has learned compassion for others who suffer from lost love. He thinks particularly of homebound ladies who lack the outlets of hunting, hawking, riding, and gambling that help lovelorn men forget their pain. Stories assuage the women's pent-up yearning while expressing their emotions relieves their loneliness. Because he recovered with the comfort offered by friends, Prince Galleoto wants to repay his survival by comforting others with stories. Similarly, Coleridge, an old sufferer, soothes the suffering and enlivens the loneliness of communities of women who have few outlets. Prince Galleoto claims that he had experienced the torments of a "love more fervent than any other, a love which no resolution, counsel, public shame, or danger which might result from it could break or bend," a source of suffering that diminished by itself over time, and left as a residue only "pleasure" and a "sense of delight" that the love had existed.[5] Similarly, Coleridge believes that his intense love for Sara Hutchinson was worth "the pain of yearning which all the pleasure on earth could not induce me to relinquish" (*CN* 3370).

At a time when Boccaccio's stock was so high that at a private auction in 1812 an edition of the *Decameron* from 1471 sold for the staggering price of 2260 pounds,[6] Coleridge on the one hand condemns Boccaccio's *Decameron* as "gross and disgusting licentiousness, [with] daring profaneness" (*Lects Lit* 2, p. 95), and on the other, praises Boccaccio for synthesizing Greek, Latin, and Christian legends. He addresses him: "O all-enjoying and all-blending Sage" (*PW* #652, l. 101). He appreciates the frame story encompassing other stories, a device perfected by Dante and used by Coleridge himself for his most famous poetic narratives.[7] He adapts his "questions of love" in his dialogues with young women. He would have been proud to know that Leigh Hunt compared his own "human plenitude" to Boccaccio's.

In this poem as in other late poems Coleridge talks with women about love. "The Garden of Boccaccio" suggests how art and companionship revive spirit and body:

> The Picture stole upon my inward Sight
> A tremulous Warmth crept gradual o'er my Chest,
> As though an Infant's Finger touch'd my Breast. (ll. 24–26)

The poem depicts Boccaccio's young men and women talking about love, Florence itself as an art work, where Coleridge had gazed at paintings and sculptures in 1805 in the company of his beloved friend, the American artist Washington Allston, and the enclosed garden with fountains. His early selves arise, and a panoramic sequence of all literature from Scalds to German women followers of Hertha to medieval minstrels to eighteenth-century satirical verse dances before him (ll. 35–45). No longer morose, he steps into the picture and participates:

> I myself am there,
> Sit on the Ground-sward, and the banquet share.
> 'Tis I, that sweep that Lute's love-echoing Strings,
> And gaze upon the Maid who gazing Sings. (ll. 65–68)

Boccaccio's spirit invigorates him: "With old Boccaccio's Soul I stand possest, / And breathe an Air like life, that swells my Chest" (71–72). The picture recalls Boccaccio's own evocation of "Gods of Greece and Warriors of Romance," Homer, and Ovid, especially his "Holy Book of Love's sweet Smart!" (l. 100), another book for lovers to read together for its wincing combination of pleasure and pain. Among the nymphs and fauns of the picture, Coleridge adds a glimpse of "that sly Satyr peeping through the leaves!" (l. 109), as if to acknowledge that the goatishness that he at first abhorred continued always in love as an underlying drive. The poem shows him moving from the outskirts back into the center, participating with lovers old and young.

When Coleridge reads Boccaccio's *Filocopo* he focuses on the wholeness of love in body and soul. In the margins he notes "how the instructor Racheo taught the prince and the beautiful girl Biancofiore to read the holy book of Ovid, in which the great poet shows how the sacred fires of Venus can speedily be kindled in the coldest hearts." Coleridge exclaims: "Deeply interesting— . . . The holy Book, Ovid's Art of Love!!—This is not the result of mere Immorality" (*CM* 1, 544). As in his poem "Love," a story is a *galleoto*, or pander, that seduces its readers.

This swooning is physical and intellectual, as Coleridge and Sara Hutchinson had similarly cooperated over *The Friend* in the comfortable room full of books and waning light. So in the *Filocopo* the lovers kindle the sacred fires of Venus by reading Ovid's *Art of Love*; the poet, like Priapus, gazes on the "lady who gazing sings," perhaps with the singing voice and gazing eyes of Anne Gillman.

* * *

Coleridge's concern for the lovelorn in his community of women leads him to discoveries about women during the last third of his life. As he had struggled over the years of composing "Christabel" to understand how young women are balked in developing as persons, often absorbed into the beings of other persons, he now watches and advises real young women, courted by men who are often unworthy of them, mulling over the single life as an alternative.

His advice can be divided into four related segments that overlap during these years: that women as well as men must take time to develop their persons and souls; that women should preserve their property by not marrying; that men and women should be careful in choosing to marry so as not to risk the pollution of their beings; and that societies that respect women are more civilized than those that do not.

Coleridge's distress at the fragility of women's personhood—the subject of the earlier chapter on "Christabel"—resumes in this late period. In an age where things and persons are measured equally on the same scale of degrees, Coleridge struggles to find grounds to preserve the uniqueness of persons, who cannot be treated as things without harm.[8] Observing that personhood diminishes with dependency, he sees that such dependencies impede women's development as persons. These dependencies arise by the force of law, property, custom, poverty, and ignorance, all combining to obliterate women's self-confidence, for as Coleridge asks in disgust, "in this age what is not property?" (*OM*, p. 146). Anne Gillman taught him much about how women can nevertheless retain their integrity as independent persons. Her "high opinion of her own sex comparatively & a partiality for female society" showed her own "womanly excellence." He admired her self-respect. He learned to share her "strongest prejudices against individual men [who profess a] Disbelief of such a thing as female friendship—or in some similar brutish forgetfulness that Woman is an immortal Soul." From his talks with Anne Gillman he has come away with "much to say on this."

"Much to say on this," especially to young men and women. Two discussions of the soul and the person with his son Hartley and his young friend Susan Steel direct the abstract ideas of personhood to the real choices that young men and women must make. In October 1815, Coleridge debates with his son Hartley about individuals in relation to others, and particularly about how one person may absorb the other as property, that is, as a thing. This topic is pertinent to both father and son who share by nature or nurture a psychological weakness of being easily absorbed by others and made to feel unworthy by contrast with their absorber. The question of persons turning other persons into things, as Geraldine reduced Christabel, as we saw, applies in a wide circle. For example, does any person have a right to prevent another person from committing suicide, if the person is choosing to end his or her life? By contrast, does a person have a right to destroy his own life if his life belongs to him? If he or she does have that right does an onlooker have the right to intervene in this destruction? Is a life a thing if it is yours to dispose of? (*SWF* 1, 405–407). Coleridge reads Blackstone, finding him weak in this area of rights and responsibilities for others. By analogy he argues that if a young helpless female is being violated a bystander has the right and the duty as well to intervene and save her; similarly the bystander has the right and the duty to save life when it is wrongly being treated as a thing by the person whose life it is. "Right is the sphere of each man's Free Agency" (*SWF* 1, 409). In reading Blackstone he thinks about "the *necessity* of individual action to moral agency, of an individual sphere to individual scheme of action, and of property to this" (*CN* 3835). How can anyone be a free agent without a sphere to act in?

Such questions about personal identity—who am I; where are my perimeters; how far does my free agency extend in my dealings with other persons—he addresses to young people, his sons and substitute daughters such as Susan Steel. Susan Steel wants to know how we know we have personal identity, an identity that young women lose legally just when they are finding it experientially. Coleridge explains the continuousness of identity despite the multiple changes in atoms and the deteriorations of old age in terms of a man's decision to leave a large sum of money to his friend's daughter when she comes of age. The man, now "this decrepit toothless wrinkled Cripple of 71," keeps his promise because his conscience "makes me know that I am one and the same Person now and 20 years back." So Susan herself remains the same through the flux and changes of life. The "I, the proper *Self*, the Self-consciousness, and the Conscience" preserve the continuity; "you affirm the *identity* of your intrinsic Being by means of *the* Unity of Consciousness." He defines her continuity further: "A self-conscious Will, Mind, and Life is a **PERSON**: an I AM." As a human person with Mind and Will, Susan acts and chooses; she lives more vividly than the Daisy, because "the Daisy does not *live* for itself." "*I* will—*I* think—*I* live—Willing, Thinking, Feeling are perfectly *distinct* each from the other; but all three are one in the 'I', or Person" (*SWF* 2, 1509). These instructions are given as they would be to a boy; they are given to Susan as to an equal, and they are given to encourage Susan to make sensible choices for herself as a willing, thinking, feeling person, not as a thoughtless daisy. Is it a coincidence that under the thought provoking and encouraging influence of Coleridge, Susan Steel rejected both her suitors (John Anster and James Gillman Jr.) and did not marry?[9] Is it a coincidence that the main example of personal identity is of a legal decision to give a young woman of 21 a substantial inheritance of her own? If property is the machine that drives the system of rank and fortune (*OM*, p. 146), then women who have property should hold on to it. Property conveys the right to be one's own proper person.

Of his own personal identity he is modest but sure. As famous as he may seem from the outside, his personal being has been distilled into a highly charged power. In a charming metaphor to Elizabeth Aders, a beautiful and accomplished daughter of the engraver Raphael Smith,[10] he describes his core self: "For in this bleak world of Mutabilities, & where what is not changed is chilled, and in this winter-time of my own Being, I resemble a Bottle of Brandy in Spitzbergen—a Dram of alcoholic Fire in the center of a cake of Ice" (*CL* 6, 532). A lover of spirits and wine, he chooses an appropriate image for his persisting identity. Elsewhere to Elizabeth Aders he sees himself humorously:

> "In truth he's no beauty!" cry'd Moll, Poll, and Tab,
> But they all of them own'd He'd the gift of the Gab.
> ("S. T. Coleridge, Aetat. Suae 63," *PW* #693)

Having made the moon cry out, "I am that I am, the jolly full moon!" he laughs about being an identity or having one. To a lady, "offended by a sportive observation that women have no souls," drawn, he says, from "Prophet Mahomet," he jokes,

> Nay, dearest Anna! Why so grave?
>   I said, you had no soul, 'tis true!
> For what you *are*, you cannot *have*:
>   'Tis I, that *have* one since I first had *you*! (*PW* #492)

He wriggles out of a politically incorrect insult by twisting the meaning of being and having.

He speaks to young men and women about questions of personal identity presumably because people over twenty-five are already fixed, committed, compromised, and as he himself became, boxed in by "the hedge-girdle of circumstance." He urges them to read, talk, judge, and become educated. He listens, he disputes, he does not condescend. To encourage the development of whole persons, Coleridge makes many plans for educating young men and women.

Taking charge of the young James Gillman Jr., he has little patience for the boy's boredom, which he mimics in his italicized phrases: "it must be evident to you, that to have no *Taste*, no *Turn*, no liking for *this* or for *that* is to confess an unfitness or dislike to a liberal Education *in toto*—And what is a liberal Education? That which *draws* forth and trains up the germ of free-agency in the Individual. . . . He alone is free & entitled to the name of a Gentleman, who knows himself and walks in the light of his own consciousness . . . all knowledge, I say, that enlightens and liberalizes, is a form and a means of self-knowledge" (*CL* 6, 629–630).

"Education draws forth and trains up the germ of free-agency in the Individual": in this illuminating formulation, which could describe the purpose of "liberal education" or "critical thinking" today, Coleridge includes young women as well. He emphasizes the flexibility exercised by thinking rather than the accumulation of information. Such flexibility would develop free choice, and thus by gradations advance responsibility in the individual person. The mentoring that Coleridge provides for young men he also gives generously to the young women who bustle in and out of Highgate,[11] and he seems to speak to them as if they had equal promise if not equal prospects in the society they are groomed to inherit. In their introduction to *Coleridge the Talker*, Richard W. Armour and Raymond F. Howes dispute the notion that Coleridge talked nonstop, paid no attention to other speakers, and did not listen to women. They write, "Coleridge politely deferred to women and gave them every opportunity to speak at length." They then quote from James Gillman's recollections of a dialogue between Coleridge and a woman musician, who played on the piano and elicited Coleridge's interpretations of the meanings of her musical phrases, an intriguing triangulation of musical lines, witticisms, and perception feelings (pp. 434–435, note 30). He had, they say "the flexibility of a true conversationalist, not the arrogance of a confirmed soliloquizer" (p. 83).

Plans to educate women percolate in several periods in his career, though he does not agree with Mary Wollstonecraft that girls and boys should be educated together. Like many modern proponents of single sex private schools, he believes that girls and boys are different (he believes that society enforces some differences that are essential to each, so that, in a gesture toward Carol Gilligan's theory, girls are more intuitive and boys more logical) and that they learn differently, but he believes that in the future they will come to be more alike: "In that future state to which we were approaching, where all were to be in common, and difference of sex would not exist, one spirit would be in all; the man would attain the tact or instinct of the woman; and the woman the courage and thought of the man."[12] This difference does not, however, relegate young women to "accomplishments," the "piano-fortery, which meets one now with Jack-o'-lantern ubiquity in every first and second story in every street" (Allsop, 1, 158–159). Even though girls do not formally learn Latin, they should be taught to read metrical poetry so as to enjoy and write it. In 1834 he publishes for young women the metrical example of his translation of Stolberg's "Hymn to the Earth," a glorification of the Earth Goddess and especially a recreation of the moment when her "lap" is inseminated by the sky God:

> Say, mysterious Earth! O say, great Mother and Goddess!
> Was it not well with thee then, when first thy lap was ungirdled,
> Thy lap to the genial heaven, the day that he wooed thee and won thee!
> Fair was thy blush, the fairest and first of the blushes of morning!
> Self- upgather'd thou shrankest! The blissful Shudder thrill'd thro' thee!
> Mightier far was the joy of thy sudden resilience: and forthwith
> Myriad myriads of lives teemed forth from the mighty embracement.
> (*PW* #257)

These lines were composed in Dec. 1799, the start of his passionate love, but his D. H. Lawrence-like praise of the copulating earth goddess must have been meant humorously. When he published these lines 34 years after their composition in *Friendship's Offering* for 1834, he directed them to young women, the readership of the volume, by explaining the metrical peculiarities of his poem:

> It may not be without use or interest to youthful, and especially to intelligent female readers of poetry, to observe, that in the attempt to adapt the Greek metres to the English language, we must begin by substituting quality of sound for quantity—that is, accentuated or comparatively emphasized syllables . . . (*PW* #618)

He continues his instructions with lively metrical examples, teaching the young women to read what their brothers had learned in their schools, and then surprising them with his lines on the "blissful Shudder" of his

Goddess (l. 25). Anne Gillman and Susan Steel may well have found these lines amusing. Thus he instructs his community of young and middle-aged women not only in metrics but in the ways of the pagan earth goddess. So, too, in "The Garden of Boccaccio" he exalts the German goddess Hertha, who dances wildly with her prophetic maids in forest glades.

Moral instructions to his young women friends are couched in gentle tales. Writing from Ramsgate in 1821, Coleridge warns Eliza Nixon in Highgate, "Be aware, how you allow a causeless Change to take place in your feelings, toward a tried Friend: lest in making hollow another's hope you undermine the foundations of your own *moral Being*. Listen to an allegoric tale. It has brevity at least to recommend it" (*SWF* 2, 959). The allegory of the flower casting off the dew drop nestling "in the pit and central Cell of her petals" so as to receive the favors of a passing breeze is so sexual that it recalls Blake's "Sick Rose." By such indirections he strives to steady Miss Nixon's fickleness. The charming Susan Steel discusses with the sage the definitions of personal identity, and, brooding on her questions, he summarizes for her a lifetime of work on this subject clearly and without pomposity.

The greatest danger to the development of each person's free agency, and ultimately to his or her soul, is any sort of dependency. For dependency warps the act of choosing. Along with the institution of slavery, along with poverty and class subservience, the institution of marriage is the most common arena where free agency is forfeited.

A paradox of marriage is that it is an institution designed to regulate human desire. But this desire is driven on many levels by an unquenchable thirst or hunger. Coleridge, the inventor of the term "self-insufficingness," knows that very often the dream of companionship with passion evaporates. Marriage and love are oxymoronic in almost all cases. "Marriage has, as you say, no *natural* relation to love. Marriage belongs to society; it is a social contract. It should not merely include the conditions of esteem and friendship, it should be a ratification of the manifestation. Still I do not know how it can be replaced: *that* belongs to the future, and is a question that the future only can solve" (Allsop, 2, 17).

When he refers to changes in social mores in the future, he means not just more liberal communities but inventions that will free women to have adventures as men do, to live fuller lives, not stuck in the homes of their husbands. Half humorously, half seriously, he mentions balloons and roads:

> When balloons or these new roads upon which they say it will be possible to travel fifteen miles an hour, for a day together, shall become the common

mode of travelling, women will become more locomotive;—and the health of all classes will be materially benefitted. Women will then spend less time in attiring themselves—will invent some more simple headgear, or dispense with it altogether. (Allsop, 2, 154)

To Mrs. Gillman he apologizes for fraternizing with her servants, since his early life as a solitary boy cast him often with servants, and he had knocked around with people of all classes, while she as a lady had been kept in confinement consorting with women of her own class (Dec. 1822; *CL* 5, letter 1321, 258–259). He notes that she "looked *down*" on servants "with the alien-like feeling of a Gentle-woman. . . . Now when you compare your Life &c with mine, can you wonder that there should be some difference both in our notions and our feelings?" What often appears to be ladylike snobbishness is caused by a social system that permits young men, especially those bred in "The Glow and Blaze of Democratic Notions," to roam about in bars, barracks, and lower class venues while it accustoms women to gracious and isolated "complacency." This lack of experience of the world may change in the future of railroads and balloons.

To an unknown correspondent, perhaps Thomas Allsop's sister, Coleridge develops a full analysis of the dangers of marriage for women. Deeply concerned with the social and legal constrictions around women, this letter, with several others, should put to rest any notions that Coleridge was frivolous about the lives and choices of girls. In advising this young woman, Coleridge asserts that for both sexes marriage "without proportionate Forethought is in both alike an act of Folly and Self-degradation. But in a Woman, if she have sense and sensibility enough to deserve the name, it is an act tantamount to Suicide." Quickly inserting Austen's 1811 title "Sense and Sensibility," he explains that marriage "fills the *whole* sphere of a Woman's Moral and Personal Being, her Enjoyments and her Duties," not because she is stupid but because the social system gives her nothing else to do and thus no other sphere for exercising what little free-agency she has. If the woman has any inclination to have more than a "Kitchen-garden" kind of marriage, "a thing of Profit and Convenience, in an even temperature between *indifference* and *liking*," if she rejects "the prospect of sinking into a lower state of moral feeling and of gradually quenching in yourself all hope and all aspiration, that looks beyond animal comforts and the outside shews of worldly respectability," then "*You* must have a *Soul*-mate as well as a *House* or a *Yoke*-mate!" Coleridge urges the young woman to find a person whom she could "love, *honor*, and *respect*." Even if this man were not actively vicious but neutral and indifferent to "the development of your moral Being, . . . still it would be a *benumbing* influence, and the Heart may be *starved* where it is neither stabbed nor poisoned." Referring directly to Milton's argument that no one is lonelier than an unhappily married person, Coleridge asserts, "God said that it was not well for the human Being to be alone," but an indifferent help-mate is worse than none and counteracts God's original reason for creating a mate for Adam (Jun. 1821; *CL* 5, 152–155).

Coleridge warns women to be wary of marriage because the decision is irreversible. If the man is even triflingly degraded he has a lifetime to get worse and to drag her down with him. Coleridge believes that a hasty choice is "criminal folly" in that it is a crime against oneself, a suicide.

The term "*Hemiplegia*" means living in half your being. "*Hemiplegia*" sounds like a disease of the blood or heart, and metaphorically it is (*CL* 5, 155). In a series of letters he argues that linking yourself to the wrong person can pollute your moral being. As you should not choose a physically sick person, so you should not choose a morally deficient or morally obtuse person. By analogies with illnesses that kill off a parent leaving the children impoverished, and with illnesses that can be inherited by children, he describes how men and women can lose their souls, gasping for air, panting, "losing all hope and all aspiration, that looks beyond animal comforts," or living in indifference and apathy, just to endure days side by side with an empty, selfish, or morally prudential person, calculating the outcomes or consequences of choices rather than their inherent worth. He asks the unknown young woman "would you surrender your *Person*, would you blend your whole personality, as far as God has put it in your power to do so, all that you call 'I', soul, body and estate, with one, the contagion of whose principles, the infection or sordidness of whose Habits and Conversation, you would [need?] to guard against in behalf of your own soul; and the insidious influence of which on the tone and spirit of your thoughts, feelings, objects, and unconscious tendencies and manners would be as the Atmosphere in which you lived?" (Jun. 1821; *CL* 5; letter 1268, p. 153).

Coleridge speaks of such a choice as a "crime," whether made carelessly out of the thoughtless and superficial desire just to be married, or to look well in the eyes of the world, or out of a foolish presumption, on the woman's part, that she could change her mate after marriage. Mimicking the voices of silly young women, he imagines the girl tapping her future husband with her fan and saying " 'For shame! You don't think so, I am sure' or 'You should not *say* so' " (*CL* 5, 157). Instead, she should take seriously the man's assertion that a law or sensibility need not apply to him, that his view of life is " 'I take care of *Number* One; hey, Neighbour! What say you?' " and she should realize how dastardly he might become as time passes, as his power grows, and as his love wanes. Not to take these revealing remarks seriously is a poor choice on her part. The crime is against herself, and her soul, selling it away for paltry gains.

In every sentence the deep self-criticism resounds. He expresses regret for how he injured his soul by allowing himself to be forced into a union with a woman who did not morally, intellectually, and emotionally support him, but blocked his spiritual development at every turn with her "dyspathy," her mockery of his immaterial values. When he agreed to a yoke-mate instead of a "Soul-Mate" he abandoned his own salvation, and succumbed to a "*benumbing* influence." Without a soul mate to help each partner "to be what *we* ought to be," "the Heart may be *starved* where it is neither stabbed nor poisoned" (*CL* 5, p. 154).

The choice to live in a state of *Hemiplegia* applies to both men and women (*CL* 5, 155). Coleridge's advice to Allsop's sister and to Allsop himself is to look for a future partner who will develop as a person and who has the rare interiority—rare in both men and women—so to develop, and only then under the right conditions. In a list of requirements for a life partner the obvious ones are health, good character, and preference; competent understanding; "competent sensibility to sympathize with her Husband's feelings . . . and the daily *Goings* on of his professional pursuits"; "competent Controll, by natural disposition no less than sense of Duty, to *fix* that sensibility, to make it converge to her Husband and diverge from him—not to be attracted by every new excellence with an enthusiasm or vivacity, innocent it may be, but yet unbecoming the *Staidness* of a Wife & Matron." Specifically would the proposed mate continue to prefer him, "if a *Shewy* Match offered?" Less obvious requirements are hidden as propensities that are poised to develop. Qualities like vanity and fickle flirtatiousness are difficult to discern and impossible to reform when they crop up. It is also difficult to know for sure whether any attractive person has the depth to develop into a good person.

Coleridge's advice on the hidden potentialities capable of unfolding in any character seems useful to men and women. As he had warned young women not to imagine that they could reform selfish or bullying young men, so he warns men and women together that the brief period between nineteen and twenty-five is the tipping point for character: it can go either way. The advice is as follows:

> If not *now*, when can she prove what she really is—19 to 25 the time when Females are most likely to manifest the depth of their nature if they

have any—A Coquette at 19 is a cold-hearted woman at 50—The question is not of little faults—tho' even these are never cured after marriage except by weariness & indifference, but the question is—Has she a *Heart* or not? Has she an inward Being, a reality more valuable & precious to her than all without? Or she is a mere Dependent on Shew, and *lives* only in the eyes and ears of others?. . . . Has she a *Heart*? What proofs of any great *depth* of affection & duty, as a Daughter, as a Sister? (*SWF* 2, 915)

A person with a heart, an inward being, and depth is a rarity; a person who cherishes his or her own inward being over outward shows is even rarer.

But Coleridge's subtle appreciation of those rare persons can be distorted by those who wish to find him minimizing the complexity of women. Out of this series of eight criteria for choosing a lifelong mate, a recent writer on gender takes two sentences and reads them as if they suggest that women as a group do not have interiority or complexity:

> He associated complex interiority—for better and worse—with men. '19 to 25 [is] the time when Females are most likely to manifest the depth of their nature if they have any.' Readers sympathetic to the depths of Coleridge's suffering may be inclined to interpret more positively his ascription of lack of interiority to women as evidence that Coleridge envied 'femininity' its relative security because of its reduced spheres of responsibility and mandated activity.[13]

The series of questions taken as a whole is designed to help a sensitive man like Allsop whom Coleridge loves with an almost trembling passion to find a woman who will be able to sympathize with him (with a hidden undertext that Coleridge himself, also sensitive, had not taken the time to search carefully for such a person). Allsop is not such a coarse gentleman to be satisfied with any pretty bed-mate and breeder. In these questions to ask himself, Coleridge develops the hope that young women are still potentially malleable before they become fixed in their constricted roles (wife, spinster, governess) after age twenty-five, and that it is possible to find a woman with potential character if one looks perceptively, assuming what most sensitive people would admit, that most people male and female do not have complexities in their interiors and that most people would not be the perfect mate having an interiority that complements one's own. We have seen him similarly warning young women not to imagine naively that they could change the moral character of men by marrying them. These are questions for each thoughtful man or woman to ask before settling down for life (with no possibility of divorce) with an incompatible person; the questions do not generalize about women's nature; they specify the qualities each person desires.

For women *hemiplegia* is even more dangerous than for men, because most women have no other outlets but the home, no verification of their being but in the home, and their identities are legally absorbed by their husbands. They lose their own names. They become their husbands. They cannot testify against them, they cannot have recourse against them. When these husbands are thoughtless, selfish, vicious, and brutal, the wives become so, too (as Maria does in Mary Wollstonecraft's novel of brutality and imprisonment) or die resisting. "O Women are hardly off!" (*CN*, 1708).

Coleridge believes that they should keep their properties, and if they have property, should have the right to exercise their free will on it as male property owners do. Working with Sara Hutchinson Oct. 12, 1809, as they pour out issues of *The Friend*, he examines the French Constitution of 1791. He notes that adult men are given the vote, under the assumption that they are creatures of reason. But Coleridge, conferring as he usually did with his amanuensis, wonders about other reasonable beings who are excluded from the vote, and about the many men whose passions and sensualities deprive them of their vaunted masculine reason. He turns from well-educated lads to Women: "Women are likewise excluded—a full half, and that assuredly the most innocent the most amiable half, of the whole human Race, is excluded, and this too by a Constitution which boasts to have no other foundations but those of universal Reason! Is Reason then an affair of Sex? No!" Shouting out against the exclusion of reasonable women from the vote, he turns to wonder why women may seem to lack reason. Dependency is the cause. Whether as daughters or wives, "women are commonly in a state of *dependence*, and are not likely to exercise their Reason with freedom." "*Dependence*" applies not only to women but also to "the Poor, to the Infirm, to Men in embarrassed Circumstances, to all in short whose maintenance, be it scanty or be it ample, depends on the Will of others." Since all these human beings live dependent on the wills of people who support them or pay them and thus are not free agents, and since their dependency and freedom vary from time to time, Coleridge concludes that a democratic government is too uncertain to function, and that only a representative government with reasonable laws will work. When he later declares that women with their own money or property should be enfranchised, he is not changing his view. He is continuing to emphasize that decision making requires independence (*Friend* 2, 129).

He dictated this long, intricately argued, revolutionary paragraph to Sara Hutchinson, so that we know these words passed through her ears and out her fingers and may have been revised or checked in the process.

Working together, Coleridge and Sara Hutchinson may well have discussed the issue together, since it applied to her own expected inheritance, her own single status, and her own free agency and responsibility.

She made a virtue of necessity by becoming "a favorer of a single life," as she wrote to console her lonely cousin Tom Monkhouse: "I have seen such misery in the marriage life as would appal you if you had seen it. Such millstones about the necks of worthy men! That I would have you be *wary*— . . . Of course you will not suppose that I think all the fault belongs to the women" (*SHL*, xxxv). Like Dorothy Wordsworth, she lived out her life caring for her brothers, also "favorers of the single life." How many have made that choice![14] Coleridge himself recommended the single life in a 1799 epigram from Lessing, satirizing a bastard:

> Bob now resolves on marriage schemes to trample
> And now he'll have a wife all in a trice—
> Must I advise?—Pursue thy Dad's Example
> And marry not. There hast thou my advice. (*PW* #228)

In the album of a young lady, Frances Sarah Bunyan, who was on the point of being married, Coleridge adapts Luther's *Table Talk* to warn first that "many thrust them selves into the state of Matrimony before they be aware & right be think themselves." But he goes on to speak generally about the state of marriage, "instituted by God before the Fall" and "an essential of our Humanity." He stresses that marriage is a discipline and a humanizing condition. Under the best circumstances it turns "the common water of our animal life to the wine of *Human Gladness*!" Even when such a miraculous transubstantiation does not quite occur, matrimony "not only preserveth human generation but it preserveth it *human* & without Matrimony there may be a Herd but a *Country a Nation* there cannot be" (*SWF* 2, 1507). After his long sorrows as a married man in love with but unable to marry another woman, Coleridge's hope for the humanizing powers of the married state can be read as either delusory or heroic.

While Coleridge invents the term *hemiplegia* for the married state in its mediocre form, he dictates to Sara Hutchinson in *The Friend* (Aug. 10, 1809) the wider context for married life and sees it as a subset of a general need for honesty in human communication. He extends the meaning of the half-life to the way many people live in half their beings and thus by their own wills become mutilated and paralyzed:

> The whole faculties of man must be exerted in order to noble energies; and he who is not earnestly sincere, self-mutilated, self-paralysed, lives in but half his being. (*Friend* 2, 42)

His goal is that all men and women should exert themselves to live whole lives of integrity, but he knows from his own life how difficult this wholeness is, how often he deceives himself, how often people choose not to engage their full powers or their spiritual and voluntary agency. Coleridge fears that starving the Heart will "disinherit the future self" (*CL* 6, 905). Thus living mutilated and paralyzed in half of one's being is a general danger, but it is a danger intensified in marriage, where *hemiplegia* runs rampant within the closed circle of lifelong bickering. The partner "surrender[s] [her] *Person*, . . . blend[s] [her] whole personality, . . . all that [she] call[s] 'I,' soul, body and estate, with one, the contagion of whose Principles, the infection or sordidness of whose Habits and Conversation, [she] would have to guard against in behalf of [her] own soul; and the insidious influence of which on the tone and spirit of [her] thoughts, feelings, objects, and unconscious tendencies and manners would be as the Atmosphere in which [she] lived" (*CL* 4, 153). Coleridge's vehemence against the sordid poisons of everyday married life, almost a pest-house in his metaphors, indicates his own pain and his fear for the souls of young women.

Critics have often called attention to Coleridge's desire for a wife to agree with him in her opinions and to learn how to be companionable and harmonious. These interests seem to require the wife's obliteration of her own personality. It is true that Coleridge's notion of marriage is based on compatibility as a necessity for peace and creativity. He learns through harsh experience that for a marriage to work as a marriage individuals must be restrained from impinging on their partners, from imposing their values on their partners, and from preventing their partners from developing as persons. Each partner must leave the other a "Sphere" in which to exercise "free agency" and thus to form the soul for its future life. Even as he suggests separate personal developments, he knows the yearning for oneness, which he occasionally achieves when he feels himself permeated by Sara Hutchinson's consciousness: "You are my better Self—I cannot see, I cannot think of you, without an intense consciousness of what I am: for what I am is only painful, is only delightful to me, by its relations to you" (*CN* 3, entry 3430; 1808–1809). Love binds identities closely, but the oneness enforced by marriage, the obliteration of one person within an other, is a completely different form of oneness.

As he ages and considers the inevitable abrasiveness of communal relations, he formulates ways of preserving individualities within various kinds of cohabitations. In the essay "Individuality" (1826; *SWF* 2, 1336–1338), he establishes first that a person's individuality is not entirely available in his or her face, but resides in some unaccountable "Treasure-vault, sunk into the foundation of the House," that "hold the Title-deeds of his Humanity." This deep place of individuality is sacred. "In the code of Conscience it is aggravated Burglary to break into it." Whatever the person's peculiarities on the surface, the other person must impose on himself "a higher Rule. Reverence the *Individuality* of those you live among." Some of the laughable peculiarities of a person's behavior may be "connected with the individuality of the Person's Being & Character—and unintelligible to you, because it[s] source lies deeper than Intelligence.—Reverence the Individuality of your friend! It is the religion of a delicate Soul" (*SWF* 2, 1337). This maxim Kathleen Coburn, with her usual intuitive understanding of her subject, paired with passages on women's freedom.[15] The maxim modifies the standard "Love thy neighbor as thyself" by detaching it from the personal affections and by eradicating the tit for tat quality that seeps into the original. The individuality of the other should be reverenced for its isolated selfhood, not for its love for the reverencer, and not for a hope of love being returned in kind. Problems in reverencing arise when the friend is not a friend, and when the friend has no individuality. In the *Opus Maximum*, syllogisms about honoring persons and others begin with the word "men" and cross out "men" to overscribe "persons." Like a politically correct modern reader, Coleridge consciously changes his nouns to include women: "It is my duty to love all men" becomes by tinkering "It is my duty to love all persons," yet loving one's neighbor as one's self continues to ring with self-love or to be difficult if one does not love oneself (*OM*, 61–63). He comments in the margins of Kant's *Anthropology*: "all morality presupposes in the Subject the faculty of regarding itself as an object—i.e. of placing the first in the ranks of the third Persons, and acting to all as one rank, me, thee, Him" (*CM* 3, 265); to reverence others one must be able to shift perspective to see from that person's point of view.

Because of this core imperative, families of all sizes and shapes should be arranged to provide private times (or we would say "space") for each person's individuality to develop. Most families would appear to be "a concentric Circle with many circumferential lines but only one center." Coleridge readjusts this circle to be a "close neighborhood of Centers within a swelling outline formed by the segments of the outer Circles." In addition, "room is allowed for every point to have a small circumference of its own, so that the contraction, to which each must consent in order to give space for the others, shall yet in no instance bring the circumferential line too close to the Centre, for any radii to be describable in the interspace." He urges "two Lovers on the point of becoming Man &

Wife" to anticipate the need for this little space, and to "invent, contrive that there shall be some points, some things respecting which you are to continue single," however "one-hearted" they may be at the beginning of their life together.

Coleridge's multifarious advice on marriage comes from the heart; it comes in the context of the law in his country which forbade divorce and made final and forever this one choice, which for innocent men and women is untested; promiscuous men can test the waters. He counsels intense scrutiny of the other's character before marriage and respectful space to develop character during marriage. His most consistent advice is: don't marry. Or do so only if all aspects of your personalities are congruent. Or do so if you make sure to keep separate spheres. If it is not good, or is actively bad, you can never escape, and over a lifetime of bickering and petty thwarting you will progressively degrade your own person and soul.

Coleridge's physicality extends to his metaphors for the soul. He questions how we can imagine a soul in the absence of physical aspects, and wittily shows how human beings have envisioned souls as "a kind of celestial poultry." Although he surmises in a lecture of 1812 on education that in the vast beyond, the souls of men and women will be identical, he occasionally wonders if there is "sex in souls," perhaps referring to the souls of living men and women who have not yet metamorphosed into generic "souls" in the world to come. In trying to clarify how he thinks about souls, he uses the analogies of insect and animal anticipations of future change, paradoxically appealing to his interlocutor's senses to convey this ultimate absence of physical being.

The self creates the person by gradual choices. If carefully made, these choices create an increasing freedom. As a free agent, the person chooses to nurture the hidden soul for a future life. This soul buds within the person as the butterfly prepares itself within the larva.

But no one knows better than STC that making the right choices is not easy. Each choice is circumscribed by circumstances beyond one's control, such as other persons, class status, gender, social custom, even weather. Thinking about how difficult choices can be for men and women, Coleridge meditates on the forces that encircle the person who attempts to exercise "free agency." When he is heart broken (1811–1816) he thinks to himself how everyone lives surrounded by a "ring-fence," a "hedge-girdle," a set of varying "circummurations" of childhood, state, and even soil, moisture, and climate. To leap out of these enclosures is almost impossible without conscious volition. Although Coleridge uses the pronoun "he" in analyzing the "Skein of necessities" that "surrounds with subtlest intertwine the slenderest fibres of his Being, while it binds the whole frame with chains of adamant," he knows that necessity applies as much to women as to men, more, because custom decreases their range of choices and thus surrounds them more tightly. When outward influences threaten to "be-thing" a person, this person must remember that without these external circumstances "his Being can not be even *thought*," and that these "labyrinthine folds belong to his Being, and evolve out of his essences." His inward being determines the forces that have power over him: "the stimulability determines the existence & character of the Stimulus" and "the temptability constitutes the temptation."

By this intricate argument, Coleridge realizes that some essential element of his own being has chosen his own weaknesses and wrong choices, and that, "in the warm & genial Light of this knowledge," he, like others, can work "to beget each in himself a new man" (*CN* 3, 4109; 1811–1816). These self-generating fates apply to women as well as to men, choosing good men, choosing solitude, choosing, as Sara Hutchinson did, the single life, supported by her own tiny inheritance from an uncle, put into stocks for an income of one hundred and ten pounds a year (*MY*, 488–489; 497): a small thing but her own.

How can men or women learn the true nature of the persons they choose to live with for the rest of their life? Anne Gillman is in Coleridge's opinion one of the good and intelligent women who can tell self-seeking and vain women in a flash; she worries with Coleridge about their dear Thomas Allsop's choice of a potentially petty wife (who does as it turns out break relations because of a clumsily addressed invitation that seemed to be just for her husband). Like his first love Mary Ann Evans, Anne Gillman shares his dread of calculating women. When Coleridge writes on October 22, 1821 to Thomas Allsop about choosing a wife, he relays Anne's intuition:

> Must not those women, who have the highest sense of Womanhood, who know what their sex may be, and who feel the rightfulness of their own claims to be loved with honor and honored with love, have likewise the keenest perception of the contrary? Understand a few foibles, as incident to humanity; take as matters of course that need not be mentioned because we know that in the least imperfect a glance of the Womanish will shoot across the Womanly—and there are Mirandas and Imogens, a Una, a Desdemona, out of Fairy Land—rare, no doubt; yet less rare, than their Counterparts among men in real life.... Can she know this and not know what a sore evil, fearful in heart-withering affliction in proportion to the capacity of be[ing] blessed, a weak, artful, and worthless Woman is—perhaps in her own experience, has been? (*CL* 5, 183, letter #1280).

In this same letter, Coleridge tells Allsop that Anne Gillman's views are deepened by her complete knowledge of Coleridge's own marital disaster (p. 182), which should be a warning to all.

His meditations about the nature of this thing called love take many forms in the absence of the infinitely beloved darling and in the close proximity of women who resemble her but are married to his friends, or who seem passionately connected with each other. Defining persons, he turns to the question of loving others; defining souls, he turns to the cultivation of love; thinking about integrity within the person, he realizes that the person knits together by loving. Love synthesizes Action and Passion, I and not-I (*CM* 3, 266). "Love is the Parent of all such sexual Desire as a pure and dignified Nature will permit itself to feel! Love alone begets it; shelters and shelt'ring at once warms and hides it; (Love) gives it nourishment & increase: and itself (in return) receives support & renewal of vivacity from its offspring! But likewise Love exerts (over Desire) the due authority of the Parent over the Child, to check, to confine, or to remove it from its Presence" (*SWF* 1, 291). Love generates well-being, friendship, and desire. It is the end and fulfillment of yearning, or "human *storge*" (*SWF* 2, 1441). Looking at others he comes to marvel at the discovery that "there is in each man and woman something 'truly lovely,' truly worthy of love, which is substantial and not accidental, a ground of personality which can make them a symbol of God to a lover," as Anthony Harding reveals.[16] Coleridge's definitions of love are grounded in his own real physical emotions of varying intensity for a variety of real women.

Coleridge's many poems about pairs of women, mothers and daughters, sisters, and friends, reveal a complex study of how women may look similar and be essentially different when they express their personalities. Poems to Bruntons, Evanses, Frickers, Hutchinsons, Morgan and Brent, and Gillman and Harding sisters participate in his larger interest in similarity and difference, imitation and copies in artistic representation. Lesbianism also gives a piquant erotic curiosity to the reduplication of beauty. Some of these pairs seem to be clones, or to lend themselves to experiments (as psychologists now do with twins) on what makes them different (*SWF* 2, 1335–1336). Beautiful women's faces, like rhymes, radiate the strange allure of similarity with difference so essential to beauty. And relationships that are too close, verging on incest, like that of his daughter Sara and his nephew Henry Nelson Coleridge, which he was powerless to stop, are disturbing. The sameness of the cousins, as much as the danger to the gene pool, merges individualities and blurs the uniqueness of identity in persons, souls, and future lives.

Gathering themes from his plans for pantisocracy, his admiration of early German egalitarian marriages, his outrage at the parliamentary debates on how to punish adulteresses, his argument in *The Friend* of 1809 that women with property should be as capable of voting as men, Coleridge sets out for young James Gillman Jr. his requirements for a civilized society. In line with his search for what makes human beings human, and how best to encourage humanity,[17] Coleridge defines civilization in opposition to barbarism as a system of government that provides "the means of National and individual Progression by the accumulation of knowledge and Experience from age to age, and of the Disposition thereto—Letters, Books, Printing, Men of Learning, Men of Science, Artists; Schools for the different Ranks of Society, and the Opportunities of *moral education and religious instruction* for all in all ranks—and last but not least the equality of Women to men in social and domestic Life, and the unconditional Sovereignty of *Law* over individual Will—these are the characters of a State that is both Civilized and Cultivated, when they are *all* found, and are organized by mutual interdependence into a System of Society" ("Lesson in Universal History for James Gillman, Jr." [*SWF* 2, 1354 (1353–1357)]). Those societies such as Russia and China that do not have "the Rational, the Moral, and the Religious Principles" do "not cease to be in a state of Barbarism, tho' . . . partially civilized." To be counted as civilized and cultivated, these societies must show "respect and reverential Tenderness toward Women, and/or the equal rights, reciprocal Benefits, and Mutual dependence of the Sexes" and "the exclusive Sovereignty of Law, so that every Individual at the Age of reason has a Sphere for the exercise of his Free-agency, into which no other Individual is permitted to intrude, in all points necessary to his Well-being and Progressive Improvement as a responsible Creature destined for a State after death." Without these principles, a nation can abound in dancing masters, cooks, and friseurs but still remain a "*state of Barbarism*." Central to a civilized and cultivated state, then, is the equality of the sexes, the "Liberty, i.e. Free-will, and Property (i.e. the right and power of exercising it withing a given sphere) [that] are like Lungs and Air" (Coleridge's note, p. 1354), a fine analogy that compares the lungs to our own selves within and the air to the conditions that permit us to inhale and exhale. Writing to this young man, the son of his protector and of one of the loved women in his life, amid a community of talking and singing women young and old, he wants him to take as his foundational principle that a society without equality for women is neither civilized nor cultivated. Though he equivocates between "reverential tenderness" "and/or" "equal rights," he uses throughout the gender-free word "Individual" so as to include all persons capable of acting as persons.

Barbaric cultures are characterized by excessive manliness. He shows remarkable subtlety in realizing that violent machismo does not express itself in sexual forms. Thinking about race in 1828, he is interested in various reports about Scythians as they resemble [native] Americans in hunting, endurance of pain, and violence. These cultures share a "deficien[cy] in sexual ardor [which] arises from the low estimation of women & the harsh bashawish contemptuous treatment of them." Scythians, Mongolians, and Native Americans show gravity and anxiety about their hunting; they experience "the absence of all the finer pleasures of the Sense . . . in addition to these the absence of all the (infinitesimal) affections and emotions of thought, conversation, and social intercourse that opens out the countenance, & distinctifies the features." Coleridge's racist views develop from his outrage at the treatment of women in these cultures. He sees the male hunters as almost beasts, their faces closed and similar because of their concentration on the unvaried actions of the hunt, their thoughts and feelings animalistic and unrefined by womanly contact, their sexuality deficient from their "low estimation of women" ("The Races of Men" [1828] *SWF* 2, 1458–1459), an insight that connects sexual energy with respect for women as opposed to predatory "bashawish contemptuous treatment of them."

"Bashawish," derives not from Scandinavian *bash* for whipping or flogging, but from the Turkish title *Pasha*, figuratively "a grandee, a haughty, imperious man" (*O.E.D.*). Coleridge extends the term to include customary treatment of women in harems and isolation at this time under control of their masters. He supposes that such tyranny gratifies power rather than desire, the kind of enslavement that Mary Shelley criticizes in the escape from the Turkish harem in the DeLacey subplot of *Frankenstein*, and that does not vary as much as one would hope from the contemptuous and punitive marriage laws of Great Britain. Perhaps these restrictive laws are even enhanced by imperial exposure to India, where suttee was common, and the Middle East, where harems still incarcerated women of all ages. From these exotic outposts British soldiers returned, when they did, with exaggerated haughtiness, dressed in turbans in London clubs as Thackeray will see them twenty years on in *Vanity Fair*. Reverence for individuality exists in communities that are civilized enough to permit personhood to all individuals.

Keen to sensuous detail in the natural world and in human bodies, ebullient in response, attuned to assorted women and alienated by few,

Coleridge had an appreciation of varying levels of love. The excitement of being in love, the loneliness of cohabiting with an incompatible partner, the crushing experience of realizing that he was forbidden to divorce, the scintillating communication of senses, feeling, and spirit in his ten years companionship with Sara Hutchinson, and the heart-wringing sorrow that followed Sara Hutchinson's departure, combined to alert him to women's lives. From these passions of looking, listening, feeling, and composing through his marrow his physically pulsing poems, Coleridge came to formulate his advice for happier freedoms for women in and out of marriage. In an era when women were prominent in tracts, novels, poems, plays, operas, pictures, and cartoons, when their voices and bodies were ubiquitous, overflowing their gowns, Coleridge participates by filling his world with female stories, songs, performances, sighs, flesh, and passion. This book has presented the movement of his experience from relishing the particularity of young women, to swooning at women's voices sung and spoken, to sympathizing with women's unique ordeals, to reverencing them as individuals, to forecasting a better civilization that would provide them with spheres for free agency.

Notes

1 Coleridge and Women's Psychology

1. J. C. C. Mays, "Editor's Introduction," *Poetical Works* 1, part 1, *The Collected Works of Samuel Taylor Coleridge* (Princeton University Press, Bollingen Series LXXV, 2001), p. xc.
2. George Felton Mathew in *"European Magazine"* (1816), in *Coleridge, The Critical Heritage*, ed. J. R. de J. Jackson (New York: Barnes & Noble, 1970), p. 241.
3. *Collected Notebooks*, 4, 5428, quoted in Michael John Kooy, *Coleridge, Schiller, and Aesthetic Education* (Basingstoke and New York: Palgrave, 2002), p. 185.
4. George Whalley, *Coleridge and Sara Hutchinson* (Toronto: University of Toronto Press, 1955), pp. 65–66, says that "he refused to consider divorce"; even the sympathetic and wise J. Robert Barth, S. J., *Coleridge and the Power of Love* (Columbia: University of Missouri Press, 1988), p. 34, writes "Divorce was for him—for religious reasons but no doubt also, unconsciously, for psychological reasons—out of the question, so a separation was arranged."
5. Leo Tolstoy, *Anna Karenina*, trans. Louise and Aylmer Maude, ed. George Gibian (New York: W.W. Norton, 1970), pp. 256–258, part 3, ch. 13, where Karenin starts planning how to punish his adulterous wife.
6. A curious example of the excision of Coleridge's adult erotic life is Jean H. Hagstrum, *Eros and Vision: The Restoration to Romanticism* (Evanston, Il: Northwestern University Press, 1989), p. 75: "To penetrate, for example, the full reasons why Coleridge denied the existence of Cupid as a separate being would take more space than we have, but it might help us understand the *shuddering withdrawals* that *everywhere* characterize his private utterances about love" (my italics).
7. In an essay, Beth Lau, "The Rime of the Ancient Mariner and Frankenstein," in *Samuel Taylor Coleridge and the Sciences of Life*, ed. Nick Roe (New York: Oxford University Press, 2000), pp. 207–223.
8. Ashley Cross, "From *Lyrical Ballads* to *Lyrical Tales*: Mary Robinson's Reputation and the Problem of Literary Debt," *SIR* 40, 4 (Winter, 2001), 571–605.
9. In Anya Taylor "Coleridge, Letitia Elizabeth Landon, and the Difficulties of Loving," *PQ* 79, 4 (Fall, 2000), 501–522, I describe the real young women who surround him in his later years and play his interlocutors in the mini-drama "The Improvisatore."

10. Joel Pace and Chris Koenig-Woodyard, "Coleridge and Divine Providence: Charles King Newcomb, Rhode Newcomb, and Ralph Waldo Emerson," *TWC* 32, 3, 138–141.
11. H. J. Jackson, "Coleridge's Women, or Girls, Girls, Girls Are Made to Love," *SIR* 32, 4 (Winter, 1993), 577–600, regales us with Coleridge's many women associates, but believes that Coleridge never met a woman whom he thought was his intellectual equal. Jackson acknowledges wittily that even she is ultimately one of the women who mop up after Coleridge. Julie Ellison, *Delicate Subjects: Romanticism, Gender, and the Ethics of Understanding* (Ithaca and London: Cornell, 1990), pp. 103–216, argues that feminine, French, and trivially minute styles were interchangeable terms in Coleridge's criticism.
12. Anne Fadiman, "Coleridge," *American Scholar*, 68, 4, 8.
13. Gurion Taussig, *Coleridge and the Idea of Friendship 1789–1804* (Newark and London: University of Delaware Press, 2002), pp. 93 and 97.
14. Camille Paglia, *Sexual Personae: Art and Decadence from Nefertiti to Emily Dickinson* (London and New Haven: Yale University Press, 1990), excitingly reveals the chthonian powers magically at work in Coleridge's great supernatural poems, but finds these powers abasing the passive poet, who is drained, dominated, raped, and silenced as "a tongueless male heroine," a "coy maid half yielding to her lover," and "the woman wailing for her demon-lover" (p. 344).
15. These foundational texts are Richard Holmes, *Coleridge: Early Visions* (New York: Viking, 1989) and *Coleridge: Darker Reflections, 1804–134* (New York: Pantheon, 1998); Stephen Potter, *Minnow Among Tritons: Mrs. Samuel Taylor Coleridge's Letters to Thomas Poole 1799–1834* (Bloomsbury: Nonesuch Press, 1934); Molly Lefebure, *The Bondage of Love: A Life of Mrs. Samuel Taylor Coleridge* (London: Victor Gollancz, 1986); George Whalley, *Coleridge and Sara Hutchinson* (Toronto: University of Toronto Press, 1955); Sara Coleridge, *Memoirs and Letters of Sara Coleridge* ed. by her daughter (New York: Harper & Bros, 1879); Bradford Keyes Mudge, *Sara Coleridge: A Victorian Daughter, Her Life and Essays* (New Haven: Yale University Press, 1989); Kathleen Coburn, *Inquiring Spirit* (rept. 1951; Toronto: University of Toronto Press, 1979); Robert Barth, *Coleridge and the Power of Love* (Columbia: University of Missouri Press, 1989); Anthony John Harding, *Coleridge and the Idea of Love: Aspects of Relationship in Coleridge's Thought and Writing* (London: Cambridge University Press, 1974); John Beer, *Coleridge's Poetic Intelligence* (London and Basingstoke: The Macmillan Press, 1977); Tim Fulford, *Romanticism and Masculinity: Gender, Politics and Poetics in the Writings of Burke, Coleridge, Cobbett, Wordsworth, DeQuincey and Hazlitt* (Basingstoke and New York: Macmillan and St. Martin's Press, 1999); Julie Carlson, *In the Theatre of Romanticism: Coleridge, Nationalism, Women* (Cambridge: Cambridge University Press, 1994); Anne K. Mellor, *Romanticism and Gender* (New York and London: Routledge, 1993); Beth Lau, *Fellow Romantics: Male and Female British Writers 1790–1830* (forthcoming); Camille Paglia, *Sexual Personae* (London and New Haven: Yale University Press, 1990); Thomas McFarland,

Coleridge and the Pantheist Tradition (Oxford: Clarendon Press, 1969) and *Romanticism and the Forms of Ruin* (Princeton: Princeton University Press, 1981); Mary Ann Perkins, *Coleridge and the Logos* (Oxford: Clarendon Press, 1994); Jean Bethke Elshtain, "Kant, Politics, & Persons," *Polity* 14, 2 (Winter, 1981), 205–221; David Clark, "Heidegger's Craving: Being-On-Schelling," *Diacritics* 27, 3, 8–33.
16. Leigh Hunt (in 1828), in Richard W. Armour and Raymond F. Howes, *Coleridge the Talker: A Series of Contemporary Descriptions and Comments* (rept. 1940; New York and London: Johnson Reprint Corp., 1969), p. 266.

2   First Loves and Flirting Verses

1. Might W. B. Yeats have borrowed and modified this phrase for his "Crazy Jane to his Bishop"? As the two epigraphs to this book suggest, Yeats often thinks and feels like Coleridge.
2. William Carlos Williams's "The Dance" catches this physical movement: "In Breughel's great picture, The Kermess, / the dancers go round, they go round and / around. . . . / . . . those / shanks must be sound to bear up under such / rollicking measures. . . ." (1944), in *The Collected Poems of William Carlos Williams*, ed. A. Walton Litz and Christopher MacGowan (New York: New Directions Books, 1986), 2, pp. 58–59.
3. For more on Coleridge's admiration of ancient German companionate marriages, see Anya Taylor, "Coleridge, Wollstonecraft, and the Rights of Women," in *Coleridge's Visionary Languages*, ed. Tim Fulford and Morton D. Paley (Suffolk: D. S. Brewer, 1993), pp. 83–98.
4. *Lects Lit* 2, 54, 60–61, and 91.
5. So, too, Coleridge's participation in manly drinking fests and drinking songs surprise many Coleridge readers; see Anya Taylor, "Coleridge and Alcohol," *Bacchus in Romantic England: Writers and Drink 1780–1830*, (Basingstoke and New York: Macmillan and St. Martins, 1999), pp. 93–125.
6. Feb. 2, 1794; Kenneth Curry, ed., *New Letters of Robert Southey*, 2 vols (New York and London: Columbia University, 1965), vol. 1, p. 48.
7. Richard Holmes, *Coleridge: Early Visions* (New York: Viking, 1990), wonders if this commitment was more in Southey's mind than in Coleridge's, pp. 75–76.
8. In *Coleridge's Poetry and Prose*, selected and edited by Nicholas Halmi, Paul Magnuson, and Raimonda Modiano (New York and London: W.W. Norton, 2004), p. 609, the single entry that is intended to encapsulate Coleridge's lifelong interest in women comes from a late conversation in *Table Talk* 1835 (1, 212–213), recorded Sept. 27, 1830, by Coleridge's conservative nephew and extracted from what may well have been a humorous context. Coleridge remarks that Shakespeare knew that it was "the perfection of women to be characterless. Every one wishes a Desdemona or Ophelia for a wife,—creatures who, though they may not always understand you, do always feel you, and feel with you." It is possible to imagine that this

comment prompted a burst a laughter from his conversational companions who knew his marital history. Suicide and suffocation are the outcomes of marrying these "ideal" wives. These five lines of print do not do justice to Coleridge's many thoughts about women.
9. See *Lects Lit* 1, 594–595: *CN* 3316, 3345, and 4013.
10. Thomas Allsop, *Letters, Conversations and Recollections of Coleridge* (London: Edward Moxon, 1836), pp. 136–137.
11. James Gillman, *The Life of Samuel Taylor Coleridge* (London: William Pickering, 1838), pp. 29, 36, 41, 49. Volume 2 was never published. Gillman does not mention his marriage, his children, his separation, or his other loves, perhaps to focus on his innocence and his achievements and thus defend him from detractors.

3   The Smoking Torch of Hymen

1. Molly Lefebure, *The Bondage of Love: A Life of Mrs. Samuel Taylor Coleridge:* (New York: Norton, 1986), p. 32. Mark Storey, *Robert Southey: A Life* (Oxford and New York: Oxford University Press, 1997), p. 7, affirms this early alliance: "there seems to have been a family understanding that it was the vivacious and beautiful Sara to whom Southey was first attracted ('He had a friendship with mama first,' recalled the young Sara Coleridge years later)." *I* thank Elisabeth G. Gitter for help in structuring the narrative of this chapter.
2. Richard Holmes, *Coleridge: Early Visions* (New York: Viking, 1989), p. 70. For formative arguments in this debate see William Godwin's *Political Justice*: *A Reprint of the Essay on Property*, ed. H.S. Salt (reprint 1949; London: George Allen and Unwin Ltd., 1890), pp. 100–105, and Mary Wollstonecraft, *Vindication of the Rights of Women*, ed. Miriam Brody (London: Penguin Books, 1985). *VRW* in text.
3. Coleridge, "Modern Patriotism," in *The Watchman*, ed. Lewis Patton (*Collected Coleridge*, 1970), no. III, Thursday March 17, 1796, p. 99. John Thelwall takes offense at the attack on their shared principles, and Coleridge responds in a letter of May 13, 1796, *CL* 1, 213.
4. Stephen Potter, ed. *Minnow Among Tritons: Mrs. S. T. Coleridge's Letters to Thomas Poole 1799–1834* (London: The Nonesuch Press, 1934), p. vii. See for troubles *The Letters of Wiliam and Dorothy Wordsworth: The Middle Years*, ed. Ernst de Selincourt and Mary Moorman (Oxford: At the Clarendon Press, 1969). *MY* in text.
5. Samuel Taylor Coleridge, marginalia to John Milton, *A Complete Collection of the Historical, Political, and Miscellaneous Works*, ed. T. Birch, London, 1738, cited in *A Book I Value: Selected Marginalia*, ed. H. J. Jackson (Princeton and Oxford: Princeton University, Press, 2003), pp. 25–27. Coleridge's description of the souls of members of Parliament as "Souls passing thro' the Stomach & Intestines of England, like Misletoe Berries thro' those of the Thrush, or Nutmegs (in the Spice Islands) thro' those of the

Eastern Pigeon, in order to be matured for germinating in France & becoming Frenchmen" is a witty example of his rabid anti-gallicism as well as his delight in humorous images for the physical body.

6. Ernest Sirluck, ed., *Complete Prose Works* of John Milton (New Haven: Yale University Press, and London: Oxford University Press, 1959), 2: 229, 235, 236, 246.
7. Dorothy and Wordsworth describe the incompatibility of Samuel and Sara Coleridge frequently in letters to Lady Beaumont and Catherine Clarkson, e.g. *The Letters of William and Dorothy Wordsworth: The Middle Years*, Part 2 1806–1811, ed. Ernest De Selincourt and Mary Moorman (Oxford: Clarenden Press, 1969), 2, pp. 78–79, 84–85, 172–173. *MY* in text.
8. Kenneth Curry, ed., *New Letters of Robert Southey*, vol. 1, pp. 102–103.
9. *Pride and Prejudice*, Book 1, ch. 8, p. 36.
10. In chapter 5, "In the Cave of the Gnome: Hartley Coleridge," *Bacchus in Romantic England: Writers and Drink 1780–1830*, pp. 126–156, I give details on this estrangement, and Coleridge's fury and anguish at his first-born son.
11. John Worthen, *The Gang* (New Haven: Yale University Press, 2002); Henry Crabb Robinson, *The Diary of Henry Crabb Robinson*, ed. Devek Hudson (London: Oxford University Press, 1967), p. 47; *HCR* in text; Sara Hutchinson, *The Letters of Sara Hutchinson 1800–1835*, ed. Kathlen Coburn (London: Routledge & Kegan Paul, 1954), p. 324; *SHL* in text.
12. Edith Coleridge, ed., *Memoir and Letters of Sara Coleridge* (New York: Harper & Brothers, 1874), pp. 40–41.
13. Bradford Keyes Mudge, *Sara Coleridge: A Victorian Daughter: Her Life and Essays* (New Haven and London: Yale University Press, 1989), describes her neglect by and adoration of her father.
14. Judith W. Page, *Wordsworth and the Cultivation of Women* (Berkeley and London: University of California Press, 1994), describes his "three wives" in his assembly line of copying and recopying his poems, and concludes that "throughout his career Wordsworth sympathizes with female characters and cares deeply about the women in his life, but he is never really able to enter into another consciousness with what Keats referred to . . . as 'negative capability' " (p. 163).
15. Percy Bysshe Shelley, "Peter Bell the Third," part four, ll. 314–317, 331, *Shelley's Poetry and Prose*, ed. Donald H. Reiman and Sharon B. Powers (New York and London: W.W. Norton & Company, 1977), p. 335.
16. Beth Darlington, ed., *The Love Letters of William and Mary Wordsworth* (Ithaca, New York: Cornell University Press, 1981), pp. 229–230. But the heat in these letters is ringed by a coldness toward others; Wordsworth seems almost pleased to be able to tell his wife that Coleridge "has a world of bitter enemies, and is deplorably unpopular . . . But you cannot form a notion to what degree Coleridge is disliked or despised notwithstanding his great talents, his genius & vast attainments" (May 17–18, 1812; p. 163). I thank Marilyn Gaull for suggesting the parallel sexualities of Wordsworth and Coleridge.

4 Blank Faces and Fear of Ruin

1. Poem #49, "A Simile; Written after a Walk Before Supper," July–early August, 1792.
2. In a paper at the Coleridge Conference, July 2000, Niccola Trott read this rousing line of verse from poem #191, "Translation of Otfrid" (1799), an example of the "reverence for the female Sex" among the "Northern Nations." John Keats enjoyed describing women's bodies, too. In a letter to George and Georgiana Keats, Feb. 14–May 3, 1819, he spins metaphors for a thin woman: she is "a lath with a boddice"; "all feathers and bone"; "a lynch pin"; "a staff," "a walking-stick, fishing-rod, tooth-pick, hat-stick," "a flag on a pole."
3. *OM*, S. T. Coleridge, *Opus Maximum*, ed. Thomas McFarland, with Nicholas Halmi (London and Princeton, N.J.: Princeton University Press, 2002), p. 126, where he claims that "we need not travel to the wastes of Africa for Fetich worshippers. . . . It is the dire epidemic of man in the social state to forget the substance in the appearance, the essence in the form."
4. Mary Poovey, *The Proper Lady and the Woman Writer* (Chicago and London: University of Chicago Press, 1984), p. 12, writes that "throughout the course of the eighteenth century, husbands were becoming more expensive, or, to reverse the formula, women were becoming less valuable."
5. Ruth Yeazell, *Fictions of Modesty* (Chicago: University of Chicago Press, 1991); Lisa Plummer Crafton, " 'Insipid Decency': Modesty and Female Sexuality in Wollstonecraft," *European Romantic Review* 11, 3 (Summer, 2000), 277–299; Sonia Hofkosh, "Introduction: Invisible Girls," *Sexual Politics and the Romantic Author* (Cambridge: Cambridge University Press, 1998), pp. 5–6.
6. Yeats, "A Prayer for My Daughter" (June 1919) wishes that his baby girl not be granted "Beauty to make a stranger's eye distraught" or to lose her own "natural kindness," *The Collected Poems of William Butler Yeats* (New York: Macmillan, 1956), p. 186. Coleridge, by contrast, wishes to protect this girl from predators.
7. Coleridge's intermittent work on "Christabel" during this three-year period suggests a continuity of worry about the obliteration of the female person, perhaps with reference also to his mother's banishment of his only sister, as I have suggested in " 'Christabel' and the Phantom Soul," in *SEL: Studies in English Literature* 42, 4 (Autumn, 2002), 707–730. In a letter to Thomas Poole Oct. 31, 1801 (*CL* 2, 772–773) he praises a "lewd Boy" for being willing to repair the damage by marrying "a wanton Girl"; "If he do not, the Girl is hunted by Infamy, & perhaps hunted by it into the Toils of Guilt & habitual Depravity." "I take it for granted," he adds, "that the Girl is with child.—" Marlon B. Ross emphasizes the force of "propriety" in *The Contours of Masculine Desire: Romanticism and the Rise of Women's Poetry* (New York: Oxford University Press, 1989), p. 199.
8. Emmanuel Levinas, "On Max Picard," *Proper Names*, trans. Michael B. Smith (London: The Athlone Press, 1996 [original 1976]), p. 95. Levinas continues, "The personality in the *face* is at once the most irreplaceable, the

most unique, and that which constitutes intelligibility itself." David P. Haney, "Aesthetics and Ethics in Gadamer, Levinas, and Romanticism: Problems of Phronesis and Techne," *PMLA* 114, 1 (Jan. 1999), 41, applies the ethical demands of the human face in Emmanuel Levinas's *Totality* to dialogues with other persons in both Wordsworth and Coleridge. The presence of a " 'face coming from beyond the world, but committing [the observer] to human fraternity,' a face whose 'destitution cries out for justice' " explains the passionate humanity of the blind beggar in Wordsworth's *Prelude*, but it eludes analysis in Coleridge, where voice, I suspect, is the core of the person. Levinas's faces pose a problem for feminists, for Levinas assumes that the female face is passive and gentle, so that he, too, is drawn up short by the female mask of modesty and propriety.

9. In "Coleridge on Persons in Dialogue," *MLQ* 50, 4 (Dec. 1989), 362–363, I suggest that Coleridge's attention to voices in dialogue resembles Mikhail Bakhtin's formulation that "an independent, responsible and active discourse is *the* fundamental indicator of an ethical, legal and political human being," a "speaking person." In a related essay, "Coleridge on Persons and Things," *European Romantic Review* 1, 2 (Winter, 1991), I address the problem of women's dependencies.

10. Mays and James Engell, ed., *The Early Family Letters* (Oxford: Clarendon Press, 1994) have slightly different dates for Ann Coleridge's exile and death.

11. Coleridge, *The Early Family Letters*, ed. James Engell, letter no. 13 (August 1, 1783), pp. 54–55. Engell's note #4 suggests that this nameless girl is their half-sister Sarah who did end up marrying her seducer. For the fierce letter to his mother, see no. 12, p. 52, same date. Engell describes this coldness and duty in his introduction, pp. 16–17. The mother seems to have been willful, truculent, and aloof, reasons for Coleridge not to go to her deathbed.

12. R. W. Armour and R. F. Howes, eds., *Coleridge the Talker: A Series of Contemporary Descriptions and Comments* (Ithaca, N.Y.: Cornell University Press, 1940), p. 327.

13. Debbie Lee narrates this story of the imposter Hatfield in her "Forgeries," pp. 521–537, in Nick Roe, ed., *Romanticism: An Oxford Guide* (New York and London: Oxford University Press, 2005), pp. 533–536.

14. Rachel Simmons, *Odd Girl Out: The Hidden Culture of Aggression in Girls* (Orlando and New York: Harcourt, 2002) began a furor on the web about teenage bullying by girls (check under "mean girls"). Simmons connects the obligation to be nice and silent with the relational aggression aimed at harming the inner selves of other girls. Gainsborough's large painting is housed in The Frick Museum, New York.

15. In "(Dis)embodied Romance: 'Perdita' Robinson and William Wordsworth" in *Women, Nationalism and the Romantic State: Theatre and Politics in Britain, 1780–1800* (Cambridge: Cambridge University Press, 2001), p. 106, Betsy Bolton shows how public women, like Emma Hamilton and Georgiana, Duchess of Devonshire, are depicted as grossly physical creatures whenever they enter the political arena.

5 "Christabel" and the Vulnerability of Girls

I wish to thank my colleagues Elisabeth G. Gitter and Judith Ryan for their help with the thought and structure of this chapter.

1. Karen Swann, " 'Christabel' and the Enigma of Form," *Studies in Romanticism* 23, 4 (Winter, 1984), 533–555, describes the reader's puzzlement: " 'Christabel' contrives to have these alternatives redound on the reader, who continually feels mad or just stupid, unable to 'tell' how to characterize the verse at any given point" (545). The poem is #176 in *Poetical Works*.
2. In his preface, Coleridge insists on the originality of his poem, and adds "that the metre of Christabel is not, properly speaking, irregular, though it may seem so from its being founded on a new principle: namely, that of counting in each line the accents, not the syllables. Though the latter may vary from seven to twelve, yet in each line the accents will be found to be only four. Nevertheless, this occasional variation in number of syllables is not introduced wantonly, or for the mere ends of convenience, but in correspondence with some transition in the nature of the imagery or passion," *PW*, preface to poem #176, 1, 482–483. Marjorie Levinson, *The Romantic Fragment Poem: A Critique of a Form* (Chapel Hill and London: University of North Carolina Press, 1986), pp. 77–94, suggests that the meter derives from Coleridge's close study of Greek meters, which he practices in his notebooks and marginalia. I discuss Coleridge's intense work with various meters in "Coleridge and the Pleasures of Verse," *Studies in Romanticism* 40, 4 (Winter, 2001), 547–569.
3. Poem #700 "E Coelo Descendit," formerly "Self-Knowledge," from his last year, recapitulates his life long questions: can one make oneself, what is one's own, can one know more than the "Dark fluxion, all unfixable by thought, / A phantom dim of past and future wrought, / Vain sister of the worm?"
4. Susan Luther, *Christabel as Dream-Reverie* (Romantic Reassessment: Salzburg Studies in English Literature 61. Salzburg: Institut für Englishche Sprachen und Literatur, Universität Salzburg, 1976) p. 11; Jonas Spatz, "Mystery of Eros: Sexual Initiation in Coleridge's 'Christabel,' " *PMLA* 90 (Jan. 1975), 107–115; H. W. Piper, "Nature and the Gothic in Christabel" in *The Singing of Mount Abora: Coleridge's Use of Biblical Imagery and Natural Symbolism in Poetry and Philosophy* (Rutherford, NJ: Fairleigh Dickinson University Press, 1987), pp. 74–79; Coleridge, *Poems*, ed. John Beer (London: Dent, 1991), pp. 256–259.
5. Stuart Peterfreund, "Coleridge and the Problem of Evil," *ELH* 55, 1 (Spring, 1988), 125–152, discovers that Geraldine is "an anagram of *Dire Angel*." Laurence Lockridge, *Coleridge the Moralist* (Ithaca: Cornell University Press, 1977), bluntly calls her "pure evil."
6. Kathleen M. Wheeler, "Coleridge and Modern Critical Theory" in *Coleridge's Theory of Imagination Today*, ed. Christine Galant (New York, AMS Press, 1989), 90–92; Wheeler argues that Coleridge deconstructs meaning by "saturating the narrative voice with Henry Jamesian-type ambiguities, avowals, disavowals, questions, uncertainties," by overlayering naive and sophisticated narrative voices, by leaving open certain elements of the

plot, by weaving stories inside stories, and by giving conflicting interpretations of the bard's dream.
7. Anthony John Harding, "Mythopoesis: The unity of Christabel," in *Coleridge's Imagination: Essays in Memory of Peter Laver*, ed. Richard Gravil, Lucy Newlyn, and Nicholas Roe (Cambridge: Cambridge University Press, 1985), 207–217. But in "The Passions," *SWF* 2, 1421, Coleridge argues that separating body and soul is "mischievous."
8. Karen Swann, " 'Christabel' and the Enigma of Form," 533–555, sees all of the figures floating in and out of "the malady of hysteria, the womb whose vaporish fantasies were thought to block the hysteric's speech" (548). Swann's discovery of hysteria has important applications to Christabel's silence. But Claire Kahane, *Passions of the Voice: Hysteria, Narrative, and the Figure of the Speaking Woman, 1850–1915* (Baltimore: Johns Hopkins University Press, 1995), defines hysteria as the repressed rage from having to reject the maternal body; since Christabel had never known her mother, she had nothing to reject and no bond to break.
9. Chris Rubinstein, "Rousseau and Coleridge: Another Look at Christabel," *Coleridge Bulletin* (Winter, 1992), 9–14.
10. Coleridge's transitions, as Heather Jackson, "Coleridge's Lessons in Transition: The 'Logic' of the 'Wildest Odes' " in *Lessons of Romanticism: A Critical Companion*, ed. Thomas Pfau and Robert F. Gleckner (Durham and London: Duke University Press, 1998), p. 220, has marvelously clarified, are "invisible, occurring in the blank spaces between sentences or stanzas. They conform to Coleridge's general preference for energy over matter in physical models of the universe and for mystery over evidence in the area of religious faith," a fine conceptualization of the "intangible powers," the subtle interconnections of thought, that characterize Coleridge's "method."
11. Tilottama Rajan, *The Supplement of Reading: Figures of Understanding in Romantic Theory and Practice* (Ithaca and London: Cornell University Press, 1990), p. 26, suggests that "meaning" that is hidden in one work may be "made explicit somewhere else in the canon." The reader, adding his "supplement," "break[s] the hermeneutic circle at the level of the oeuvre, projecting into the individual text a set of meanings that it does not have in isolation, and perhaps even reversing the reading that emerges when the text is made its own context." In applying to "Christabel" themes and ideas that appear in Coleridge's own earlier and later writings I hope to be bringing to the surface meanings hidden in this one poem that are apparent elsewhere.
12. As in an 1811 essay in *The Courier*, in *EOT* 3, 235 and *BL* 1, 205.
13. As in his 1795 lecture on the slave trade, Lewis Patton and Peter Mann, eds., *Lectures 1795 On Politics and Religion*, pp. 242–243; in R. J. White, ed., *LS*, pp. 207, 218–220; and in *Constitution of Church and State*, ed. John Colmer, pp. 15–16.
14. As in *The Friend*, 2, pp. 44, 71, 125. Other references to persons and things can be found in Anya Taylor, *Coleridge's Defense of the Human* (Columbus, OH: Ohio State University Press, 1986); Anya Taylor, *Coleridge: On Humanity* in *Coleridge's Writings*, ed. John Beer (London and New York: Macmillan and St. Martin's, 1994); and Anya Taylor, "Coleridge on Persons

in Dialogue," *MLQ* 50, 4 (Dec. 1989), 357–374 and "Coleridge on Persons and Things," *European Romantic Review*, 1 (Winter, 1991), 163–180.

15. John Beer, *Coleridge the Visionary* (New York: Collier, 1962), pp. 150–152, explains that "the word 'preternatural' seems with him to carry a certain pejorative force, from which the word 'supernatural' is exempt, and it is not unlikely that he intended, when he wrote his poems, to distinguish between literature which simply made use of supernatural 'machinery' for the sake of sensationalism, and that which was concerned with the possible significance of extra-sensory phenomena as a revelation of the metaphysical."

16. Later in life he continues to believe that his weakness is "a readiness to believe others my superiors and to surrender my own judgment to their's" (*CL* 5, 231).

17. Marlon B. Ross, *The Contours of Masculine Desire: Romanticism and the Rise of Women's Poetry* (New York: Oxford University Press, 1989), pp. 93–108, where he writes, for instance, that "As the 'active' agent asserts its power by permeating the 'passive' medium, it also gives itself to that medium and becomes possessed by it" (95) and "What Wordsworth joins, Coleridge subtly tears asunder" (101).

18. Donald-Reiman, "Coleridge and the Art of Equivocation," *SIR* 25 (Fall, 1986), 325–350.

19. Diane Long Hoeveler, *Romantic Androgyny: The Women Within* (University Park and London: Pennsylvania State University Press, 1979), pp. 176–188. She finds that the poem "reveals a fear and hatred of women" and "his conscious and unconscious opinion of them as perverse, sexually voracious, predatory, and duplicitous" (176). By contrast, Tim Fulford, *Romanticism and Masculinity*, interprets Coleridge's androgyny as an impulse toward inclusiveness.

20. Madelon Sprengnether, *The Spectral Mother: Freud, Feminism, and Psychoanalysis* (Ithaca and London: Cornell University Press, 1990) illuminates the power of the mother. Countering Freud's attention to the father and the phallus, she turns to the biologism of the mother's body: "No longer an exile from the process of signification, the body of the (m)other may actually provide a new, material, ground for understanding the play of language and desire" (10). Sprengnether writes, "Whereas object relations theory stresses maternal presence (and plenitude) through the concept of mother-infant fusion, Lacan downplays the role of the biological mother to the point where she barely seems to exist in a corporeal sense" (183). The recognition that the mother is a real body with a face and a breast, a being whose absence would be a deprivation, fulfills Coleridge's insights, and shows his connection to John Bowlby, D. W. Winnicott, and other Object Relations psychologists.

21. Here again Sprengnether helps to explain Coleridge's work on the loss of the mother and the crisis that forces identity. She writes, "the loss that precipitates the organization of a self is always implicitly the loss of a mother . . . The mother's body becomes that which is longed for yet cannot be appropriated, a representative of both home and not home, and hence, in Freud's terms, the site of the uncanny" (8).

22. David L. Clark, "Heidegger's Craving: Being-on-Schelling," *Diacritics* 27, 3, 8–33, writes of Schelling in a way that can be applied to Coleridge's "Christabel": "Primal craving is an important part of a more extensive rhetoric of affective states and borderline conditions (including melancholy)—in other words, a body language of 'flesh and blood' " (17).
23. His capacity for friendship with women is in dispute. Heather J. Jackson, "Coleridge's Women, or Girls, Girls, Girls Are Made to Love," *SIR* 32, 4 (Winter, 1993), 577–600, argues that he takes a dim view of female intelligence, while Reggie Watters, "Coleridge, Female Friendship, and 'Lines Written at Shurton Bars,' " *The Coleridge Bulletin* (Spring, 2000), 1–16, believes that he welcomes companionate love.
24. Julie Carlson, "Gender," in *The Cambridge Companion to Coleridge*, ed. Lucy Newlyn (Cambridge: Cambridge University Press, 2002), p. 213.
25. Camille Paglia, *Sexual Personae: Art and Decadence from Nefertiti to Emily Dickinson* (London and New Haven: Yale University Press, 1990), pp. 331–346.
26. To borrow a term from Mark M. Hennelly, Jr. " 'As Well Fill Up the Space Between': A Liminal Reading of *Christabel*," *SIR* 38 (Summer, 1999), 203–222, a witty application of Victor Turner's anthropological work on initiations.
27. *CM* 2, 131, notes that Coleridge borrowed Henry Boyd's translation of the *Inferno* from the Bristol library in late June 1796. "Soon after, he noted a project for a 'Poem in one Book in the manner of Dante on the excursion of Thor—' " (*CN* 1, 170). Ralph Pite, *The Circle of our Vision: Dante's Presence in English Romantic Poetry* (Oxford: Clarendon, 1994), mentions Coleridge's use of Henry Boyd's translation in 1796 (p. 69), but finds Dantean images only in the late poems such as "Ne Plus Ultra" and "Limbo." I believe that "Christabel" shows the influence of the 1796 reading of Dante.
28. Jack Stillinger, *Coleridge and Textual Instability: The Multiple Versons of the Major Poems* (New York: Oxford University Press, 1994), p. 80, writes "While the numerous substantive differences among the texts have their local effects and exemplify Coleridge's rhetorical skills as reviser, none of the rewritten passages alters the plot (such as it is), the characters, or the themes of the fragment. The most interesting revisions occur not in the verse but in a series of *Mariner*-like glosses that Coleridge added in the margins of one of the annotated 1816s at Princeton." For the smudging of the details about Geraldine's breast or side, see p. 88. In *Revision and Romantic Authorship* (Oxford: Oxford University Press, 1996), p. 142, Zachary Leader argues against Stillinger that Coleridge's revisions are efforts to achieve perfection rather than signs that the text is unstable and the meaning uncertain.
29. Percy Bysshe Shelley, *The Cenci* 3, 1, lines 26–28, in Donald H. Reiman and Sharon B. Powers, eds., *Shelley's Poetry and Prose* (New York: Norton, 1977), p. 262.
30. Both Coleridge and Shelley may also draw from Dante's Vanni Fucci as he stumbles blinking and stupefied from his solitary prison (*Inferno*, 24, 112–118).
31. My understanding of the yearning and loneliness of daughters who lose their mothers comes from Hope Edelman, *Motherless Daughters: The Legacy*

of Loss (Reading, MA: Addison-Wesley Publishing Company, 1994). But even Edelman has no chapter on girls who never know their mother. Coppelia Kahn explores the effect of the absent mother on the hysteria of King Lear himself, but not on the daughters left in his erratic care in "The Absent Mother in 'King Lear' " in *King Lear: Contemporary Critical Essays*, ed. Kiernan Ryan (New York: St. Martin's Press, 1992), pp. 92–113.

32. After arguing into the night with Southey about incest and other taboos, Coleridge writes in his notebook that the so-called crime against Nature is in many countries "a bagatelle, a fashionable Levity" (Nov. 1803; *CN* 1637).
33. John Beer, *Coleridge's Poetic Intelligence* (New York: Barnes and Noble, 1977), p. 233, writes that "if the acting self has lost contact with its own organic centre, it will be at the mercy of the energies that have invaded it, able only to mirror back a reflection of their form."
34. Alice Miller, *The Drama of the Gifted Child: How Narcissistic Parents Form and Deform the Emotional Lives of their Talented Children* (originally published as *Prisoners of Childhood*), trans. Ruth Ward (New York: Basic Books, 1981).
35. I have described these spells and incantations, and their relation to passions, in "Coleridge and the Potent Voice," *Magic and English Romanticism* (Athens, Georgia: University of Georgia Press, 1979), pp. 99–133.
36. In Samuel Hearne, *A Journey to the Northern Ocean* (1795); Coleridge's copy is from Dublin, 1796, noted in *CN* 1637 note (Nov. 1803).
37. I discuss the father and son interchange in chapter five, "In the Cave of the Gnome," of *Bacchus in Romantic England: Writers and Drink 1780–1830* (Basingstoke and New York: Macmillan and St. Martin's Press, 1999), pp. 126–156.
38. Lyn Mikel Brown and Carol Gilligan, *Meeting at the Crossroads: Women's Psychology and Girls' Development* (Cambridge: Harvard University Press, 1992), describe the "self-silencing," fear of conflict, and "corrosive suffering" of girls at the onset of puberty.
39. Karen Horney, "The Flight from Womanhood" (1926), "Inhibited Femininity" (1926–1927), and "The Denial of the Vagina" (1933), in *Feminine Psychology*, ed. Harold Kelman (New York: Norton, 1967), tries to readjust the study of woman's development from a woman's point of view. Coleridge in "Christabel" seems to be struggling with some such realization that male and female developments are not identical.
40. Cited by John Beer, "Coleridge and his Critics," *Samuel Taylor Coleridge: Poems* (London: Dent, 1993), pp. 505–506.
41. George Felton Mathew in *European Magazine* (1816), in *Coleridge, the Critical Heritage*, ed. J. R. de J. Jackson (New York: Barnes & Noble, 1970), p. 241.
42. James Engell, ed., *Coleridge: The Early Family Letters* (Oxford: Clarendon Press, 1994), pp. 52–55, 96.
43. Meena Alexander, *Women in Romanticism: Mary Wollstonecraft, Dorothy Wordsworth, and Mary Shelley* (Basingstoke: Macmillan, 1989), pp. 86, 87, 103, 118.

44. Jessica Benjamin, *Like Subjects, Love Objects: Essays on Recognition and Sexual Difference* (New Haven: Yale University Press, 1995), p. 150.
45. Including the motherless heroine of "Ruth," a poem Coleridge wished that he had written. Judith W. Page, *Wordsworth and the Cultivation of Women*, reveals a wealth of information on Wordsworth's women friends and helpers.
46. Coleridge's notebooks for this hike record detailed vistas but do not mention the treasure tucked in his pocket.
47. Mary Moorman, ed., *Journals of Dorothy Wordsworth* (Oxford and New York: Oxford University Press, 1971), p. 43.
48. Richard Holmes, *Early Visions* (New York: Viking, 1989), pp. 281–286; Holmes, *Coleridge: Darker Reflections, 1804–1834* (New York: Pantheon, 1998), p. 458: Might Wordsworth's complete silence about "Christabel" after its 1816 publication hint at a resentment at some reference to his own absorption of his sister?
49. Susan Eilenberg, *Strange Power of Speech: Wordsworth, Coleridge, & Literary Possession* (New York: Oxford University Press, 1992), pp. 87–107, p. 99.
50. With some ironies Coleridge calls this interloper poem "mild" and "unassuming" but "full of beauties to those short-necked men who have their hearts sufficiently near their heads—the relative distance of which (according to Citizen Tourdes, the French Translator of Spallanzani [a work on circulation]) determines the sagacity or stupidity of all Bipeds & Quadrupeds" (*CL* 1, 649).
51. Jack Stillinger, *Coleridge and Textual Instability: The Multiple Versions of the Major Poems* (New York: Oxford University Press, 1994), pp. 78–91 and 189–215.
52. Tilottama Rajan, "Coleridge's Conversation with Hermeneutics," in *The Supplement of Reading* (Ithaca: Cornell University Press, 1990), p. 114, writing about Coleridge's effort to understand Charles Lamb's experience in "This Lime Tree Bower My Prison."
53. This malaise is probed by Julia Kristeva, *Powers of Horror: An Essay on Abjection*, trans. Leon S. Roudiez (New York: Columbia University Press, 1982), pp. 1–90, as a turmoil.

6 Sara Hutchinson: Love and Reading

1. *CL* 3, 76, #682; Feb. 18, 1808.
2. Southey, explaining his fondness for Caroline Bowles, tells his grown daughter Bertha that "since Miss Hutchinsons death there has been no woman with whom I have been so intimate, or for whom I have entertained so high a regard" (Oct. 1838; *CL* 2, 479). He, too, seems to have come to favor Sara Hutchinson over his original girlfriend Sara F. Coleridge.
3. John Worthen, *The Gang* (New Haven and London: Yale University Press, 2002), pp. 93–95. But see Mays, *PW*, headnote to #605.
4. In *Lyrical Ballads 1800* Coleridge calls the poem "Love" and detaches it from its original genesis as "The Introduction to the Tale of the Dark

Ladie." This "introduction" does not describe the poem "Love" at all, since it promises "cruel wrongs" rather than mutual passions; see R. L. Brett and A. R. Jones, eds., *Wordsworth and Coleridge, Lyrical Ballads*, 2nd edition (London: Routledge & Kegan Paul, 1991), pp. 119–123 and note pp. 298–299. The "pernicious wrongs" mentioned in the attached material in *Poetical Works* apply to "Christabel," "The Ballad of the Dark Ladie," and "The Three Graves" but not to "Love." To embed "Love" in "The Introduction to the Tale of the Dark Ladie" as the new edition does is to warp the meaning, to darken the joy.

5. J. C. C. Mays, "Coleridge's 'Love': All he can manage, more than he could," in *Coleridge's Visionary Languages*, ed. Tim Fulford and Morton D. Paley (Cambridge: D.S. Brewer, 1993), pp. 49–66, p. 53. Tim Fulford, *Romanticism and Masculinity* (London: Macmillan Press, 1999), pp. 108–110, mentions "Love" briefly, saying that the "knight is a chivalric defender of chastity and propriety—a hero for middle class respectability. The narrator, however, does not act. The poem as a whole is consequently a commentary on Coleridge's need to derive his masculine authority from another, and it shows that it is by poetic imagination that he can do so." Morton D. Paley, *Coleridge's Later Poetry* (Oxford: Clarendon Press, 1996), starts too late to mention the 1799 "Love," and is too general to note the tangles of passion and jealousy in the later love poems discussed in his chapter four, entitled "Love," pp. 91–113.

6. Although the editor's note to line 41 suggests that the knight is suffering from an inward scorn akin to Godwin's intellectual pride, the scorn may instead be the Lady's cruelty to him for ten long years, and he is "craz'd" by her "cruel scorn" (ll. 41–42). As he lay dying after rescuing her "from outrage worse than death" (l. 55), she wept, "And ever strove to expiate / The scorn that crazed his brain" (ll. 59–60). She nursed him in a cave, and his madness went away before he died. This Lady's scornful rejection and loss rouse the woman in the frame to show her love and carpe diem.

7. Mays's headnote to the poem, *PW* 2, #605. Avi Sharon, "Touching Words: Finding Tradition through Translation Among Seferis, Eliot, and Keats," *Arion: A Journal of Humanities and the Classics* 11, 3 (Winter, 2004), narrates the sequence of events between meeting Coleridge on Hampstead Heath, April 11, 1819 and writing the first draft of "La Belle Dame Sans Merci," April 21. He writes, "Four days later, on April 15, Keats read to Fanny from the fifth Canto of Dante's *Inferno* of the doomed and damning love of Paolo and Francesca, and that very night Keats dreamt of himself in the same nether region, afterward recalling that 'it was one of the most delightful enjoyments I ever had in my life.' " Inspired by this dream, Keats wrote a sonnet which Fanny later copied into the flyleaf of his Dante and which concludes with these lines:

> Pale were the sweet lips I saw
> Pale were the lips I kiss'd and fair the form
> I floated with about that melancholy storm.

Just days after this vision, on April 21, in a letter to his brother George, then in America, Keats copied out the first version of that dreamlike poem that would so ominously express his helpless attraction to Fanny Brawne, 'La Belle Dame Sans Merci' " (pp. 52–53). The intertexual play of love poems branching out from Dante's fifth canto reaches on to Leigh Hunt's "Story of Rimini."

8. Eric C. Brown, "Boyd's Dante, Coleridge's *Ancient Mariner*, and the Pattern of Infernal Influence," *SEL* 38 (1998), 649–655, 647–667. Brown argues that "the inattention to Boyd's translation is remarkable" (648).

9. Henry Boyd, A. M., *A Translation of the Inferno of Dante Alighieri, in English Verse, with Historical Notes, and the Life of Dante, to which is Added a Specimen of a New Translation of the Orlando Furioso of Ariosto* (London: C Dilly, 1785), 2 vols., canto the fifth, pp. 249–261.

10. Paolo Valesio, "Canto V," in Allen Mandelbaum et al., eds., *Inferno: A Canto-by-Canto Commentary* (Berkeley: University California Press, 1998), pp. 71–72.

11. Jacqueline Pearson, *Women's Reading in Britain: 1750–1835* (Cambridge: Cambridge University Press, 1999), p. 112.

12. In chapter 10 we see that Coleridge turns in late middle age to model himself on Boccaccio's Prince Galleoto, continuing his Italian theme of love.

13. This hair art is analyzed in Elisabeth G. Gitter, "The Power of Women's Hair in the Victorian Imagination," *PMLA* 99 (October 1984), 936–954.

14. Morton Paley, *Coleridge's Later Poetry* (Oxford: Clarendon Press, 1996), p. 100, mentions the use of courtly love tropes.

15. S. T. Coleridge, ESQ, *Sibylline Leaves: A Collection of Poems* (London: Rest Fenner, 23 Paternoster Roe, 1817), p. 118. Petrarch's letter appears in long form in *CN* 1478 from Feb. to June 1813; Kathleen Coburn translates it in her note to 1478. I thank Nicholas Halmi for help in piecing together this information.

16. See Lucy Newlyn, *Coleridge, Wordsworth and the Language of Allusion* (Oxford: Oxford University Press, 2001), pp. 61 and 70. Paul Magnuson, *Coleridge and Wordsworth: A Lyrical Dialogue* (Princeton: Princeton University Press, 1988), pp. 289–308, places Sara at the center of the poem to her.

17. Michael Camille, *The Medieval Art of Love: Objects and Subjects of Desire* (New York: Harry N. Abrams, 1998), pp. 78–79.

18. See *CN* 3, entries 3284, 3442, 4036; but cf 1, 1065 and 3, 4297.

19. *The Letters of Charles and Mary Lamb*, ed. Edwin W. Marrs, Jr., 3 vols (Ithaca and London: Cornell University Press, 1978), pp. 3, 160–162.

20. Richard Holmes, *Darker Reflections, 1804–34* (New York: Pantheon, 1998), pp. 176–199, only imagines the simmering desires and frustrations as the hopeless lovers lean together near the lamp in the dark room night after night. George Whalley in *Coleridge and Sara Hutchinson*, pp. 73–74, claims: "That she loved him and had a sympathetic understanding of his condition—an understanding unclouded by illusions—is made clear by her later correspondence with Crabb Robinson," 1811–1813.

7 Hearkening to the Voices of Women

1. *SWF* 1, 358. This is the movement from "Behold!" to "Listen!" to apply the later 1805 formulation in Wordsworth's "The Solitary Reaper" and to anticipate John Hollander's division of poetry in *Vision and Resonance: Two Senses of Poetic Form* (New York: Oxford University Press, 1975).
2. Jonathan Ree, *I See a Voice: Deafness, Language and the Senses—A Philosophical History* (New York: Metropolitan Books, Henry Holt, 1999), p. 61. Ree quotes Hegel's *Philosophy of Mind*, 401: " 'It is primarily through the voice that people make known their inwardness, for they put into it what they are.' " The voice objectifies subjectivity (p. 60). I thank Professor Elisabeth Gitter for this reference.
3. In "From *Lyrical Ballads* to *Lyrical Tales*," *SIR* 40, 4 (Winter 2002), pp. 590–593, Ashley Cross outlines a tradition, begun by Mary Robinson herself, of seeing the woman singer as marginal to the inspired poet, whereas I argue here that he is humbly scribbling in her margin.
4. Ashley Cross, "Harping on Mary Robinson," discusses the interplay of Coleridge and his friend Mary Robinson in this poem, in *Fellow Romanticists*, ed. Beth Lau, forthcoming.
5. Amanda Foreman, *Georgiana, Duchess of Devonshire* (New York: Random House, 1988).
6. Betsy Bolton, *Women, Nationalism, and the Romantic Stage*, pp. 30–39, 45–48, describes the focus on Georgiana's sexuality as a way of undermining her intelligence.
7. Duncan Wu, ed., *Romantic Women Poets: An Anthology* (Oxford: Blackwell Publishers, 1997), p. 176, ll. 93–96.
8. For authenticating emotion by means of quotations, see Adela Pinch, *Strange Fits of Passion: Epistemologies of Emotion, Hume to Austen* (Palo Alto: Stanford University Press, 1996), p. 169.
9. Eric Griffith, *The Printed Voice in Victorian Poetry* (Oxford: Clarendon Press, 1989), pp. 95–96.
10. Matthew Campbell, *Rhythm and Will in Victorian Poetry* (Cambridge: Cambridge University Press, 1999), p. 5.
11. Marilyn Gaull, *English Romanticism: The Human Context* (New York: W. W. Norton, 1988), p. 98. Chapter 4, "The Theater," initiates the interest in theatricality and melodrama in recent writing on the Romantic period. See her earlier "Romantic Theater," *The Wordsworth Circle* 14 (1983), pp. 255–263.
12. In her chapter "Sarah Siddons and the Performative Female," in *Romantic Theatricality: Gender, Poetry, and Spectatorship* (Ithaca and London: Cornell University Press, 1997), p. 21.
13. Judith, Pascoe, "Embodying Marie Antoinette: The Theatricalized Female Subject," pp. 95–129. For the influence of Mrs. Siddons on Mary Robinson, see Pascoe's chapter "The Spectacular Flaneuse," p. 120.
14. Julie Carlson, *In the Theatre of Romanticism: Coleridge, Nationalism, Women* (Cambridge University Press, 1994), pp. 117–122; 29. For more on the large new field of women and theater see also Tracy C. Davis and Ellen Donking, eds., *Women and Playwrighting in Nineteenth Century Britain*

(Cambridge: Cambridge University Press, 1999) and Catherine Burroughs, ed. *Women in British Romantic Theatre: Drama, Performance, and Society 1790–1840* (Cambridge: Cambridge University Press, 2000). Coleridge also praises the actress "Miss Hudson" to Lord Byron, noting particularly her skill in balancing the metrical line with natural rhythms of speech (*CL* 4, 599); from a skilled metrist, this praise is supreme.

15. Iain McCalman, ed., *The Oxford Companion to the Romantic Age* (New York: Oxford University Press, 2001) has done a great service to the field in enumerating these divas.
16. Susan Levin, "The Gipsy is a Jewess: Hariett Abrams and Theatrical Romanticism," in Paula R. Feldman and Theresa M. Kelley, eds., *Romantic Women Writers: Voices and Countervoices* (Hanover and London: University Press of New England, 1995), pp. 236–251 and notes 312–314.
17. Coleridge admires Mr. Dibdin's "excellent songs" as Mays shows in the headnote to poem #321, 1799–1802, "Westphalian Song."
18. Angela Esterhammer, "The Practice of Improvisation in European Romanticism," examines this Italian facility and its skeptical reception in northern Europe. In "Romantic Improvvisatori: Coleridge, L. E. L., and the Difficulties of Loving," *PQ* 79, 4 (Fall, 2000), 501–522, I show how Coleridge engaged the women poets of his day in a dramatized drawing room.
19. Rachel Cowgill, Paula Gillett, and Simon McVeigh, Music entries in *An Oxford Companion to the Romantic Age: British Culture 1776–1832*, ed. Iain McCalman (New York: Oxford University Press, 1999).
20. *Lects Lit* 2, 210.
21. Gary Schmidgall, *Shakespeare and Opera* (New York: Oxford University, Press, 1990), pp. 34, 20, 39. See Elisabeth Bronfen, " 'Lasciatemi Morir': Representations of the Diva's Swan Song," *MLQ* 53, 4.
22. Wayne Koestenbaum, *The Queen's Throat: Opera, Homosexuality, and the Mysteries of Desire* (New York: Poseidon Press, 1993), pp. 42–43, 183–184.
23. Charles Lamb warns him about this potential calumny, which might be against "Mrs. Gertrude Elizabeth Mara (1749–1833), a popular singer who performed in London from 1784–1787 and from 1790–1802," *The Letters of Charles and Mary Anne Lamb*, vol. 1, p. 42 and note 12.
24. Theodor W. Adorno, "Some Ideas on the Sociology of Music," *Sound Figures*, trans. Rodney Livingstone (Stanford: Stanford University Press, 1999), p. 2, writes that performances such as those of Beethoven "supply consumers with prestige and even with emotions that they do not themselves possess but to which their nature cannot remain immune."
25. Amanda Eubanks Winkler, "Madness and the Prophetic Voice: Musical Prognostication on the Late Seventeenth-Century English Stage" (delivered at NEASECS conference 2002), cites a well-known song by Henry Purcell, "Beneath a poplar's shadow" (1702), where the diva sings "I swell . . . and am bigger, I swell. . . .," with trilling between words. Coleridge tells his interlocutors (July 6, 1833), "I like Beethoven and Mozart. . . . And I love Purcell" (*TT* 2, 244).

26. To use part of the title of Bruce R. Smith, *The Acoustic World of Early Modern England: Attending to the O-Factor* (Chicago: University of Chicago Press, 1999).
27. For a close analysis of how technique reflects consciousness, see Marshall Brown, "Mozart and After: The Revolution in Musical Consciousness," in *Turning Points: Essays in the History of Cultural Expressions* (Stanford, CA: Stanford University Press, 1997), pp. 138–155; Brown describes Mozart's "new way of thinking or, yet, of dreaming in musical forms, a mood of intense self-absorption that is favored even in the operas" (p. 153).
28. In the version of the poem printed in the *Morning Post,* Sept. 24, 1799, three additional stanzas of irregular length turn this accomplished music toward political activism, marching together "with trump and timbrel clang, and popular shout, / To celebrate the shame and absolute rout," perhaps, E. H. Coleridge conjectures, at the battle of Novi over Napoleon's troops led by Joubert. See Ernest Hartley Coleridge, ed., *The Poems* (London: Oxford University Press, 1960), pp. 324–325.
29. Graham Davidson,"Coleridge in Malta: Figures in a Landscape," *Coleridge Bulletin* 19 NS (Spring, 2002), 84–85.
30. J. Robert Barth, S. J., *Coleridge and the Power of Love* (Columbia: University of Missouri, 1988), pp. 91–97; "Whatever else it is, the 'Letter to Sara' is a poem about love and its loss" (p. 94); " 'Dejection' . . . becomes a love power in a broader and deeper sense—not merely the lament of a frustrated lover but an ode to the power of love itself" (p. 97).
31. Michael John Kooy, "The Clerisy and Aesthetic Education," in *Coleridge, Schiller, and Aesthetic Education* (New York: Palgrave, 2002), pp. 178–179.
32. Paul H. Fry, "The Wedding Guest in 'Dejection,' " in *The Poet's Calling in the English Ode* (New Haven: Yale University Press, 1980), pp. 175 and 178.
33. Edward Kessler, *Coleridge's Metaphors of Being* (Princeton: Princeton University Press, 1979), pp. 24 and 50.
34. Zachary Leader, *Revision and Romantic Authorship* (Oxford: Oxford University Press, 1996), p. 138; for revisions from Letter to Ode, see pp. 150–154.

8 Divorce and the Law

1. The debates are recorded in *Parliamentary History of England from the Earliest Period to the Year 1803* (Peterborough Court: T. C. Hansard, 1819), vols. 34 and 35. Individual bills for divorce—Addison's and *Eeson's*—seem to have aroused the lords to address the Standing Order 142 at length, beginning on March 21, 1800 (vol. 34, column 1552–1562). Vol. 35, columns 226–326, recounts the continuing debate (going to May 19, 1800), under the title "Adultery Prevention Bill." Standing Order 142 requires the aggrieved husband to repeat his charges a third time. This Standing Order is the pretext for a comprehensive scheme to stop adulteresses from making such humiliation necessary in the first place.

2. *England and Wales Parliamentary Proceedings 1660–1796, 3 vols; Eighteenth Century*, reel 4815, no. 03. London: J. Debrett, 1797; Microfilm. Woodbridge, Ct. Research Publications, Inc., 1986. Vol. 3, p. 592, June 10, 1773. After refusing to hear a particularly seamy divorce case (Eeson's divorce bill, *Parliamentary Debates,* vol. 33, Mar. 2, 1798, column 1306–1310), Lord Chancellor Lloyd Kenyon promised to create a resolution to control the grossest collusions between parties, and this promise resulted in Standing Order 142, virtually a repetition of the 1773 Standing Order. Thus the debates at the turn of the century began in an effort to control the males, and ended with bills to punish the female at the center.
3. Samuel Taylor Coleridge, "Lecture on the Slave-Trade," *Lects 1795*, p. 244 and note 5. The Duke's maiden speech on May 3, 1792 showed little fairness to African slaves traded on British vessels.
4. Molly Lefebure, *The Bondage of Love: A Life of Mrs. Samuel Taylor Coleridge* (New York: Norton, 1986), pp. 52–53, believes that they were exultantly happy.
5. To Southey, for example, he writes that she is a good mother but as a woman has no sympathy for his ideas or infirmities. I thank Michael Gitter for help in translating this passage.
6. *CN*, 650, Feb. 1800. Kathleen Coburn comments that "from April to June the papers were full of it." Coburn intuits that the pregnant Sara may have regarded these months as "crucial in her marriage" (note to entry 712).
7. See Anya Taylor, "Coleridge, Wollstonecraft, and the Rights of Women," pp. 83–98.
8. Godwin published this two volume fiction in 1798, see *Maria or The Wrongs of Woman*, introd. Moira Ferguson (New York: Norton, 1975), p. 16. Coleridge does not mention this fiction but, visiting William Godwin's home often during his stay in London, he must have seen these volumes published the year before.
9. Might his reference to the use of great endowments to undermine a community's trust suggest his reading of Dante's cantos on Fraud including fraudulent seduction, so much lower in hell than lust and adultery? His early knowledge of Dante through Boyd's translation has been discussed in chapter 6.
10. Lawrence Stone, *The Road to Divorce* (Oxford University Press, 1990), p. 26.
11. Such love is evident in the case of Middleton versus Middleton narrated by Lawrence Stone in *Broken Lives: Separation and Divorce in England 1660–1857* where Clara Louisa Middleton made overtures of love to her young Mellors-like groom John Rose and pursued him in secret meetings for the next decade, while household spies vied to inform her innocent husband William. As Stone summarizes, the results were "ironically a tragedy for all parties involved. By the time William Middleton had completed his fanatical vendetta in 1796, he was a broken-hearted recluse. He had killed his wife's favourite dog and horse, destroyed her reputation by publicly exposing her as an adulteress with a stable boy, closed up his country seat, discharged most of his servants, and sent his [eight] children off to boarding

school." Clara Louisa was ruined and lived another 38 years in "obloquy" (246–247). Carlisle mentions Mrs. Middleton with disgust (col. 280).
12. Keith Thomas, "The Double Standard," *Journal of the History of Ideas* 20, 1 (1959), 195–216, cites prostitution, divorce, and the laws related to property of married persons as the chief categories for the exercise of the double standard.
13. Debbie Lee, *Slavery and the Romantic Imagination* (Philadelphia: University of Pennsylvania Press, 2002) sets this disturbing aspect of Romanticism in a philosophical context of looking at alterity; Jon-Christian Suggs, *Whispered Consolations: Law and Narrative in African American Life* (Ann Arbor: University of Michigan Press, 2000), pp. 19–30, uses the words of slaves to describe what it feels like to be property; Anya Taylor, *Coleridge's Defense of the Human* (Columbus: Ohio State University Press, 1986), pp. 14–16 and 35–60, sets slavery in the context of Coleridge's rage at the dehumanization of persons.
14. Blackstone writes, "By marriage, the husband and wife are one person in law: that is, the very being or legal existence of the woman is suspended during the marriage; or at least is incorporated and consolidated into that of the husband; under whose wing, protection, and cover, she performs everything; and is therefore called in our law—French, a feme covert, and is said to be under the protection and influence of her husband, her baron, or lord, and her condition during her marriage is called her coverture. . . . For this reason, a man cannot grant anything to his wife, or enter into covenant with her: for the grant would be to suppose her separate existence; and to convenant with her, would be only to covenant with himself," in J. W. Ehrlich, *Erlich's Blackstone: Part One, Rights of Persons, Rights of Things* (New York: Capricorn Books, 1959), 78–86.
15. *The Essay on Property*, ed. H. S. Salt (London: George Allen and Unwin Ltd. 1890; rept. 1949), pp. 103–104.
16. Samuel Pyeatt Menefee, *Wives for Sale: An Ethnographic Study of British Popular Divorce* (New York: St. Martin's Press, 1981).
17. Amy Louise Erickson, *Women and Property in Early Modern England* (New York: Routledge, 1995).
18. Barbara J. Harris, *English Aristocratic Women 1450–1550* (New York: Oxford University Press, 2002), pp. 82–87.
19. A similar degeneration had occurred in classical Athens, where women lost the freedoms that their foremothers had enjoyed in the Archaic period; autonomous persons in the eighth century B.C.E, women in the fifth century were enclosed in their homes, their names not used in public. See Elaine Fantham, Helene Peet Foley, Natalie Boymel Kampen, Sarah B. Pomeroy, and H. A. Shapiro, *Women in the Classical World: Image and Text* (New York: Oxford University Press, 1994), pp. 39, 79, 101, 109–112, 113–115.
20. April London, *Women and Property in the Eighteenth-Century Novel* (Cambridge: Cambridge University Press, 1999), pp. 2 and 8.
21. This unique injunction was, ironically, instituted by Henry VIII, who in fact "never did obtain a divorce." For a summary of the stages of court

appearances in this complex process, see Allen Horstman, "The Origins," *Victorian Divorce* (London and Sydney: Croom Helm, 1985), pp. 1–5.
22. Allen Horstman, "The Origins," *Victorian Divorce*, p. 13.
23. Debate in the Lords on Taylor's Divorce Bill, March 19, 1801, Parliamentary Debates, vol. 35, cols. 1248–1264. This adultery was flagrant in that Mrs. Taylor's lover for four years was the clergyman in their obscure country town in Devonshire.
24. David Erdman calls this poem a new ascription, not a conjectural one. Fulford places the poem in the context of the new science in "Coleridge, Darwin, Linnaeus: The Sexual Politics of Botany," *TWC* 28, 3 (Summer, 1997), 124–130.
25. William Wilberforce orates passionately on May 30, 1800, cols. 320–322.
26. Dickens saw the burdens of the law against divorce from a husband's point of view. See *Hard Times*, chapter 11, "No Way Out," and see Margaret Simpson, *The Companion to Hard Times* (Westport, CT: Greenwood Press, 1997), pp. 8–9, 132–138, for his collaboration with Caroline Sheridan Norton on what eventually became the Married Women's Property Bill in 1857.
27. Tim Fulford discusses the Queen Caroline Affair with its sordid spies, green bags, and rerouted corteges in *Romanticism and Masculinity*, pp. 156–176.
28. Dorothy Wordsworth quotes SFC to Catherine Clarkson, " 'Well,' she replied, 'he may stay away if he likes I care nothing about it if he will not talk of it'; and then she began again about disgrace, and the children," *MY* 2, 177–178, Dec. 2, 1807.
29. Coleridge advocates women's education, Lect. 1, 594–595; *SWF* 2, 1354, *TT* 1, 462.
30. Kathleen Coburn, *Inquiring Spirit: A New Presentation of Coleridge from his Published and Unpublished Prose Writings*, ed. Coburn, revised (Toronto: University of Toronto Press, 1979; original in 1951), p. 307, saw long ago Coleridge's enlightened interest in women's lives, and grouped some of his comments together in pages 303–309.
31. William Galperin, "Lord and Lady Byron and Mrs. Stowe," paper at North American Society for Romanticism conference, July 2003, New York.
32. Andre Maurois, *Byron* (New York: Ungar, 1930), p. 322. See Malcolm Elwin, *Lord Byron's Wife* (New York: Harcourt Brace, 1962).
33. Marilyn Butler, *Jane Austen and the War of Ideas* (Oxford: Clarendon, 1975), cited in *Sense and Sensibility*, ed. Beth Lau (Boston: Houghton Mifflin, 2002), p. 344, declares that "Willoughby's crime proves after all not to have been rank villainy, but expensive self-indulgence so habitual that he must sacrifice everything, including domestic happiness to it."

9 "A Kite's Dinner"

1. Stephen Gill, *William Wordsworth: A Life* (Oxford: Clarendon Press, 1989), p. 256.
2. Mays's translation in *PW* #430, pp. 842–843, is slightly different from Kathleen Coburn's in the note to *CN* 3231. This dark version of

"Ad Vilmum Axiologum" contrasts with the first version, which praises Wordsworth's *Prelude*, which he had chanted aloud soon after the scene in the bedroom: "This be the meed, that thy Song creates a thousandfold Echo!" (*PW* #429, pp. 841–842). Where one praises Wordsworth's immortal words, the other bitterly reviles his low notions of love.
3. Richard Holmes gives a sense of the merriment and ease of the Morgan home in Hammersmith and later in Calne in *Coleridge: Darker Reflections: 1804–1834* (New York: Pantheon, 1998), pp. 220–264. Amid jokes and riddles and excursions, Coleridge "had fun with the Morgans" (p. 262).

10 Communities of Women: Developing as Persons

1. I discuss this poem in connection with Laetitia Elizabeth Landon's poem "The Improvisatrice" in "Romantic *Improvvisatori*: Coleridge, L. E. L, and the Difficulties of Loving," *PQ* 79 4 (Fall, 2000), 501–522, in the context of Coleridge's knowledge of the women poets of his day.
2. J. M. W. Turner also painted this subject: "Boccaccio Relating the Tale of the Bird-Cage," exhibited in 1828 at the Royal Academy, in the style of Antoine Watteau. Turner refers to the work of Thomas Stothard, who had illustrated the *Decameron* in 1825 (Tate Britain, room 41).
3. Graham Davidson, " 'The Garden of Boccaccio': Coleridge's Recovery of Romance," Coleridge Conference 2004 paper. Davidson cites the introduction to the poem "Work without Hope"—"THE ALONE MOST DEAR: a complaint of Jacob to Rachel as in the 10th year of his Service he saw or *fancied* that he saw Symptoms of Alienation" (headnote to *PW* #606). Davidson has found that Anne Gillman wrote beside this phrase: "it *was* fancy." She is thus privy to his notebooks and she frankly acknowledges her role as his Rachel as well as his devotion as her Jacob. She ushers him into a world of "joyaunce" and glee.
4. "The Lost Garden of Coleridge," 1990 Coleridge Conference.
5. *The Decameron*, trans. Mark Musa and Peter Bondanella (New York: Signet, 2002), pp. 3–4.
6. Venetia Murray, *An Elegant Madness: High Society in Regency England* (New York: Penguin, 1998), p. 165.
7. Thomas G. Bergin, *Boccaccio* (New York: Viking Press, 1987), p. 87, see for questions of love, pp. 78–81.
8. David Hume popularized the fragmentation of *person*; subsequent philosophers and poets from Kant and Coleridge on, struggled to reconstitute its cohesion. For discussion of personal identity in relation to Coleridge, see Thomas McFarland, *Coleridge and the Pantheist Tradition* (Oxford: Clarendon Press, 1969), pp. 289–297; Thomas McFarland, "Prolegomena," to *Opus Maximum*, ed. Thomas McFarland with Nicholas Halmi, pp. cxiv–cxix; Anya Taylor, *Coleridge's Defense of the Human* (Columbus, OH: Ohio State University Press, 1986), pp. 13–33; Mary Anne Perkins, *Coleridge's Philosophy: The Logos as Unifying Principle* (Oxford: Clarendon Press, 1994), pp. 223–254, with an emphasis on the Divine Man, the person as Christ.

The fragile personhood of women is rarely discussed. I do so briefly in "Coleridge on Persons and Things," *European Romantic Review* 1, 2 (Winter, 1991), 163–180.
9. Coleridge wrote to both men in July 1829. He told John Anster that he was too old, too poor, and too nervous to marry Susan (CL 6, 793). He told James Gillman Jr. that he and Susan needed to get to know each other more seriously, for "what but misery and discomfort can be expected, when a union so intimate has begun and been completed in passion, or caprice, or error from imperfect knowledge?" (*CL* 6, 795–796).
10. Mays's headnote to poem #613.
11. Anthony John Harding, "Coleridge as Mentor and the Origins of Masculinist Modernity," *European Romantic Review* 14, 4 (Dec. 2003), 453–466, describes Coleridge's mentoring as exclusively for young males as a means of passing along political power, but in fact Coleridge's female households in this late period of his life included many young women whose intellects and life choices he discussed and guided.
12. *Lects Lit*, 1, 594–595.
13. Julie Carlson, "Gender," in *The Cambridge Companion to Coleridge*, Lucy Newlyn (Cambridge: Cambridge University Press, 2002), p. 210.
14. Bridget Hill, *Women Alone: Spinsters in England 1660–1850* (New Haven: Yale, 2001), shows that despite the "scoffs that are thrown on superannuated virgins" (pp. 8–9), many women lived as spinsters and pursued work in agriculture, manufacture, business, and education, thus preserving their properties.
15. Kathleen Coburn's *Inquiring Spirit* (1957)—now revised to *Inquiring Spirit: A New Presentation of Coleridge from his Published and Unpublished Prose Writings* (Toronto: University of Toronto Press, 1979), pp. 304–310—proved the groundbreaking pedecessor or to all her later delving.
16. Anthony John Harding, *Coleridge and the Idea of Love: Aspects of Relationship in Coleridge's Thought and Writing* (London: Cambridge University Press, 1974), p. 90.
17. He outlined this system of cultivating human beings in 1830 in *On the Constitution of Church and State*, ed. John Colmer, pp. 71–76.

Index

Abrams, Harriet, 111
Aders, Elizabeth, 48, 160, 161, 168
Adorno, Theodore, 203n24
Adulteresses, 125–30
Adultery: as only grounds for divorce, 28, 125–8, 136–7; punishments for, 127, 129, 130
Adultery Prevention Bill, 204n1
Agency, 129, 167; in civilized cultures, 183; forfeited in marriage, 171; in voice, 108
Alexander, Meena, 73
Alighieri, Dante, 64, 82–5, 89, 94, 163, 164, 200–1n7, 205n9
Allsop, Thomas, 6, 20, 61, 155, 160, 181; and C's letter to his sister, 172–4
Allston, Washington, 6, 165
Armour, Richard, 169
"Asra Poems," 85–9; second wave of, 150–2
Austen, Jane, 4, 7, 35, 36, 52, 54, 134, 161, 172; and divorce in *Sense and Sensibility* and *Mansfield Park*, 141, 142–4

Bacon, Ann, 10
Bacon, Dashwood, 10
Baillie, Joanna, 110
Barbarism, 185–6
Barbauld, Anna, 43, 47
Barth, J. Robert, 6–7, 187n4, 204n30
Bedford, Grosvenor, 16, 31–3

Beer, John, 5, 7, 196n15, 198n33
Benjamin, Jessica, 73
Bertolossi, Cecilia, 117, 145, 148
Betham, Mathilda, 109–10
Billington, Elizabeth, 111–12, 115
Blackstone, William, 131, 167, 206n14
Blake, William, 36, 84, 143, 145, 171
Blushes, 2, 49, 93, 99, 158
Boccaccio, Giovanni, 7, 85, 161, 162, 163–5; Prince Galleoto as Coleridge, 163–4
Bolton, Betsy, 56, 193n15, 202n6
Boutflower, Elizabeth, 10
Boyd, Rev. Henry, 82–4, 154, 197n27
Breasts, 9, 10, 11, 17, 43, 81, 85, 86, 103, 106–7, 114–15, 147
Brent, Charlotte, 77, 99, 100, 101, 147, 156–8, 160
Brown, Eric C., 82
Brown, Marshall, 204n27
Browne, Thomas: annotations and letters in, 94–9, 118
Brunton, Ann, 16–17, 111
Bunyan, Frances Sarah, 177
Butler, Marilyn, 207n33
Byron, George Gordon, sixth Baron Byron, 14, 41, 74, 141–2

Camille, Michael, 94
Campbell, Mathew, 108
Carey, Rev. Henry, 82

Carlson, Julie, 7, 63, 110, 175, 209n13
Catalani, Angelica, 111–12
Cavendish, Georgiana, Duchess of Devonshire, 106–9, 136
Chapman, George, translation of Homer, 99
Clark, David, 7, 197n22
Coburn, Kathleen, 6, 147, 205n6, 207n30, 209n15
Coleridge, Anne (Nancy) (C's sister), 51–4, 73–6, 89–92, 116, 119, 120
Coleridge, Hartley (C's older son), 34, 37, 38, 39, 40, 61, 71, 127, 155, 167, 191n10
Coleridge, John (C's older brother), 53–4
Coleridge, Mrs. Anne (C's mother), 53–4, 193n11
Coleridge, Samuel Taylor: admiring grand ladies, 105–13; advises young women and men, 166–84; affinity with women, 61–3; and Ann Brunton, 16–17; attending debates in the House of Lords, 125–30; and child development, 62; declarations of love in poems, books, and notes, 78–101, 139–40; develops ethics of reverencing persons, 179–80; dislikes prudish gossips, 44, 55–7, 108; falls in love with Sara Hutchinson, 77–79, 88; fears to imagine the death of his wife, 138; "four sorrows," 155; and Godwin, 29–30; humor, 11–14, 15, 43, 74, 128, 158, 190–1n5, 199n50; and listening to women's voices, 103–6; looking at women, 43–50; loves Mrs. Gillman, 159–61; and Mary Ann Evans, 16–20, 30, 31, 33; and Mary Wollstonecraft, 18, 47–8; and Milton, 28–9; and naked women, 13–14; and opera, 111–18; resilience, 156; resists Italian diva, 117–18, 148; and Sara Fricker, 22–8, 30–1, 35–7, 43–4; sensuality, compared to Wordsworth's, 41–2; separates from his wife, 139–40; from SH, 152–3, 155; suffers "the Epoch," 145–56; and Southey, 3, 16, 22–37; sympathizing with women's plights, 49–57, 164–7; and unchastities, 14–15; understanding girls, 59–70, 72–5; and youthful vitality, 3, 7, 11–15, 18; see also jealousy; love; marriage; soul
Coleridge, Samuel Taylor: works:
"An Essay on the Adultery Bill," 129–30, 133
The Friend, 100, 141, 167–8
"Individuality," 178–9
"Lesson in Universal History for James Gillman, Jr.," 183–4
Opus Maximum, 61–2, 75, 179, 192n3
"On the Passions," 63, 163
"The Races of Men," 184
"Uterine Disorders," 45

Poetical Works:
"Absence," 10
"Ad Vilmam Axiologum," 122
"Ad Vilmam Axiologum (Latin version)," 149–50
"After Bathing," 85–6
"After Marino," 150–1
"Alice du Clos," 84, 153–4, 164
"Alternative Stanzas," 151
"An Anagram of Mary Morgan's Face," 158

"To Ann Brunton," 16
"Answer to a Child's Question," 87
"The Ballad of the Dark Ladie," 49–51, 59, 79, 199–200n4
"Balsamum in Vitro," 49
"The Blossoming of the Solitary Date-Tree," 150–1
"Christabel," 3, 58, 59–73; copy to Sara Hutchinson, 99; and "Love," 77, 79; its meter, 194n2; as recitative, 113; and "The Rime of the Ancient Mariner," 63, 68, 71, 74, 75; and persons, 167; and sex, 63–5; and "the song of her desolation," 75
"On the Christening of a Friend's Child," 44–5
"Couplet on Lesbian Lovers," 159
"Cupid Turn'd Chymist," 9
"A Day Dream," 101
"The Day Dream," 87
"Dejection: an Ode," 63, 97, 116, 117; and "Letter to . . . SH", 118–22; and "Lines Composed in a Concert Room," 118–21
"Destiny of Nations," 70–1
"Duty, Surviving Self-Love," 155
"E Coelo Descendit," 71, 194n3
"To Eliza Brunton," 16
"The Eolian Harp," 25
"Epigram from Lessing," 108
"Epigram of a Maiden," 52
"An Extempore," 10
"Extremes Meet," 158
"Fears in Solitude," 3, 115
"Fragment in Blank Verse," 153
"Fragments of an Unwritten Poem," 155
"Fragments written in February," 151
"To a Friend," 53

"The Garden of Boccaccio," 163–6, 171
"Genevieve," 9, 103
"Glycine's Song," 156
"The Happy Husband: A Fragment," 152
"Hexameter Lines to Mrs. Coleridge," 36–7
"Human Life, or the Denial of Immortality," 153
"The Improvisatore," 161–3
"The Keepsake," 86–7
"The Kiss," 23–4
"The Kiss and the Blush," 49
"Kubla Khan," 6, 27; women's voices in, 104–5, 118, 148
"To a Lady, Offended," 168
"Letter to . . . SH," 91–3; and "Dejection: An Ode," 118–22; and "Lines Composed in a Concert Room," 118, 120; and love, 92–3
"Lewti," 17
"Limbo, A Fragment," 153
"A Line from a Lost Poem," 151
"Lines Composed in a Concert Room," 113–19; extra stanza, 204n28
"Lines on Aurelia Coates," 158
"Lines on Wordsworth and Coleridge," 149
"Love," 52; as bold triumph, 78–82; and Dante's Paolo and Francesca, 82–92; and "Rime of the Ancient Mariner," 3, 68, 78, 79, 80, 82
"To Matilda Betham from a Stranger," 109–10, 122
"To Miss Dashwood Bacon," 11
"Names," 46
"To the Nightingale," 103
"Not at Home," 154–5

Coleridge, Samuel Taylor:
  Poetical Works—continued
  "Ode to Georgiana, Duchess of Devonshire," 106–9
  "Ode to Sara, Written at Shurton Bars," 25
  "To a Painter," 10
  "Philosophical Apology for the Ladies, An Ode, addressed to Lord Kenyon," 135–37
  "On Presenting a Moss Rose," 9
  "Religious Musings," 46
  Remorse, 110, 156
  "The Rime of the Ancient Mariner," 3, 68, 71, 74, 75, 82, 104–5, 122–4, 127, 167, 168
  "Separation, after Cotton," 152
  Sibylline Leaves, 89, 164, 201n15
  "A Simile; Written after a Walk Before Supper," 43
  "Soliloquy of a Full Moon," 86
  "Sonnet on Receiving an Account," 52
  "Sonnet to Sarah Siddons," 110
  "Sonnet to Sara Hutchinson," 87–8
  "Sonnet to William Linley," 104
  "S. T. Coleridge, Aeta Suae, 63," 168
  "A Stranger Minstrel," 105–6
  "The Suicide's Argument," 153
  "The Three Graves," 70–1
  "Translation of Otfrid," 190
  "Translation of Stolberg's 'Hymn,'" 90, 170
  "The Two Founts," 161
  "The Two Sisters: a Wanderer's Farewell," 27, 45, 157–8
  "To an Unfortunate Woman," 45–6
  "Verse Letter," 86
  "The Visionary Hope," 152
  "Westphalian Song," 203n17
  "Willow," 100
  "Work without Hope," 208n3
  "Written in Dejection," 152
  Zapolya, 110
Coleridge, Sara (C's daughter), 38–40, 182
Coleridge, Sara Fricker (C's wife), 16–17, 19–20; early love of Robert Southey, 21–2, 27–9, 31–3, 37–8; her letters, 26–8; in London, 127–8; and negation, 23–6; on opera, 112; resemblances to Southey, 33–6; and separation, 139–40; her special language, 36–8; her values, 27, 31–7
Coverture, 133, 206n14
Cross, Ashley, 5, 202nn3–4
Crouch, Anna Maria, 112
Cruikshanks, Anna, 44–5, 116

Davidson, Graham, 4, 117, 163, 208n3
Dependency, 176–7
Dibdin, Thomas, 111, 203n17
Dickens, Charles, 35, 137–8, 207n26
Divorce; among peerage, 134; assumptions about, 4–5, 91; in Austen, 142–4; debates on, 125–34; "easy divorces," 139–40; procedures for, 134–5; in other Romantic writers, 141

Edelman, Hope, 197–8n31
Education, for women, 19, 169–71
Edwards, Jenny, 9
Eilenburg, Susan, 74
Ellison, Julie, 188n11
Elshstain, Jean Bethke, 7
Engell, James, 53–4
Erdman, David, 135, 207n24

Erickson, Amy Louise, 132–3
Evans, Mary Ann, 11–13, 17–19, 22, 84, 97, 99, 112

Faces: C's own, 5; covering individuality, 179–80, 192–3n8; frowning, 24–6; opaque, 48–9; and persons, 48–9; sameness of, 158–9; seen by the eye, 103
Fadiman, Anne, 5
Fetish-worshippers, 44
Fry, Paul, 120
Fulford, Tim, 7, 135, 196n19, 200n5, on "Love," 207n24, and, 207n27

Gainsborough, Thomas, 56, 193n14
Galperin, William, 142
Gaull, Marilyn, 110, 202n11
Gill, Stephen, 148
Gillman, Anne (nee Harding), 5, 27–8, 48; advice for Allsop, 181–2; C watches, 159–60; and "Garden of Boccaccio," 162–5; knows C's marital history, 182; and music, 160; as Rachel to C's Jacob, 159, 163, 207n3; and self-respect, 166, 171; and servants, 172; and swimming, 160
Gillman, Dr. James, 20, 27–8, 138, 145, 156, 159, 160, 169, 190n11
Gillman, James, Jr., 168, 169, 183–4, 209n9
Girls: absorption of identity, 68–73; dangers for girls, 48–55; development of, 59, 60, 68–71; mean girls, 56–7, 193n14; at puberty, 59, 72; studies of, 196nn20–1, 197nn38–9; and suicide, 54
Gitter, Elisabeth G., 87, 201n13

Godwin, William: at home, 5; on marriage as property, 22, 28, 29, 30, 56, 90, 128, 131; publishes Wollstonecraft's *Maria*, 205n8
Goethe, Johann Wolfgang von, 149–50
Griffiths, Eric, 108

Hagstrum, Jean H., 187n6
Halmi, Nicholas, 189–90n8, 192n3, 201n15, 208n8
Hamlet, 19, 84, 95
Haney, David P., 193n8
Harding, Anthony, 19, 195n7, 209n11, 209n16
Harding, Lucy, 156, 160
Hardy, Thomas, 131
Harris, Barbara J., 132
Hatfield, John ("The Keswick Imposter"), 54–5
Hazlitt, William, 60, 72, 91, 140, 144
Heart, as physical thing, 155, 175
"Hemiplegia," 173–4, 177, 178
Hill, Bridget, 209n14
Hoeveler, Diane, 62, 196n19
Hofkosh, Sonia, 44
Holmes, Richard, 6, 22, 100, 145–7, 158, 189n7, 199n48, 201n20, 208n3
Homer, 99, 100, 165
Horney, Karen, 198n39
Horstman, Allen, 134
Howes, Raymond F., 169
Human, 206n13
Hunt, Leigh, 7, 84, 164, 201n7
Hutchinson, Sara, 30, 36; appearance, 77–8; her breasts, 87, 147; C's letters to, in Thomas Browne's *Works*, 95–98; C's passion for, 77–90; departure, 100; her voice, 87, 105; feelings for William Wordsworth, 146–9;

Hutchinson—*continued*
hears C playing with children, 40; her income, 181; letters burned, 95; her letters to C, 90–4; on Mrs. C, 38–40, 177; newly discovered poem to her, 87–8, 99; on opera, 111–12; poems to her, 85–94, 150–6; reading "Christabel" aloud, 74; reading with C, 84, 89, 94–9; reciprocity in love, 86–94, 121, 153; on the single life, 177; visited by C, 90, 128; working with C, 86–9, 100, 140, 146–7, 176–7
Hutchinson, Thomas, 85

Identity, 167–9
Inchbald, Elizabeth, 110
Individuality, 178–9; separateness, 183–4, 185

Jackson, Heather, 188n11, 195n10, 197n23
Jealousy, 146–8, 153–5
Jordan, (Mrs.) Dorothy, 110
Joyce, James, 12, 123

Kahane, Claire, 195n8
Kahn, Coppelia, 198n31
Kant, Immanuel, 179
Keats, John, 3, 4, 12, 41, 81–2, 84, 151, 192n2, 200–1n7
Kisses, 10, 23–4, 49
Koenig-Woodyard, Chris, 5
Koestenbaum, Wayne, 114
Kooey, Michael John, 120, 122

Lamb, Charles, 52, 94–5, 99, 144, 159
Lamb, Mary, 33, 54, 99
Landon, Letitia Elizabeth, 161–3
Landor, Walter Savage, 142

Lau, Beth, 5, 7
Lawrence, D. H., 5, 170
Leader, Zachary, 121–2, 197n28
Lee, Debbie, 191n13, 206n13
Lefebure, Molly, 6, 21, 23, 36–8
Levin, Susan, 111
Levinas, Emmanuel, 26, 48, 192n8
Levinson, Marjorie, 194n2
Lockridge, Laurence, 194n5
London, April, 133
Love, 77–89; as absence, 163; bold assertion of, 78, 81, 82; defined, 82, 89, 162–3, 182; as hunger, 63; love for one woman, 97; and music, 105, 121, 122; and rapture, 85–94; and reading together, 83–5; right to love freely, 89–90; and self-insufficingness, 162–3; tumults, 89; "united souls," 96; as volcano, 148; wholeness of love, 165; *see also* yearning
Luther, Susan, 64, 163, 194n4

Magnuson, Paul, 189n8, 201n16
Maiden-names, 141
"Maid of Buttermere," 54–5
Mara, Gertrude Elisabeth, 112
Marriage, 22–30; advice: avoid marriage, 180; advice: choose carefully, 181–2; changes in 18th century, 132–4; dangers for women, 172–4; debasing, 28–31, 40–1; difficulty of choosing partners for, 173–5; happy, 96–9; and "hemiplegia," 173–5; humanizing spheres, 178–80; kinds of, 172–3; "a meet and happy conversation," 100; as poison, 178; and property, 133–5; as regulative institution, 171; of soul-mates, 172–4

Married Woman's Property Act, 41, 207n26
Mathew, George Felton, 3, 72
Mays, J. C. C., 1, 2, 9, 10, 19, 49, 52, 78, 135; discovers sonnet to Sara Hutchinson, 87–8; on "Love," 82, 85, 199–200n4, 200nn5–6, 207n2
McCalman, Iain, 203n15, 203n19
McCarthy, Desmond, 1–2, 146
McFarland, Thomas, 7, 208n8
Medieval imagery, 78, 82, 94
Mellor, Anne, 7
Menefee, Samuel, 131–2
Milton, John, 28–29, 31, 56, 77, 100; "Treatise in Favor of Divorce," 28–9, 100, 163, 173
Modiano, Raimonda, 189n8
Monkhouse, Tom, 177
Montagu, Basil, 147, 153
Morgan, John, 100, 155–6, 157, 208n3
Morgan, Mary (nee Brent), 155
Mothers, 68, 70–1, 196n20–1
Mudge, Bradford, 6
Music, 103–5; as female, 109, 111–15, 122, 160; and love, 119–22; and primary feelings; 104–5; and selfhood, 108; women's song and James Joyce, 123

Nesbitt, Fanny, 9–11
Newcomb, Rhoda, 5
Newlyn, Lucy, 201n16
Nixon, Eliza, 160, 171

Object relations, 57, 196n20
Opera, 110–18
Ovid, Publius Naso, 64, 135, 153–4, 164, 165, 166

Pace, Joel, 5
Page, Judith, 191n14
Paglia, Camille, 6, 7, 64, 188n14
Paley, Morton, 200n5
Pantisocracy: and free love, 22
Parliamentary Debates 1799–1800, 125–30, 132–6, 204–5n1, 205n2
Pascoe, Judith, 110, 202n13
Pearson, Jacqueline, 84
Perkins, Mary Anne, 7, 208n8
Personhood: in face, 26, 48; surrendered in marriage, 170–4, 178, 184; in voice, 103–5, 192–3n8, 193n9
Persons: absorption of, 64–7; complex persons, 175; defined for Susan Steel, 167–9; degraded by unworthy mates, 172–5; in "Dejection: An Ode," 122; in families, 178–80; fragility in women, 166–8; incoherence of, 60–3; from infancy, 62; and things, 166–7
Peterfreund, Stuart, 194n5
Petrarch, Francesco, 89, 94, 164, 201n15
Piper, H. W., 105
Pite, Ralph, 197n27
Plato, 162–3
Poole, Thomas, 6, 27, 51
Poovey, Mary, 44
Potter, Stephen, 6, 19, 26–8
Pregnancy, 44–5, 51–2, 55
Primogeniture, 133
Property, 130–3, 140–1, 166; inheritance for young women, 168, 176–7
Propriety, 133
Prostitutes, 13–15, 56, 127, 130
Prudentialism, 32–6
Puberty, 59, 63, 71, 72
Purcell, Henry, 104, 203n25

"Queen Caroline Affair," 7, 137–8

Rajan, Tilottama, 195n11
Ree, Jonathan, 104, 202n2
Reiman, Donald H., 62
Reverence for individuals, 72–3, 179–80; in free civilizations, 184
Rickman, John, 34, 139
Robinson, Henry Crabb, 38, 91, 101, 144
Robinson, Mary, 5, 56, 105–6, 108, 109
Ross, Marlon, 62, 192n7, 196n17

Same-sex love, 6, 159, 198n32
Schiller, Friedrich, 120, 122
Schmidgall, Gary, 114
Self, and choices, 160–1, 180–2
Sensuality, 3, 5, 6, 11–14, 17, 18; about daughter's "sweet flesh," 39, 41, 49, 77, 146–9, 158–9
Separation, 139–41, 152–3
Sex, 22–3; aroused through eyes, 52; "best reason to esteem her," 54–5; in "Christabel," 63–8; coition "taken by itself," 98–9; desires, 89, 90, 93, 94; and insects, 135–7; in souls, 180; through texts, 84; "warmth of constitution," 51–2; without love, 18, 29–31
Shakespeare: *Hamlet*, 19, 84, 95; heroines, 189n8; *King Lear*, 26, 108
Sharon, Avi, 200n7
Shelley, Mary Wollstonecraft Godwin, 5, 44, 73, 184
Shelley, Percy Bysshe, 4–5, 41, 66; and Dante, 197n30
Shepherd, Mary, 160
Siddons, Sarah, 110

Simmons, Rachel, 193n14
Singers, 110–23
Single women, 59, 132–3, 209n14
Slaves, 125, 131–2
Smith, Charlotte, 43, 72, 195n13
Soul-mates, 172–4
Souls: metaphors for, 180; polluted in marriage, 28–41, 172–4; spheres to develop, 178–80
Southey, Edith (nee Fricker), 21–2, 27, 32–3, 38
Southey, Robert, 3, 16; helps C's children, 38; on C's ideas of easy divorces, 139–40; marries Edith, 32; and melancholy, 31–2; pressures C to marry, 22–30; relations with Sara Fricker, 21–4; his values, 31–37
Spatz, Jonas, 194n4
Sprengnether, Madelon, 196nn20–1
"Standing Order 142," 126
Steel, Susan, 167–8, 171
Stillinger, Jack, 197n28
Stone, Lawrence, 130–1, 205nn10–11
Storey, Mark, 190n1
Suicide, 54, 138, 153, 172–3
Swann, Karen, 59, 194n1, 195n8
Swinburne, Algernon, 72

Taussig, Gurion, 6
Temple, Laura Sophia, 99
Theatre, 110
Thelwall, John, 22, 44
Thomas, Keith, 206n12
Tolstoy, Leo, 4
Turner, J. M. W., 208n2

Valesio, Paolo, 84
Voices, 103; "Dejection: An Ode," 118–121; identity in, 103–8; "irreducibly individual," 108; operatic, 110–20; and

persons, 104; in poems, 104–6; voice, not face, as core of person for C, 192–3n8

Watters, Reggie, 197n23
Whalley, George, 6, 86, 90, 91, 201n20
Wheeler, Kathleen, 194n6
Wife-sale, 131–2
Wilberforce, William, 125, 137
Will, 66–7, 73–5
Williams, William Carlos, 189n2
Wives: demanding to be exclusive, 89–90; as non-persons, 132–3; as slaves, 130–1
Wollstonecraft, Mary, 18, 36, 47; on education, 169–70; and heartbreak, 145; her *Maria*, 129, 133–4, 136, 139–40, 176; her reputation, 56; and women's souls, 47–8
Women: abandoned, 49–55; in ancient world, 206n19; choices for, 172–6; in civilizations that reverence them, 183–5; dancing, 13–14; free agency for, 176–80; German, 14; loose, 14–15, 46; love between, 158–9; mobility for, 171–2; and moral law, 120; as music, 122; naked, 13; in opera, 111–14; and ownership of property, 176–7; in pairs, 45, 72, 182; and passivity, 44–7, 75; poor, 15; and property; 140–1; as property, 131–4; sameness of, 44–6, 48–9, 157–8; scheming, 36, 181; in theatre, 109–11;
Wordsworth, Dorothy, 27, 30, 73–4, 77, 85, 100, 139, 140, 177, 191n7, 207n28
Wordsworth, Mary (nee Hutchinson), 42–3, 77, 147
Wordsworth, William, 41–2; "baseness," 155; betrayal in "Alice du Clos," 153–4; C's anger at, 207–8n2; C's jealousy of, 146–9; on C's unpopularity, 191n16; disparages "Love," 89; and "Michael," 199n50; minimizes C's love for SH, 95; and poems about women, 73; quarrel with C, 101, 155; rational view of love, 149–50; reads some of their letters, 91; rejects "Christabel," 73–4; relations with SH, 146–8; and "Solitary Reaper," 202n1; his "three wives," 147; and women, 199n45
Worthen, John, 38

Yearning, 62–3, 89, 101, 162–3
Yeats, William Butler, 1, 45, 189n1, 192n6